RECORD OF A SCHOOL.

RECORD OF A SCHOOL:

EXEMPLIFYING

THE GENERAL PRINCIPLES

OF

SPIRITUAL CULTURE.

———————————

He that receiveth a little child in my name, receiveth me.—*Jesus Christ.*

———————————

APPLEWOOD BOOKS
Bedford, Massachusetts

Record of a School was originally published in 1845 by James Munroe and Company.

Thank you for purchasing an Applewood book. Applewood reprints America's lively classics— books from the past that are still of interest to modern readers. For a free copy of our current catalog, write to:

Applewood Books
P.O. Box 365
Bedford, MA 01730

ISBN 1-55709-959-6

INTRODUCTION

As you read Elizabeth Peabody's *Record of a School*, imagine that you are seated on a green velvet couch under a cathedral window that takes up much of an entire wall of the most unusual classroom you have ever seen. You have just walked across the tree-lined Boston Common and climbed a flight of stairs leading to an airy loft space that fills the upper story of Boston's new Masonic Temple on Tremont Street, a Gothic Revival structure considered "one of the chief architectural ornaments of the city." There you find roughly two-dozen children, boys and girls aged five to fifteen, busily occupied at work stations arranged through the sixty-foot-long schoolroom. Some are studying quietly at desks lining one wall, others are refreshing themselves at a "table of sense," where a pitcher of water awaits any thirsty scholar. But most are seated in chairs arrayed in a semi-circle in front of the teacher's own u-shaped desk, custom-designed so that his pupils can imagine he is always available to them, engaged in an intense discussion.

All of this is new to you, and would be to anyone else in this time and place: Boston, 1835. Work stations, water table, chairs arranged in anything other than straight rows. But newest of all is the notion of teacher and pupils conversing. This is what you have come to see and hear.

In all the schools you know, particularly those for boys, lecture and recitation is the order of the day, discipline with the rod the only sure guarantee that students will pay attention and learn their lessons. Yet in this classroom, with no rod in evidence, the children attend to their teacher's every word. And then, more astonishing, the small pupils utter their own thoughts in response. Clever, insightful, eloquent; hesitant, childish, or prosaic—no matter, each student's remarks are received with sincere interest by the ebullient, rangy figure seated behind the u-shaped desk, a blue-eyed blond-haired man named Bronson Alcott. Indeed, at times it seems as if this open-hearted teacher has permitted the children themselves to lead the discussion.

Simply by virtue of the curiosity that has brought you to the visitors' couch at Bronson Alcott's Temple School, you are a member of a small but influential band of New England freethinkers dedicated to "the newness": men and women, as Alcott's partner and promoter, Elizabeth Palmer Peabody, would write, "who have dared to say to one another . . . Why not begin to move the mountain of custom and convention?" You might be joined by other seekers after innovation—the British journalist Harriet Martineau, for example, who would describe the school in her 1837 travelogue *Society in America*. There she summarized

Bronson Alcott's unorthodox methods, his belief that "his little pupils possessed . . . all truth, in philosophy and morals," and his view that it was "his business . . . to bring it out into expression; to help the outward life to conform to the inner light." Or you might find yourself seated next to Ralph Waldo Emerson, who visited the Temple School with his bride Lidian. When Elizabeth Peabody sent Emerson her draft of *Record of a School*, he wrote that he'd read it "with greatest pleasure" and hoped that "it may be printed speedily" so that its usefulness could be tested. The finished book, he said, was "beautiful . . . certain true & pleasant." It read like a novel.

But at this particular historical moment, Emerson's word counts for little beyond a small circle of admirers in Boston and nearby Concord. He has delivered only one complete series of public lectures, downstairs in the main hall of this same Masonic Temple, and he has published nothing. On this day, Bronson Alcott seems to hold just as much promise, and he is the man you have come to see in action, invited by one of Boston's most prominent women of letters, Elizabeth Palmer Peabody.

"Alcott is a man destined . . . to make an era in society, *and I believe he will*," Elizabeth Peabody wrote in July, 1834, scarcely a month into her acquaintance with the thirty-four-year-old idealist. She had just read through the journals his students had written in an experimental school Alcott kept for a short time in Germantown, Pennsylvania, before moving to Boston with his wife Abigail and their two young daughters, Anna and Louisa May. Elizabeth Peabody found the children's writing skills, along with the self-inquiry they exhibited, remarkable. At thirty, Peabody was a teacher herself and a woman of prodigious learning—Alcott said she possessed "the most magnificent philosophic imagination" of any person he ever knew. She was also well-connected and ready to do anyone she admired a good turn. Peabody offered to help Alcott start a school in Boston where he could test his theories more effectively. She would even teach Latin and mathematics, subjects in which Alcott had no expertise, free of charge until Alcott began to make a profit.

By September, 1834, just in time for the fall semester, Peabody had found Alcott his pupils and the classroom in the Masonic Temple. And she helped him furnish it, supplying her own green velvet couch for the visitors she hoped would broadcast the school's innovative methods to the world at large. Recording Alcott's dialogues with his pupils was Peabody's idea as well. Initially she did it for the students' benefit: she read the conversations out loud to them at the end of the school day so that they could review and consolidate their thoughts. But as Peabody saw Alcott's experiment begin to succeed, she became more ambitious for the pages she was rapidly accumulating. One small boy told her, "I never knew I had a mind till

I came to this school." In the classroom dialogues, she boasted to her sister Mary, the children don't just talk, "*they create.*" She decided to publish her record.

Peabody added her own commentary to Alcott's dialogues, explaining the purpose of the school: to prove that the "innocence" of childhood was a "positive condition," one that "comprehends all the instincts and feelings which naturally tend to good, such as humility, self-forgetfulness, love, trust." In a young America, only beginning to shake off the constraints of a strict Calvinism which taught that children were born sinners, this was a radical agenda. Although they did not yet call themselves by this term, Peabody and Alcott were transcendentalists who subscribed to a romanticism that idealized childhood as offering wisdom for adults, rather than the other way around. Like Wordsworth, whose poetry they taught in the Temple School, Peabody and Alcott believed "the child is father to the man." Peabody's *Record of a School* would be the first book of transcendentalist ideas to be published in America.

As Peabody and Alcott read over the proofs of the book during the summer of 1835, they felt a growing excitement. "How much life you can breathe into me from your sympathy in my pursuits and purposes," Alcott wrote Peabody in gratitude, "I know not that I have another to whom I can truly apply the name of friend as yourself." In return, Peabody praised Alcott's "genius for education," admitting, "I am vain enough to say, that you are the only one I ever saw who, I soberly thought, surpassed my gift in . . . the divinest of all arts."

To Peabody, Alcott, Emerson, and their circle, education *was* a divine art. Peabody's mentor, the Boston minister Rev. William Ellery Channing, considered his preaching—which made him the most charismatic liberal theologian of his day— to be educating his flock. Emerson viewed his lectures the same way. Elizabeth Peabody's *Record of a School* should be read as the first in a long line of books that attempt to reform not just schools, but society as a whole, by considering the classroom a microcosm of the human community. *Record of a School* was nothing less than Peabody's account of the "unfolding" of the human spirit. It was written with the same evangelical fervor as the 1960s classic *Summerhill*, which spoke for a similar historical moment of intellectual ferment and social turmoil with its own record of an experimental school.

The first edition of a thousand copies sold briskly during the fall of 1835 to Boston's intelligentsia— until a warehouse fire destroyed half that number. Peabody arranged for a second edition of *Record of a School*, with an expanded "Explanatory Preface," to be published early in 1836. By then the popular novelist Catharine Maria Sedgwick had given the book the lead review in the February issue of the New York magazine *The Knickerbocker*. Sedgwick noted, with some reservation, that "Mr. Alcott rejects all previous systems," and she complained of his "tendency to *ultraism*, to go beyond not only all customary and prescribed, but ... all practicable limits." But she applauded his results: "Mr. Alcott has shown, how much more intelligent [children] are—how much more capable of thought, and reflection, and of moral and intellectual discrimination—than has been generally supposed." As for the recorder, Elizabeth Peabody: "She is evidently a woman of genius, and her remarks, when not too deeply *spiritual* . . . are very fine." Sedgwick was not partial to the "mystical" philosophy that underlay the Temple School experiment; but she was sympathetic to its liberation of its pupils from drudgery and harsh discipline.

That *Record of a School* found this measure of acclaim in the mainstream New York press was remarkable; that news of this tiny free school on Boston Common reached England with Martineau's book a year later was astounding. Peabody herself sent the book to Wordsworth, completing the circle of influence.

In September of 1835, as *Record of a School* went to press, enrollment in the Temple School for its second year was high, and Peabody and Alcott's hopes for continued success seemed justified. But just as quickly, it all melted away. Within the year, Alcott created a scandal by issuing his own second volume of classroom conversations, ignoring Peabody's advice to delete certain controversial passages that she knew would offend even the school's supporters. This was the beginning of the end of a fascinating story that can be read in most Alcott biographies and books about Peabody as well. By 1838, the school was shut down, and Alcott never taught children again. Peabody, more resourceful and less easily discouraged, took up a series of professions—bookseller, editor, publisher—before returning to the cause of education in the 1860s as founder of kindergartens in America.

What remains of the Temple School experiment is a set of core beliefs that still appeal to progressive educators and enlightened parents today: a commitment to honor the spirit of childhood in the classroom; an expectation that the imagination can be "called into life" in school. Looking back on their work together, Peabody always maintained that Alcott's teaching contained "a current of the true method—an infusion of Truth." Read her *Record of a School*, and see if you think she's right.

MEGAN MARSHALL
Newton, Massachusetts
July, 2005

Ms. Marshall is the author of The Peabody Sisters: Three Women Who Ignited American Romanticism *(Houghton Mifflin, 2005)*

RECORD OF A SCHOOL.

ERRATA.

The author not being skillful in correcting proofs, must ask the reader to correct with his pencil the following errors.

Page 59 line 6th, for *in* read *is*.
" 72 " 13th, for *expressing* read *explaining*.
" 73 " 17th, omit *but*.
" 77 " 35th, for *them* read *thoughts*.
" 101 " 5th, for *conduct* read *conflict*.
" 114 " 11th, for *said* read *told*.
" 114 " 20th, for *doings* read *doing so*.
" 116 " 12th, for *claim* read *charm*.
" 117 " 7th, for *obstruction* read *abstraction*.
" 117 " 35th, for *often* read *after*.
" 143 " 14th, omit *and reason*.

ENTERED according to Act of Congress, in the year eighteen hundred and thirty-four, by JAMES MUNROE & COMPANY, in the Clerk's office of the District Court of Massachusetts.

PREFACE.

WHEN the author of the following pages commenced the journal, which makes the staple of this book, it was with the idea of collecting more facts than she already had in her recollection, wherewith to illustrate some general views, which she deems of great importance. Being engaged in teaching, an hour or two each day, in Mr. Alcott's school; and being led, by her confidence in his general principles, to look with interest upon the details of his instruction—she found that so much of children's minds were brought out upon moral and intellectual subjects *in words,* that she was induced to keep a Record, by way of verifying to herself and others the principles acted upon.

This Record she has received Mr. Alcott's permission to print in this volume. He, indeed, is not without the hope, that these slight details, published in connection with a discussion of principles, may lead to a better appreciation of his own views and plans, than could be otherwise brought about; ex-

cepting, indeed, by the slow process of waiting results in the children's ultimate experience; which
method of verification might perhaps leave him, in
the interval, without a sufficient number of pupils on
whom to exert his influence : or, to speak more accurately—the influence of those great principles of
spiritual culture, of which he would fain be the me-
diator, by removing inward and outward obstacles to
their full and harmonious development, in the individuals committed to his care. The author, therefore has availed herself of the advantage of bringing
this practical and obvious illustration of principles,
which she has never before seen systematically applied to any school of children under ten years of
age; and which she has only, in the course of her
own duties, had an opportunity to test on individuals.

For it is well known, that even in our cultivated
community, vague ideas prevail of a truly spiritual
education. The most enlightened people rarely
think of sending their children to school, except to
make attainments in this or that branch of intellectual
culture; as if any full, complete, and lifely intellectual
culture could take place, without constant reference,
on the part both of teacher and of pupil, to that
spiritual nature, a consciousness of which precedes
the development of the understanding, and is to out-
live and look back on the greatest attainments of
natural science, as the child looks back on his picture

alphabet, from the height of communion with the highest expression of genius in human language.

The author, however, is not going to complain of the want of confidence and coöperation with a teacher, which must flow from such inadequate views. For she has to be grateful, individually, to many who trusted her for many years, when she was almost afraid to trust herself; and never could have done so, with any steadiness, unless aided by that generous sympathy, which overlooked her fluctuations of spiritual strength, and forgave her mistakes of detail. Besides, she is well aware that the profession of teaching has not deserved more faith than it has obtained, taking it as it has been, at least for the last century. It is perhaps not easy to say where, originally, the fault lay. But the fact cannot be denied, that this employment has been too often assumed, on the part of teachers, with avowedly mercenary ends, or at least, for secondary purposes: and that, on the part of parents, there has not been an importunate demand for a better spirit, where it was wanting; nor always a ready sympathy and appreciation of it, where it existed; not even in a community, where the teachers of adults—the clerical profession, have been held up to an almost ideal standard.

This little book makes no high pretensions. It is an address to parents, who are often heard to express their want of such principles, and such a plan, as it is even in the author's power to afford. It will perhaps be more useful than if it were a more elaborate performance; for many will take up the record of an actual school, and endeavor to understand its principles and plans, who would shrink from undertaking to master a work, professing to sweep—from zenith to nadir—a subject, which has its roots and its issues in eternity; as this great subject of education certainly has.

RECORD OF A SCHOOL.

SCHOOL ROOM.

Mr. Alcott re-commenced his school in Boston, after four years interval, September, 1834, at the Masonic Temple, No. 7.

Considering that the objects which meet the senses every day for years, must necessarily mould the mind, he felt it necessary to choose a spacious room, and ornament it, not with such furniture as only an upholsterer can appreciate, but with such forms as might address and cultivate the imagination and heart.

In the four corners of the room, therefore, Mr. Alcott placed upon pedestals, fine busts of Socrates, Shakspeare, Milton, and Sir Walter Scott. And on a table, before the large gothic window by which the room is lighted, the God of Silence, " with his finger up, as though he said, beware." Opposite this gothic window, is his own table, about ten feet long, whose front is the arc of a circle, and which is prepared with little desks for the convenience of scholars. On this table he placed a small figure of a child aspiring. Behind him is a very large bookcase, with closets below, a black tablet above, and two shelves filled with books. A fine cast of Christ, in basso-relievo, is fixed into this bookcase, so as to appear to the scholars just over Mr. Alcott's head. The bookcase itself is surmounted with a bust of Plato. On the northern side of the room, opposite the door, is the table of the assistant, with a small figure of Atlas, bending under the weight of the world. On a small bookcase behind the assistant's chair, are the figures of a child reading, and a child drawing. Two old pictures; one of Harding's portraits; and some maps hang on the walls. The desks for the scholars, with conveniences for placing all their books

in sight, and with black tablets hung over them, which
swing forward, when they wish to use them, are placed
against the wall round the room, that when in their seats
for study, no scholar need look at another. On the right
hand of Mr. Alcott, is a sofa for the accommodation of
visitors, and a small table, with a pitcher and bowl; and
underneath the "table of sense," as this cold water table is
called, is a small figure of Bacchus, riding on a barrel.
Great advantages have been found to arise from this room;
every part of which speaks the thoughts of Genius. It is
a silent reproach upon rudeness.

About twenty children came the first day. They were all
under ten years of age, excepting two or three girls. I became
his assistant, to teach Latin to such as might desire to learn.

Mr. Alcott sat behind his table, and the children were
placed in chairs, in a large arc around him; the chairs so
far apart, that they could not easily touch each other. He
then asked each one separately, what idea she or he had of
the object of coming to school? To learn; was the first
answer. To learn what? By pursuing this question, all
the common exercises of school were brought up — suc-
cessively — even philosophy. Still Mr. Alcott intimated
that this was not all; and at last some one said "to behave
well," and in pursuing this expression into its meanings,
they at last decided that they came to learn to feel rightly,
to think rightly, and to act rightly. A boy of seven years old
suggested, and all agreed, that right actions were the most
important of these three.

Simple as all this seems, it would hardly be believed
what an evident exercise it was to these children, to be led
of themselves to form and express these conceptions and
few steps of reasoning. Every face was eager and interested. From right actions, the conversation naturally led
into the means of bringing them out. And the necessity
of feeling in earnest, of thinking clearly, and of school discipline, was talked over. School discipline was very carefully considered; Mr. Alcott's duty, and the children's
individual duties, and the various means of producing attention, self-control, perseverance, faithfulness. Among these

means, punishment was mentioned; and after a consideration of its nature and issues, they all very cheerfully agreed, that it was necessary, and that they preferred Mr. Alcott should punish them, rather than leave them in their faults, and that it was his duty to do so. Various punishments were mentioned, and hurting. the body was decided upon, as necessary and desirable in some instances. It was universally admitted that it was desirable whenever words were found insufficient to command the memory of conscience. After this conversation, which involved many anecdotes, many supposed cases, and many judgments, Mr. Alcott read from Krummacher's fables, a story which involved the free action of three boys of different characters, and questioned them respecting their opinion of these boys, and the principles on which it was seen by analysis that they acted. Nearly three hours passed away in this conversation and reading; and then they were asked, how long they had been sitting? None of them guessed more than an hour. After recess Mr. Alcott heard them read; and after that, spell. All present could read in such a book as Miss Edgeworth's Frank. Then each was asked what he had learned, and having told, they were dismissed one by one. The whole effect of the day seemed to be a combination of quieting influences, with an awakening effect upon the heart and mind.

The next day, a conversation somewhat like the former was commenced; but Mr. Alcott showed that he intended to have profound attention. When any one's eyes wandered, he waited to have them return to him, and he required that they should sit very still in their comfortable chairs. The questions, however, by interesting them very much, aided them in this effort. After recalling the conclusions of the day before, he read them more fables from Krummacher, paraphrasing, and interrupting himself constantly, to enforce what he was saying, by addressing it particularly to individuals; and requiring them now to guess what was coming next, and now to tell what they thought of things said and done. They then all read, and spelled, and, after recess, were placed in their seats, where each found a ruled

blank-book and a lead pencil; with a printed volume, from
which he directed them to copy a passage. Only half a
dozen could write. He told the rest, even the youngest, to
copy in printed letters, and this occupied them very dili-
gently until school was done.

I will here speak somewhat at large of Mr. Alcott's mode
of teaching the art of writing; as it is the result of a good
deal of thought; and has grown out of his own experience
as a teacher. For he early discovered how to obtain a
remarkable command of his pen without instruction from
others; and, having reasoned on the methods which necessity suggested to himself, he has reduced them very happily
to their principles and constructed them into a natural system, whose results have perfectly satisfied him.

When children are committed to his charge very young,
the first discipline to which he puts them, is of the eye;
by making them familiar with pictures. The art of drawing has been well called the art of learning to see; and
perhaps no person ever began to learn to draw, without
astonishment at finding how imperfectly he had always
been seeing. He finds that the most common forms are
not only very falsely defined on his sense, but a vast deal
that is before the eyes, is entirely overlooked. The human
mind seems very gradually to descend from its own infinity
into the details of the finite; and the senses give but little
help when unaided by a developed mind. It has been
demonstrated, not only by the acute reasonings of philoso-
phers, but by observations made on persons,* who have
begun to see at late periods of life, that the eye sees scarcely
any thing but what the mind has suggested beforehand.
Yet by a reciprocal influence of the mind and the organ,
this "avenue of wisdom," may become very broad. By a
little attention to children's habits, and by exercise, their
minds may very early attain great perfection in the use of
this instrument, than which none is finer of all that are
given to us; and none more effective in bringing to our
fixed point in the universe that variety of the Almighty's

* The Scotch boy Mitchell and Casper Hauser, for instance.

manifestation of himself, to which it is necessary for us to have access, in order to be able to clothe our inward life with forms, by which it may manifest itself to kindred beings; carrying them and ourselves on, into harmony with the Divine intellect, and sympathy with his spirit. The Phrenologists say it was their first discovery, that persons who had prominent eyes were remarkable for their powers of learning and using language. Now, as all language is founded on imagery, it follows that fine and perfect organs of sight, giving to the mind vivid impressions of the forms· of things, would make the language of the individual picturesque and lifely, and thus, even without resorting to the theory of Phrenology, the fact of prominent or fine eyes, connected with great powers of language, has an explanation. But without reference to the influence of clear vision upon expression in this way, there can be no doubt of its effect upon thought. The forms of things are God's address to the human soul; they are the first incitement to activity of mind; or, to speak more accurately, they are the first supporters of that activity which is the nature of mind, and which can only be checked by the soul's being starved of nature.

It is from considerations of this kind, that Mr. Alcott very early presents to children pictured forms of things; and he selects them in the confidence that the general character of these forms will do much towards setting the direction of the current of activity, especially if we attend to and favor those primal sympathies, with which nature seems to wed different minds to different portions of the universe.

To aid the practice of the eye, in looking at forms, the practice of the hand in imitating them should soon follow. Mr. Alcott thinks the slate and pencil, or the chalk and black board, can hardly be given too early. The latter is even better than the former; for children should have free scope, as we find that their first shapings are always gigantic. And is it not best that they should be so? Miniature, when it appears first in the order of developement, seems to be always the effect of checked spirit or some artificial influence.

1*

With such education of the eye, as a preliminary, reading and writing may begin simultaneously; and the former will be very much facilitated, and the latter come to perfection in a much shorter time, than by the usual mode. By copying print, which does not require such a sweep of the hand as the script letter, a clear image of each letter is gradually fixed in the mind; and while the graceful curves of the script letter are not attained till afterwards, yet they are attained quite as early as by the common method of beginning with them; and the clearness and distinctness of print, is retained in the script, which, from being left to form itself so freely, becomes also characteristic of each individual's particular mind.

When the pages were presented to Mr. Alcott after their first trial, the hieroglyphics were sufficiently unintelligible it must be confessed. But, (what is another proof of how slowly the mind appreciates the arbitrary and finite,) the serious looks of the children, especially of the younger ones, as they exhibited their strange copies, betrayed no misgiving as to the want of resemblance; nor did Mr. Alcott rudely point it out. He took the writing for what it was meant to be; knowing that practice would at once mend the eye and the hand; but that criticism would check the desirable courage and self-confidence.

In the course of a few days, cards were placed at the desk of each child, on which were very large forms of the letters; and they were encouraged to imitate them. It soon became a regular arrangement for the children to pass their first school hour at this employment, and to return to it after the recess. After some weeks spent in this way, Mr. Alcott taught them the small script letter, but not to supersede the exercises in printing. Indeed, throughout the whole teaching, he recommends that this system of printing should be retained, especially in all those written exercises, which children are tempted to slight; for it prevents the habit of indistinct writing, by keeping the imagination wonted to the original forms of the letters. The ultimate and sure result of this plan, is a simple unflourishing chirography, whose great and characteristic merit is intelligibleness; and constant practice in writing the script, gradually adds to this merit the grace of beauty. When a child begins on this plan of writing at five years of age, by the time he is seven or eight, he has much of the ease of a practised penman, combining considerable rapidity with perfect intelligibleness, and a fair degree of beauty. Mr. Alcott has verified this in many hundreds of instances in his own schools, within ten years. There is a vast deal of difference, however, in the improvement of individuals; and the matter cannot be hurried. Time will accomplish it, in all instances.

It was soon found that Mr. Alcott, with all his mildness, was very strict. When sitting at their desks, at their writing, he would not allow the least inter-communication, and every whisper was taken notice of. When they sat in the semi-circle around him, they were not only requested to be silent, but to appear attentive to him; and any infringement of the spirit of this rule, would arrest his reading, and he would wait, however long it might be, until attention was restored. For some time the acquirement of this habit of stillness and attention was the most prominent subject, for it was found that many of the children had very little self-control, very weak attention, very self-indulgent habits. Some had no humility, and defended themselves in the wrong; a good deal of punishment was necessary, and some impressions upon the body (on the hand;) but still, in every individual instance, it was granted as necessary, not only by the whole school, but I believe, no bodily punishment was given without the assent of the individual himself; and they were never given in the room. In many of the punishments,—in the pauses of his reading, for instance, the innocent were obliged to suffer with the guilty. Mr. Alcott wished both parties to feel that this was the inevitable consequence of moral evil in this world; and that the good, in proportion to the depth of their principle, always feel it to be worth while to share the suffering, in order to bring the guilty to rectitude and moral sensibility.

On all these occasions, he conversed with them; and, by a series of questions, led them to come to conclusions for

themselves upon moral conduct in various particulars;
teaching them how to examine themselves, and to discriminate their animal and spiritual natures, their outward and
inward life; and also how the inward moulds the outward.
They were deeply interested in these conversations, and
would constantly declare this; although, at first, some, who
were very often revealing to themselves and others their
hitherto unrecognized weaknesses and faults, were so
deeply mortified, that it was constantly painful.   The
youngest scholars were as much interested as the oldest,
and although it was necessary to explain language to them
rather more, it was found less necessary to reason on moral
subjects.   They did not so often inquire the history of an
idea, or feeling; but they analysed the feelings which
prompted action better.   It was very striking to see how
much nearer the kingdom of heaven were the little children,
than were those who had begun to pride themselves on
knowing something.   We could not but often remark to
each other, how unworthy the name of knowledge was
that superficial acquirement, which has nothing to do with
self-knowledge; and how much more susceptible to the
impressions of genius, and how much more apprehensive
of general truths were those, who had not been hackneyed
by a false education.

A great deal of time was given to explaining the philosophy of expression.   They were taught to see that sculpture,
painting, and words, were only different modes of expression; and the casts in the room, were spoken of, and they
were led to explain those that were ideal.   Then they were
led to consider gestures, and the *rationale* of manners; and
they were shown that the positions and motions of their
bodies were produced by the mind, and that the mind could
control them, and therefore they were responsible for the
impressions they conveyed in this way, especially while
they were forming their habits, and had not yet become
wonted to any particular ones.   Lastly, they were led to
consider how words bodied forth thoughts, signing external
objects, and suggesting internal facts of the spirit.   External
fact was discriminated from internal truth, and the young-

est children were exercised on such questions as these : Is *love* in the mind, or out of the mind ? Is *size* in the mind, or out of the mind ? Is *a book* in the mind, or out of the mind ? Is *a table* in the mind, or out of the mind ? &c. They soon were able to answer, and seldom made a mistake, especially the younger ones.

One great means, however, of making this subject thoroughly understood, was by reading to them, and fastening their attention ; and then bringing them to attend to the fact of having been thus chained to their chairs by thoughts and feelings in their own minds, which words ha'l waked up. As Mr. Alcott read, his eyes sought all their faces ; a wandering mind was immediately detected, and its sign pointed out ; and he required them, at any moment that he chose to stop, to repeat what he had last said in their own language, to describe the picture he was calling up, or to give the meaning of the allegory. And as the matter was intensely interesting, taken from the master-works of genius, he succeeded in gaining attention, and also its outward signs. They were soon able to catch the meaning of emblems, &c. so as to preclude the necessity of explanations : indeed, from the first, explanations were elicited from themselves, and not given dogmatically.

"Emblems," (to quote Mr. Alcott's own words in a letter to myself,) "I have found to be extremely attractive and instructive to children. I could not teach without them. My own mind would suffer, were it not fed upon ideas in this form ; and spiritual instruction cannot be imparted so well by any other means. The universal spirit flows into nature, whether material or human, through these media ; and sense and imagination are the faculties that receive the divine stream—the one from without, and the other from within—and pour it upon the soul. The manner of Jesus and of Plato is authority, were any needed on this subject, to show what the mind requires in order to be quickened and renewed. *"Without a parable,* spake he not unto them." Neither should the teacher of spiritual truth now-a-days. From neglecting this mode of instruction, we have shorn the young mind of its beams. We have made it prosaic, literal, worldly. We have stripped truth naked, and sent her cold into the world, instead of allowing her to clothe herself with the beautiful associations in which she presents herself in infancy and childhood."

It was in pursuance of these ideas that Mr. Alcott took so much pains at first, to bring out clearly in the children's consciousness, a conception of the spiritual world, as alone having permanence and reality, notwithstanding its invisibleness. And when he read, he constantly asked questions, calculated to keep attention on the ideas in the author's mind, that were clothed with imagery, and signed by words. So successful was he in fixing attention on the spiritual part of any matter, that not only the imagery of poetry, but every incident of a narrative was listened to with an air of thought and investigation, not always seen in adult hearers of reading. To illustrate this fact, I will make an extract in this place from the Journal of February 12th, when Mr. Alcott read from Krummacher, "the birth of the caterpillar."

What is in your mind? said he, to a boy of eight years old, as soon as he had finished. I cannot express it, he replied. Is it a thought, or a feeling?—Both—it is a belief. What have you learned from this story? said Mr. Alcott to another boy of the same age. It reminds me that when the body dies the soul will live and go to heaven. How long have you had that thought? Ever since I was four years old. Do you remember the time when you did not have it? Yes, when I was very little I thought we did not live after our bodies died. Another boy of the same age said, he never remembered the time when he did not believe in life's going on. Do all believe without a shadow of doubt that they shall live after death has taken place? I believe it, said a boy of nine, but not without a shadow of doubt. A boy of six said, when we die, an angel comes from heaven, and takes us—the shell and all. What is the shell? said Mr. Alcott. The body, said another child of the same age. Do you want to stay in your bodies a-while? Yes, said both, with a smile. What did you think while I was reading this story? said Mr. Alcott to a thoughtful little boy of five. I thought God changed the caterpillar into a butterfly, and then there was an angel that went in, and ascended into heaven, and when it got to heaven the butterfly's body fell again to the earth. But where did the butterfly come from? God changed the caterpillar into a butterfly; the body of the caterpillar was changed into the form of a butterfly. Who made the caterpillar? God. What did God make it of? He made it out of dust. Nothing but dust? Nothing but dust. When did the angel go into the butterfly? When it began to move. Where did the angel come from? I did not think—I must stop to think, said he. In a minute he went on. The angel must have been in the worm— some of it. Where did the angel come from? God sent it. Did the angel help to make the caterpillar into a butterfly? No, but God made the body of the caterpillar into the body of a butterfly, and covered over the angel with it. You see it was not a real butterfly but it seemed so to the eyes. It was made to carry the angel up to heaven with its wings. Do you think every butterfly has an angel in it, like that one? Oh no! Well how came it to be so, that particular time? Why God wanted to show Adam and all of them, an angel going to heaven, and he could not do it without something for their eyes. Why did he want to show them an angel going to heaven? Oh! so that they need not mourn any longer for their brother Abel. I think, said I, that God means to put us in mind of the soul's going to heaven by every butterfly that he makes. *Do you?* said he very slowly, his thoughtful countenance lighting up into a bright smile. (Is not that a mind in the kingdom? said Mr. Alcott to me, after this conversation was over.) What does this story bring to your mind? said he to a girl of twelve. The life of the senses—the change of death—and immortality. In the Bible some one says, *I die daily :*—do you understand that? Yes—It means you daily go more and more away from the senses, into the inward life.

Their own reading lessons were also made subservient to this object. Thus, in reading in Frank, the passage beginning, "There was one part of a winter's evening, which Frank liked particularly, &c." Mr. Alcott, called on each one to describe the room, as it pictured itself out in his thoughts ; asking questions about the curtains, chairs, tables, situation of the persons in the rooms, &c. Every one made a different, but each a complete picture.

And here I will give the record that I made of one of the reading lessons of the first class. It was "an address to a dying child," in the Common Place Book of Poetry, and selected by one of the class, eight years old, who began with reading it all through.

Which verse do you like best? said Mr. Alcott. The boy read,

> "Yes, thou art going home,
> Our Father's face to see."

I like those lines very much. Why—what sentiment do they awaken ? The pleasure of seeing God ; dying and going up to stay with God. Have you never seen God here ? Yes, in one way, but I like to think of dying and going up to God ? Which way do you suppose is *up* ? *Up* is by the sun—higher than the sun. Do the people on the other side of this round earth say *up* ? This led to considerations on the illusions of the senses, and what that idea was which was signified by this emblem of place. The idea seemed to be gained ; and the boy paraphrased the lines thus :

> You are going within yourself
> Your Father's face to see thro' your own spirit.

Do you know, said Mr. Alcott, you never would have seen the outward world, except by first going within yourself ? After a long pause of thought, the boy replied, Yes, I see how it is. Why is it said Father's *face* ? I don't know why they say *face*. What do you see in any person's face ? The mind—the expression of the soul,—said he after some hesitation. And if God expresses himself in any way to us, when we go inward, and think over our own faculties and feelings, which are his expressions of love to us, is it not very natural to say we have seen his *face* ? Yes. I cannot help thinking God has a real face, said another boy of the same age. Can you think of your own spirit without thinking of a face ? Yes. Then why not of God's spirit ? I can. Do you think you see more of your brother, when you see his body with your eyes, or think about him in your mind ? said Mr. Alcott to the reader. I realize him when I think of him, sometimes more than when I am looking at him.

Each of the class then read the verse that they liked best. One boy, who had been punished considerably since he came to school, read the verse beginning,

> " Oh Father of our spirits,
> We can but look to thee ;
> Tho' chastened, not forsaken,
> Shall we thy children be." &c.

What is meant by chastened ? said Mr. Alcott. Punished—disciplined. Can one be punished and not forsaken ? Yes. Did you not think when I first punished you, that I hated you ? Yes. You thought I forsook you ? Yes. Do you think so now ? I have not thought so for a great while. You understand now that it was just the contrary of forsaking and hating you, to punish you ? Yes. It was you that forsook me and not I that forsook you ? Yes. Read the two last lines.

> " Teach us to say with Jesus
> Thy will, not ours, be done."

What do these lines express ? Self-sacrifice—self-surrender. One of the girls read the third verse as the most beautiful.

> " Soon shall thy bright young spirit
> From Earth's cold chains be free." &c.

What does it express ? Liberty, said one. Blessedness, said several. What was the leading idea of the first verse ? The expression of the eye ; the appearances of death ; it is descriptive ; picturesque ; were the several answers. What is the idea of the second verse ? The pains and pleasures of this earth, said one. Cannot you express it in one word ? This life ; said he after a pause. What is the object of this life ? said Mr. Alcott. To make us better ; to try us. Oh, the idea of this verse is the trials of life. What is the idea of the fourth verse ? It compares Heaven and Earth, said one. What of the last ? Devotion—faith, said a boy of ten. Well, said Mr. Alcott. Death—human life—heaven, a comparison of the two, and the principle by which we rise from the human to the heavenly life :—this is a beautiful

2

range of thought, is it not? Beautiful, said several. They
were then sent to their seats to write a paraphrase.

This is a fair specimen of the readings. It is plain that
not a great deal of ground can be passed over, but the effect
is to make the reading very expressive, by keeping the
Author's mind constantly before the reader, and interesting
him in the thoughts. There is no greater illusion than the
common idea of the method of learning to read, by pronounc-
ing pages of matter, which is not moving the heart and mind
of the reader. Mr. Alcott's method, in this particular, is so
different from the common one, that it is common to hear
that his scholars do not read at school.

In teaching reading, in the first instance, Mr. Alcott's
method has also been much misunderstood; and because
he thinks a child should never be hurried into or over the
mechanical part of the process, many say and perhaps think,
that he does not think it important for children to learn to
read at all! It will probably, however, be difficult to find
children, who know so well *how to use a book*, when they
are eight years old, as those who have been taught on his
method, which never allows a single step to be taken in any
stage of the process, without a great deal of thinking on the
part of the child. Perhaps a general adoption of Mr. Alcott's
ideas on this subject, would lead to some check upon the
habits of superficial reading, which do so much to counterbalance all the advantages arising from our profusion of
books.

It is a common remark, that the age of much reading is
not an age of creative power. Yet why should it not be?
Would the human mind cease its own appropriate action,
if fed with proper food, in the proper way? We should
not doubt that there is some error in the general method of
acquirement, when it is accompanied by a growing inaction
of the highest, that is, the creative faculties of the soul.
Mr. Alcott thinks that every book read, should be an event
to a child; and all his plans of teaching keep steadily in
mind the object of making books live, breathe, and speak;
and he would consider the glib reading which we hear in
most schools, as a preventive, rather than as an aid to his

purposes. He has himself no doubt as to the ultimate result, not only upon the intellectual powers, but upon the very enunciation of the words; which cannot fail to borrow energy and life from the thoughts and feelings they awaken within the soul of the reader.

But the best reading which children can do for themselves, in the early stages of their education, cannot supersede the necessity of the teacher's reading a great deal to them; because it is desirable that they should early be put in possession of the thoughts of genius, and made to sympathise in the feelings inspired by their master works; as well as have their taste formed on the highest models.

In one of Mr. Alcott's letters, from which I have already quoted, he says, " To form a library, suited to the wants of the young, from modern works, would be impossible. We have few, very few, that nurture the spiritual life. A dozen volumes would include all that are of a quickening and sustaining power. On subjects of mere fancy, and of the understanding, we have many ; but these too often tend to dissipate the wants of the young, and materialize their spirits. I have been seeking works for my purpose for the last ten years, and my library is still scanty ; yet within this period, hundreds of volumes have been contributed to our juvenile literature.

" Indeed, modern works, whether for children or adults, are greatly deficient both in depth and purity of sentiment: they seldom contain original or striking views of the nature of man, and of the institutions which spring from his volition. There is a dearth of thought and sterility of sentiment among us. Literature, art, philosophy, life, are without freshness, ideality, verity, and spirit.

" But the works of some of the more ancient writers are of a more vivid and spiritual character. They are not however to be found in our book stores. Seldom do we see a copy even of Spencer, Jeremy Taylor and Dr. Henry More, to say nothing of other writers of a highly spiritual character, whose names are not so familiar. The age of spiritualism seems to be past, and few are the representations of that age which have come down to us; they are generally only to be found in the libraries of collectors, who value them for their scarcity, or peculiarities of exterior, rather than for their intrinsic merit. In truth, we have fallen so far below the high standard of these authors, both in thought and style, that we do not appreciate their transcendent power. We do not rise to the apprehension of their beauties of language, their richness and profoundness of thought, their delicacy and humanity of sentiment. We are less of metaphysicians than they; i. e. we know less of man; we have less faith in humanity. How affluent are those deep-thoughted minds! How full of wisdom and love! Their thoughts flow from the heart; they are clear, strong, quickening, effective; unlike the sterile notions of modern minds. Open any of these works, and you are upon a deep, rich, fresh thought, clad in imagery all a-glow with life; you feel you are at once in communion with a great spirit; your spiritual faculties are quickening into being, and asserting their prerogative of insight. You are charmed into reflection. But I do not at this moment think of any writers, since the days of Milton, excepting Coleridge and Wordsworth, whose works require a serene and thoughtful spirit, in order to be understood. Most works since this date, require little thought; they want depth, freshness; the meaning is on the surface; and the charm, if there be any, is no deeper than the fancy: the imagination is not called into life; the thoughts are carried creepingly along the earth, and often lost amid the low and uncleanly things of sense and custom.

" In the discharge of my duties as a teacher, therefore, I have found few works to aid me. I have been thrown mostly on my own resources, to create from circumstances, and the ideal of my own mind, the material for the intellectual and spiritual nurture of children. Of the few works that have become established favorites with my scholars, works containing thoughts to which they recur with delight, and which awaken, as it were, a brood of other thoughts in their minds, I can only recollect the Bible, Pilgrim's Progress, The Fairy Queen, Krummacher's Parables—English Translation and Edition, The Story without an End,

Coleridge's Poems, Wordsworth's Poems, Milton's Paradise Lost, Quarles' Emblems.*

"I have this day sent to England for Bunyan and Spencer, as fine copies cannot be procured in this country; and I wish I had added Quarles. It is from these books that I generally read; for, although imagination is acknowledged to be the shaping power of the soul; and, when rightly nurtured by meditation and observation, she clothes the spirit in the chaste and beautiful robes of truth, how seldom is it cultivated among us! I seldom hear any one speak of cultivating this faculty. And yet if there is any fact settled by the history of our race, it is, that imagination has been the guiding energy of light and life to humanity. For what is genius but this faculty in its most vivid action? and genius has shaped the institutions of society in all past ages. We need schools not for the inculcation of knowledge, merely, but for the developement of genius. Genius is the peculiar attribute of soul. It is the soul, indeed, in full and harmonious play; and no instruction deserves the name, that does not quicken this its essential life, and fit it for representation in literature, art, or philosophy."

Pilgrim's Progress, (read with omissions and in paraphrase,) was for the first three months, the greatest favorite of all the above-mentioned books in the school I am describing. The Bible was the next favorite; and in March, the test being made, it was found that they were less willing to give up the readings in the Bible than any thing else. The readings of the Bible are not confined to particular seasons, being constantly called to meet the occasions of the moment; but they come regularly on Saturdays.

Krummacher also comes at no regular periods, but is taken

* Light & Horton have in contemplation, to publish a series of books of a more spiritual character for children, than has yet been attempted. This will include Shoberl's translation of Krummacher, (for the American translation falsifies, as well as abridges the original;) Pilgrim's Progress, prepared by Mr. Alcott, for children; Story without an End; Quarles Emblems; and Pictures of Thought, which is a work Mr. Alcott already has in manuscript, and which will probably be the first of the series.

2*

up whenever the influence of his beautiful spirit, is needed, to give life and power to the moral discipline, or to illustrate the subject of thought which is on hand. Mr. Alcott also read to them the allegory of the cave from Plato, which they themselves explained, and which they admired very much. He also read the death of Socrates, from the Phædo, which called forth their tears; and was only second in effect to the story of the Crucifixion; which was very powerful, not so much by its pathos, as by its life-enkindling sublimity. But I am anticipating results.

The spiritual eye when it had been closed was not immediately opened. At first we had some trouble with the older scholars, who affected to laugh at the simplicity of the incidents in Krummacher; but when they found afterwards, that they had included, unawares, some of the standard works of literature, and even some of the history and words of Christ in what they called Mr. Alcott's "baby stories," they were shamed into silence, and their next step was to endeavor to follow lead, and interest themselves as much as they could in the spiritual things that, in spite of themselves, they found most interesting.

The first two months were given up almost entirely to this preliminary discipline. Two hours and a half every day were divided between the readings and conversations on conduct, and the comparative importance of things within and without. The government was decided and clear from the first; but was not hurried beyond the comprehension of the children; for Mr. Alcott is so thoroughly convinced that all effectual government must be self-government, that he much prefers that all the operations of school should obviously stand still, than that they should go on *apparently*, while standing still or going back *really*, in any individual instance. If it should be objected to this principle, that the good are here made to wait upon the bad; it may be answered, that the good are learning the divinest part of human action, even the action of Christ, when they are taught to wait upon the bad for their improvement; and that there are seldom such actual discrepancies in children of but a few years difference of age, as that any harm can result to the best, from being brought to the contemplation of the worst; especially when the worst, as in every case in this school, express themselves sincerely desirous of becoming better; and not one is so bad as not to have been able to ask for punishment, at some gracious season.

One thing, however, should be remarked, as a caution to young teachers. It will be seen in the subsequent journal that Mr. Alcott is very autocratic. But it must be remembered that this is dangerous ground for a young, or rather for an inexperienced teacher, to take. It is not, in this instance, taken by an inexperienced teacher. Mr. Alcott has taught school for twelve years. During the first several years, he felt himself hardly any thing but a learner, on this sacred ground.—He did not, for many years, enforce authority in any instance, unless it was sanctioned by the unanimous voice of a school, sometimes of a school of an hundred pupils. So reverent was he of the voice of nature, that he chose to hear all its varying tones, before he ventured to feel that he sufficiently understood what he was dealing with, to raise his own voice above theirs, in confidence of harmonising them. That time of self-reliance, however, came at last; and he now is able to have faith in the moral response from the heart of the child, which he once only hoped for. This autocracy, therefore, is not derivative but original. It is drawn from experience and observation; and, I should add that it continually takes counsel from these, its sources. And is not this legitimate, in the moral sense of the word? Are not the laws of human nature sufficiently intelligible, to enable sensibility, and observation, and years of experience at last to construct a system, whose general principles need not to be reviewed, in every instance of application to every scholar? It is true that every scholar may afford new phenomena; and that the teacher who does not observe these as materials of thought, in private review of the principles on which he acts, thereby to enlarge them or rectify such small errors of application, as the wisest may fall into, omits the best means of perfecting himself and his art. Besides, a teacher never should forget that the mind he is directing, may be on a larger scale than his own;

that its sensibilities may be deeper, tenderer, wider ; that its imagination may be infinitely more rapid ; that its intellectual power of proportioning and reasoning may be more powerful; and he should ever have the humility to feel himself at times in the place of the child, and the magnanimity to teach him how to defend himself against his own (i. e. the teacher's) influence. By such humility, he will also be in the best road towards that deeply felt self-reliance, which is founded on sober self-estimation, although entirely removed from vanity. And I believe I do Mr. Alcott no more than justice when I say of him—that he answers Wordsworth's description of the man—

> " Who in the silent hour of inward thought,
>   Can still suspect, and still revere himself,
>   In lowliness of heart."

From the commencement of the school, an hour every day was given to the Latin class, which included about one third of the scholars. They commenced with Walker's Latin Reader, at the beginning of the Historiæ Sacræ, and were required to learn by heart both Latin and English. In order to facilitate this, I would read over a sentence with the English meaning to each word, and let each one repeat it, with the English ; and by the time I had arrived at the end of the class, with the sentence, those who sat at the head could say it without the book. One or two, who had studied Latin before, used the Latin Tutor, and wrote the first exercises ; and when some of the brighter ones would get ahead of the others in the translation, I gave them lessons in the Grammar—the paradigms of the verbs and nouns. By these means, in a few months they had laid quite a foundation of translated Latin in their minds, on which to erect a knowledge of the principles of the language.

At the end of December, it was astonishing to see what a change had taken place in the pupils; what self-control, attention, intelligent ways of doing what was to be done, what thoughtfulness, what knowledge of language, and what understanding of Mr. Alcott's views, had been produced. He then thought it best to suspend the daily reading to them for a while: and to require more exercises to be performed by themselves independently. The older children commenced the keeping of journals. A course of lessons was given to the whole school, on the science and art of Numeration, from Lovell's Arithmetic; and a course of lessons on the Map of Massachusetts, which they were required to draw. We were however dissatisfied with our method of teaching Geography, and concluded to lay aside this study for some weeks. And when the lessons on Numeration, and some of the first rules of Arithmetic had been given, on their black-boards and their slates, they all returned to Colburn's Mental Arithmetic. English grammar lessons were also introduced, which will be explained in the journal.

But before making any more remarks, I will proceed to give a few weeks of the Journal continuously. I do this, because I wish to show the school, as it is; and to let be seen what proportion of time and attention is given to each study. I have not entered into the details, it is true, of the Arithmetic, Geography, and Latin lessons; although nearly two hours of every day are given to these. The spelling, and reading, and parsing of English, are the lessons which more especially cultivate the spirit; and therefore they come first in the morning; and occupy more than half the school hours. The other lessons come in the latter half of the day.

Before beginning the Journal, I must premise, in justice both to the school and to myself, that the record being made at the moment, a great deal was omitted, for it was impossible to seize and fix with the pen, many of the most beautiful turns, and episodes of the conversation; especially as I often took part myself; and the various associations of thought in so large a company often produced transitions which seemed very abrupt.

JOURNAL—When I arrived at the school-room just after nine o'clock, December 28th, I found all the children studying a spelling lesson in Lee's Spelling Book. They were in the words of four letters. This lesson is studied by their writing a given number of words on their slates, or in their manuscript books; those who do not yet write the script hand, printing them. After writing the words, they spell them

to themselves, and when they think they can arrange the letters rightly, they look out the meanings of each word, in their
dictionaries : a copy of Johnson's Dictionary being placed
at each desk.   Mr. Alcott has chosen Lee's Spelling Book,
because it has in it all the primitive words of the language ;
and the derivatives which are roots in relation to other words.

During this time of silent study, Mr. Alcott walks
about, preparing pencils and pens at each seat, and making
remarks.   For the study of this lesson, an hour is generally
appropriated ; which gives time for the journalists, also, to
learn it.   About a quarter before ten, Mr. Alcott takes the
seven younger members of this spelling class, as they cannot use a dictionary very intelligently, and lets them spell
the words over to him, and he tells them their meanings.
Of this, the rest of the class can take advantage, if they
choose.   All, however, are thrown into one class at ten o'-
clock ; when two concentric semi-circles are formed in front
of Mr. Alcott's table, and the spelling, defining, and illustration of the words commence.   The arrangements are made
without words on the part of the scholars.   The division
which sit at the table, merely push back their chairs, so as
to be a little farther apart ;—and the others, who sit generally with their faces to the wall, turn round in their seats quietly ; and are almost a semi-circle before they draw up behind the smaller arc.   Every chair is at a little distance from
its neighbor's, of which the size of the room admits, and
which is an easy mode of preventing intercommunication.
Mr. Alcott shows much judgment in diminishing temptation
by his arrangements.   And every day before they turn in
their seats, he reminds them that it can be done without
noise.   It is very desirable to speak to children before hand,
in regard to all such things ; for they fail in such duties from
want of forethought, rather than from insensibility to the
obligations of duty ; and they are always grateful for being
prevented from doing wrong ; but are often depressed by
being reproved for it, when it was inadvertent.

After they were arranged to spell, the question arose
whether any thing would be wanted before eleven o'clock ?
Several answered, that they should wish to go to the fire.

Mr. Alcott talked to them a while to convince them, that all could not go to the fire; that it would be unjust for some of them to be selected for the purpose; and that all could bear without injury, any degree of cold they might be subjected to this morning. He added, moreover, that the stove was to be altered, and made to give forth more heat, and that it was worth while to make the present an occasion for the exercise of self-control. One boy said that he did not see any use in having self-control; but from the manner as well as the matter of this remark, Mr. Alcott concluded it was made in sport; he could not believe that this boy really thought that fortitude was not a virtue. He therefore passed it over, saying he had no time except for serious conversation.

Thirty words were spelled; and then they were taken up, one by one; and not merely defined, but illustrations of all their meanings, literal and imaginative, were given, either by original or remembered sentences, which contained the word in question. This course led often to disquisitions on the subject to which the word was imaginatively applied.

During this lesson on words, which Mr. Alcott considers one of the most important exercises in the school, he requires profound attention from every scholar. A whisper, a movement, a wandering look arrests him in what he says, and he immediately calls the scholar by name. When he asks a question, all who can answer it must hold up their hands, and he selects one,—sometimes he asks every member of the class,—to give what is in his mind upon the word. The most general and strict attention is the result.

Lone was the first word defined. Did you ever feel *lone, lonely?* said Mr. Alcott. Yes. Always, when there was no person present?—No. Ever, when there were people present?—Yes. This led to the conclusion that loneliness was in the mind, a feeling independent of circumstances; as one could be alone in a crowd; (Lord Byron was quoted on this subject;) but that the feeling could not exist when the soul was conscious of the omnipresent friendship of its Father, as it may always be.

Look was defined. How does the soul *look out?* said Mr.

Alcott. Through the eyes. How does the soul *look in?* A very little boy said, by the thoughts turning round. A large boy said—the soul looks in with the eyes, as well as out. Mr. Alcott said, is not the soul itself an eye? And what are conscience and reflection? The soul's looks upon itself? *Reflection,* said a girl, twelve years old, seems to imply a looking-glass. Mr. Alcott replied, it is not a good name for the act of mind I was speaking of; and I seldom use it. Conscience is the soul's knowledge of its moral laws; reflection, is the soul's knowledge of its intellectual laws; but there is a better word for this;—which has gone out of use, —intellection. One of the little boys asked what was the name of the soul's *look* upon things? Mr. Alcott said it was commonly named perception ; but he added, *I* believe that all the shapes we see without, exist within the mind first ; and when the shape that is without, comes before us, the shape which is within, wakes up out of its sleep : and I believe the shape within us is perfect, whether the shape without is so or not. He illustrated this, by asking them if the man who made the Temple, did not have a picture in his mind of the Temple, before it was made, &c.?

Meek was defined, and Mr. Alcott described a meek character, and said there were some meek ones in school, and asked if they knew who they were; but they need not say. He should like to have each one think for himself, if he was meek. One boy said, if I thought I was meek I would not say so, lest the other boys should say I was proud. Eighteen hundred years ago, there was a meek one on earth, said Mr. Alcott. They all exclaimed, I know who that was. He passed on, and they defined more words, which were talked over in the same way.

Then there was recess half an hour. And after recess I took my Latin scholars into the anti-room ; and Mr. Alcott heard the rest read in Frank, and parse English. The latter exercise was conducted in this way. He divided his black-board into three parts thus :

Persons.	Things.	Actions.

And then asked them what words out of the page they had read, he should put down in these several compartments. This was an exercise in which he had drilled them before.

December 30th.—When I came to school, I found all the children in their seats, at their lessons. Mr. Alcott, who was walking round as usual, was saying to one of the journalists: You are engaged in recording what happens *out of you*; its advantage is to make you feel and remember what *effect* all outward events, and your action on what is outward, may have on your inward state of mind.—You write down the picture made on your mind by things. I hope you will soon write the thoughts and feelings that come up from your soul about these things. These thoughts and feelings are your inward life. Do you understand this;—the spiritual world is the inward life of all beings? All the journalists were looking at him as he asked this question; and they replied very animatedly, yes; and then turned back to their writing.

It was sometime, however, before the journals which were commenced by those who could write the script hand, became any record of the inward life. The children were entirely unused to composition, and for some time they only set down circumstances, and the most dry and uninteresting ones. Mr. Alcott, however, contented himself with expressing the hope that bye and bye, we should have more thoughts mingled with the record of facts; and he made no criticisms on the language, or even on the spelling; knowing that courage is easily checked, in these first efforts, by criticism; and wishing to produce freedom as a condition of free expression. He did not expect interesting views from them, until their minds were more thoroughly trained to self-inspection and inward thought. He has little reliance on any method of producing the impulse to composi-

3

tion, excepting on the indirect one of leading children to think vividly and consecutively, which leads of itself to expression. And still less has he any reliance upon the power of a composition which was not the result of an inward impulse. A mere mechanical exercise, leads to a tame and feeble style, which it is a misfortune to acquire, and which generates no desire to write more; but it is spontaneous to endeavor to express energetically, what one feels vividly and conceives clearly; and any degree of success in this, inspires ardor for new attempts.

In some of Mr. Alcott's former schools, he has tested this theory by trial, and found the result satisfactory. Very interesting composition had come out of the boys' journals, and in correspondence with him, of which some specimens will be given in this volume.*

Instructors are not, perhaps, aware how much the art of composition is kept from being developed in children, by petty criticism. Children have a great deal to contend with, in the attempt to express their thoughts. In the first place, they find it more difficult than better trained minds do, to preserve their thoughts in their memory; while the mechanical labor of holding the pen, of seeing to the spelling, of pointing, and all such details, interferes with the purely mental effort. And even when all this is mastered, and they express original thought, it is like putting out a part of themselves, and they are intensely alive to its reception, in proportion to its real originality, and if it is misunderstood, or its garb criticised, they shrink more than they would at a rude physical touch, and will be very much tempted to suppress their own thoughts, on another occasion, and only attempt the common places, for which they have *heard* expressions.

For there seems to be in all finely attempered spirits, a natural modesty, sometimes even a shrinking delicacy, which instinctively forbids exposure of the invisible exercises of the mind and heart, except to the eye of a generous liberality and a tender love: and it is only time for reflection and

* See Appendix.

a fully realised faith, which gives the strength of mind that may separate the sense of personality from the expression of general truth and beauty; and make clear and possible to them the duty of reposing on the intrinsic worth of what is said, and at all events frankly to express themselves.

And is there not a beautiful cause for the modesty of childhood and genius? Is not the ideal, in these instances, more vivid, to which their own actual creation is so painful a contrast, that if they are forced to attend to the discrepancy, they are discouraged? It has been remarked that the first essays of high genius are seldom in perfect taste, but exhibit "the disproportions of the ungrown giant." This can be easily explained. Genius is apt to feel most deeply the infinite, and never losing sight of even those connections which it does not express, is unaware of the imperfections of what is seen by others, which is only a part of what is created in its own being. But if left to a natural development, and unhindered by internal moral evil, the mind always works itself out to perfect forms; while premature criticism mildews the flower, and blasts the promised fruit.

This case of genius is not irrelevant. Intellectual education, as an art, is an embodiment of all those laws and means, which the development of genius manifests to be the best atmosphere for the production of creative power. For all minds are to be cherished by the same means by which genius is developed. In the first place, we never know but we have genius to deal with among our pupils, and should therefore always make our plan with reference to it; knowing that the smallest degree of mind is also benefited in its due proportion, by the discipline which brings out the highest, and is certainly quenched by those processes from which genius suffers. It would not perhaps be going too far to say, that the period of school education is too early a period for criticism on any original production.— There is only one fault which may be excepted from this rule, and that is affectation, a style which proceeds from want of the sentiment of truth. Even this, however, should not be taken up as literary blunder, but as moral evil, of which it is an expression, quite as much as affectation of manners, and want of veracity.

Thursday, December 31st.—When I came into school a few minutes after school began, the children were all writing in their seats, either their journals, or their spelling lessons.

While attending to the smaller division to day, Mr. Alcott was once or twice interrupted by the speaking in a whisper of some of the girls, and by one of the boys' making a noise with his book; he spoke to them to show them that they interfered by this thoughtlessness with his hearing the lesson, and he contrasted their noisy movement with his own quiet ones, in making his arrangements. Mr. Alcott requires profound quietness in school. He thinks that children are morally benefitted by being obliged to exercise such constant self-control; and he presents to them this as a motive, not less frequently than the convenience of others. In giving to the smaller division instruction upon the spelling lesson, he showed to them how the words might be pronounced wrong, and spelled wrong, and thus fixed their attention upon the precise letters used, and their sounds in each particular instance.

When it was ten o'clock, Mr. Alcott observed that the hour for spelling was arrived; but that they could not turn round quietly without thought. They turned round very quietly. Some remarks were made to some boys, because they had made a noise with their books; he said it could be avoided by arrangement. He illustrated the subject by referring to what was a good machine. A perfect machine, he said, was one which made the least noise. Every wheel moved so as not to interfere with the other parts in a perfect machine. When the machine of this school was perfect, *every wheel*, that is, *every boy* would move without jarring against any other. Two boys said they were not wheels, they were very sure, and one added that he did not know what Mr. Alcott meant. Mr. Alcott, who doubted his ingenuousness, expressed surprise at his want of imagination, but very carefully explained his figurative language. All the rest seemed to understand.

He asked if any body would want any thing during the hour of recitation. One boy asked for some water to drink, but soon after acknowledged that he did not need any, and he would not take it when Mr. Alcott told him he might. Mr. Alcott had suggested that when one boy went for water, it excited the desire in a half dozen, which, perhaps, led him to feel that it was wrong to ask for it. Some of the younger boys asked to go out, and were allowed to do so, and Mr. Alcott waited for them to return, making remarks all the time. He then put out the words, which were all spelled right.

In hearing the definitions, he gave the meanings and asked them to guess what the words were. Some considerations were thus brought up in regard to words nearly synonymous, and the discriminations between them. A good deal was said about the word *nice*, which was decided as meaning *attention to small things*. The word *node* was referred to its latin original, and the figure, by which the intersection of the moon's orbit with the earth's is called a *node*, was explained.

The word *none* was referred to its origin in the words *no-one*. Mr. Alcott asked them if they could think of *nothing at all*, or if they did not think of *some* or *one* in order to be able to get the abstract idea of nothing. I cannot remember this metaphysical disquisition, which, of course, consisted of questions, calculated to give them a realising sense of their not *understanding* unity, and which probably conveyed nothing more. Mr. Alcott thinks it wise to let the children learn the limits of the understanding by occasionally feeling them.

Afterwards Mr. Alcott remarked that when they obtained one thought, they got more than a person who had earned five thousand dollars. The oldest boy said he thought five thousand dollars was better than a thought. Mr. Alcott said that thoughts were the wealth of heaven. Another boy said that he should rather have five thousand dollars than all the thoughts he had this last hour. Mr. Alcott said, here is a boy that prefers five thousand dollars to his mind. The boy replied that he did not do that, but only to the thoughts of this last hour. Mr. Alcott replied that the thoughts even of this hour were mind. The boy replied

3*

that the thoughts of the last hour were not all his mind. Mr. Alcott said that was very true; and possibly he had thought no thoughts in the last hour; but he was going on the supposition that he had had thoughts, when he said that the last hour was worth more to him than five thousand dollars. One boy said he should prefer five thousand dollars to the thoughts of this last hour, even if he had had any. Mr. Alcott said, " Lay not up for yourselves treasures on earth, where moth and rust do corrupt, but lay up treasures in heaven, (that is *thoughts* in your mind; feelings in your soul,) where moth and rust do not corrupt." They all said they should prefer the treasures of heaven to money; but some thought they might have the treasures of earth also. Mr. Alcott said it was very often the case that the desire for the latter interfered with that of the former; Jesus had said, it was easier for a camel to go through the eye of a needle than for a rich man of his time to be a Christian, which involved giving up his riches, and putting them in a common stock. One boy said he wanted money for his relations. Mr. Alcott said, that was a very good object; but the " Meek One," they had spoken of, once said to a young man who had kept the commandments from his youth, " One thing thou lackest," and had bid him go and sell all that he had; and then this *good* young man found his treasure was on earth, a piece of self-knowledge which Jesus meant to convey. (This story was told because one boy had said he could be good enough even if he were engaged in getting riches.) There was a good deal of conversation on this subject, and as it closed, Mr. Alcott asked them if they were sorry to hear such kind of conversation? If any of them did not like it, he wished they would hold up their hands. No one held up his hands.

The word *pall* led to the consideration of the source of *palling*. It was explained as arising from previous self-neglect when life palled upon the soul. It was because the soul was not alive and active.

The word *palm* led to the word palmistry and its absurdity; and to a consideration of the true sources of knowledge, which opened out an interesting field of thought.

The word *pain* led to a consideration of the uses of pain. He spoke of Pain as a good angel with a mask.

The word *pang* led to a consideration of the word *sensation*, for it was defined a sudden sensation, and sensation the boy said was a feeling. One said a pang is a sudden sensation of pain. Another said, two boys were swimming, one had a sudden pang of the cramp. Another said, when a master says he is going to keep me after school, I feel a *pang*. Mr. Alcott quoted Coleridge's "keen pangs of love." It was decided that pang did not refer to bodily pain, so often as to mental, and especially to moral pains. One boy said that men felt pangs when they were turned out of heaven. Mr. Alcott asked him if he thought God *turned people* out of heaven? A little girl said *that* was a pang that came when one told a lie. A boy said a murderer felt a pang. Mr. Alcott then returned to the turning out of heaven. He said whenever you are angry, you turn yourself out of heaven. The boy said *he* did not mean heaven in *that* sense. Mr. Alcott asked him if heaven was a place, and God sitting there, tumbling people out of heaven; is that the picture in your mind? All the boys seemed to feel the absurdity of this. Mr. Alcott said wicked things turn the soul out of heaven, for heaven is a state.

Pant led to a consideration of the state of mind described in the sentence "As a hart panteth after the water-brooks, so doth the soul after God;" and he asked one boy if he ever desired goodness enough to be said to pant after it? While talking of this, he interrupted himself and said, but you are tired of this conversation: they all burst forth that they were not. Show it to me then by your attentive looks.

Mr. Alcott then told a short story which had the word *pelt* in it, in order to illustrate the word, and which seemed to amuse them very much. *Pelt* was defined as being struck on the *skin*. The story was of a boy stealing apples. The three oldest boys seemed to think they should have done as the boy did, because they thought the stealing showed the boy's courage and spirit. And his impudence to an old man in the story, seemed to be more admirable

still, in their eyes; and they said they would not have acknowledged the fault and asked pardon. Mr. Alcott made
some remarks to lead them to think that it was really magnanimous to ask pardon when in the wrong; but they
were not, or affected that they were not convinced.

One of the larger boys remarked that the recess-hour
was come. Mr. Alcott said that boy was particularly *nice*,
always, about every moment of recess, and not equally nice
about the school hours; he took time out of school hours to
speak of the recess-time; and Mr. Alcott observed that he
should not let this boy go out for a quarter of an hour to
day. Another boy said *that* was not just. Mr. Alcott
asked the rest, if they thought it just. Almost all held up
their hands deciding that it was just. Mr. Alcott then
asked the young judge why he thought it not just? He
said he did not know. Mr. Alcott told him that he might
sit also and think a quarter of an hour, and perhaps he
would find out. He told two younger boys also that they
might sit a quarter of an hour too, because they had been
so inattentive, and had moved about so much during the
recitation. In order to amuse them, I proposed to read the
journal written above. When the time was out, the two
older boys both jumped up, to go out, with a very peculiar
air. Mr. Alcott said that he thought their remaining a
quarter of an hour had not done them any good, and he
told them to remain the rest of the time. This was on account of observations he had made upon them while I was
reading the journal, and which consequently I did not
make, and cannot put down. Some conversation ensued,
in which Mr. Alcott endeavored to make them understand
why and how it was his duty to keep them within during
this recess; and they professed to acquiesce in his views.

After recess, I took my Latin scholars into the other
room, and Mr. Alcott heard the others read and parse, and
gave them arithmetic lessons.

January 1st. 1835.—I arrived a few minutes past nine,
and found most of the children at the school. There were
many exclamations as the children entered, one by one, of
" Happy new year!" which Mr. Alcott allowed, although it
is generally the rule that not a word should be spoken.

The older scholars were writing their journals, and the younger were writing the words of the spelling lessons.

As Mr. Alcott was walking round, mending the pens, and preparing the pencils, he talked to the children as he passed them, about happiness and pleasure; the difference between them, and the sources of happiness. Pleasure, he said was bodily, happiness was mental. One of the little girls brought to me, and also to Mr. Alcott, little pieces of her handy-work as new year's gifts.

At about ten minutes before ten o'clock, Mr. Alcott very quietly moved back the chairs of the little boys, who sit round his table, making them form an arc of a circle, of which he was the centre. Then he told the other children, (who had learnt their spelling lessons) to arrange the words in separate columns, according as they expressed objects, actions, qualities, or relations. This is an exercise in grammar, in which Mr. Alcott had before assisted them. The scale for this morning was

Objects.	Actions.	Qualities.	Relations.

The boys copied the scale from the black board on their own slates, and were allowed to take the spelling lesson for their vocabulary.

This is the true way of beginning to study English Grammar. In all sciences, the principles of classification should always be understood, before the nomenclature is presented; but in none is it so important as in the science of grammar, whose very material requires an effort of abstraction in order to be apprehended, and whose nomenclature is particularly hard, being composed of foreign words; or of English words in obsolete meanings, or most awkwardly figurative; a nomenclature, which instead of helping the mind to the acquisition of the science, as the nomenclature of chemistry does, really interferes with the progress of acquisition, by seeming so entirely extraneous to the subject in hand. Were it not for the convenience of understanding the grammars of foreign languages, it would be better to have the whole nomenclature of English Grammar given up.   English Grammar can be taught, however, before the nomenclature is attended to; and then the nomenclature may be learnt as a separate affair, merely for the purpose of leading into foreign languages.

Having suggested this grammatical exercise to the elder scholars, as a means of filling up the hour, if they should learn their lesson in spelling and defining, before he was ready to hear it, Mr. Alcott attended to the division of the class before him. First, he pronounced all the words in the lesson, and then each of the class pronounced them. Having done this, he directed their attention to the marks of accent, sound, and quantity over the words, and asked them if they knew what they meant; they said, No. He said, sometime he would tell them what they meant. He then described these little marks, and led them to observe their forms, and told them he should ask them to describe them to him another day.

It is very important in teaching young children to direct their attention very carefully to things in detail, and to each detail at a separate time, for the synthetic is the first mode of perception; it is an effort for the mind to analyse the tout-ensemble of sensation or of thought into the parts. The intuitive act of the mind puts things together. A child not only associates outward things with each other very rapidly, but associates the actual picture with the ideal whole; and merges the boundaries of the finite in the great infinite from which it has lately drawn its being. Other people cannot aid the intuitions of the mind, so much as its analyses, and its understanding. In one sense, however, the intuitions of the mind may be aided: they may be helped by sympathy, and by removing all the hindrances of development. But the understanding process can be helped a good deal, and it must be done by directing the attention to details, by directing *the senses*, for (although this is a fact that teachers do not generally advert to,) the education of the senses in children is naturally *behind* that of the higher faculties of the soul. Emotions, feelings, intuitions, come first, and interfere with the perceptions of the external world, by their over mastering predominance.

At ten o'clock, Mr. Alcott told the rest of the school to turn round; but not until he had remarked that there was a wrong and a right way of doing it. He then told the small division of the class to open their books, and look upon them while he heard the older division spell. He first himself spelled the words and required them to pronounce them, and this led to some remarks upon particular words whose pronunciation is disputed. He required them afterwards to spell the words to him.

After the words were spelled, Mr. Alcott asked those to hold up their hands, who had been as attentive as they would have been to a *coasting* frolic. Some held up their hands and some did not. He then said that whoever interrupted him while the definitions were talked about, should be deprived of the pleasure of recess. He asked if that was *just*, they all held up their hands that it was just.

The word *nook* was put out and defined *corner*. He then asked if there was a nook in the room, which led to a doubt of the perfect accuracy of this definition. He asked if any one remembered a line of poetry in which the word nook occurred, for it was a word oftener used in poetry than in prose. One boy remembered a line. Mr. Alcott asked if they had any *nooks* in their minds. Some said they had. Mr. Alcott said he was sorry,—that a perfect mind had no nooks, no secret places.

The word *nose* led to a consideration of its uses; and its convenient situation in our own faces, and also in the heads of those animals, who need a still more perfect organ for their purposes. There was a long conversation about cultivating the senses, and on the abuse of the senses by cultivating them too much.

The word *note* was referred to its Latin original *to know.* Mr. Alcott said he should like to have them give a practical definition of it, he wished they would *note him and his instructions.* All the derivatives, *notion, notice, notary,* &c. were considered.

The word *noun* was referred to its Latin original *nomen*.
Mr. Alcott defined *noun* as the name of any object *in* the
mind, or *out* of the mind; the verbal type of the object of
thought, whether *existing in*, or *shaped out* of the mind;
and then he asked each one to tell him what a noun was,
and they all gave answers, some of which he corrected,
filling up those that were inadequate. He then took up a
book, and asked what that was; some said a book, and
some said a noun. He said, what! is *this* book a *noun?*
they replied, no, the *word* book is a noun. He asked if
the book was *existing in* or *shaped out* of the mind, they
replied, *shaped out*. He asked if the hour-glass was *existing in* or *shaped out?* they said *out*. He asked how it
was with virtue? and they said *in the mind*. *New year*
they said was both *out* and *in*. He then took up Frank
and read words which they referred to the right classes,
whether denoting *in* or *out* of the mind.

The word *null* was defined as annihilate, but the word
annihilate was not pronounced right, and it was evidently
a mere dictionary definition. Mr. Alcott said *null* meant
void, without force or meaning: some people's words are
null; some people's whole characters are *null*. He then
spoke of the derivations *nullify* and *nullification*, but he did
not enter into them.

It was eleven o'clock, and they began to fidget; Mr.
Alcott asked who was tired of explaining these words, and
one of the boys held up his hand. Mr. Alcott asked
another boy what a *word* was? He replied, something
made out of letters. The next boy said, a word is a
thought shaped out by letters. Mr. Alcott replied, or a
feeling; feeling may be denoted by inarticulate sounds
also; as oh! ah! &c. Why do you come to school? To
learn, said several. Yes, said he, to learn *words;* to learn
to *word* your thoughts; this is a *word shop*. What do you
come to school for, then? he repeated. To *buy* words,
said one. I said, to *word your thoughts*. *Words*, then, are
the signs of *thoughts*. What great things *words* are! a
word has saved a life when spoken at the right time.
Mary, said he, do you remember that it is said somewhere,

In the beginning was the Word, and the Word was with God, and the Word was God :—What does Word mean there? It means God, said she. Yes, language is a sign of God, a representation of God in the world, said he : how important then are *words ;* how sacred should be our use of them ; how carefully should we learn them ; how carefully should we express our thoughts in words, in order to have them what they should be. Don't you know how painful it is to hear people *swear ?* That is a wrong use of words. He added, that he was sorry he had not time to talk longer of the passage of the Bible he had quoted, as it had a great deal of meaning. I was sorry he did not take time to observe to them, that *word,* in that passage was probably used in a still more general sense than *Language,* meaning *the expression of Truth in all ways,* including action as the highest.

The word *park* led to a description of the chase, which afforded many animating pictures. These were the most important words defined, before recess.

At twelve o'clock, all the children came in, and found their slates ready ; those around Mr. Alcott's table had sums to do from Fowle's Child's Arithmetic. The rest, except the seven oldest, found their slates ready for the grammatical exercise, for which the words were to be found in Frank.

The reading class consisted of the seven oldest. They took the A. C. P. B. of Poetry. The reading lesson was Pinckney's *Evergreens.*

Mr. Alcott asked, what is the subject? Evergreens. Whose thoughts are these? Pinckney's. What are evergreens? Plants which are green all the year. Have you seen any in any house or church lately? Yes, in the Episcopal churches. Can evergreens be made to mean any thing? There was no answer, and he added ; I suppose there is nothing in the external world, but it will suggest to us some thoughts. Before we observe what thoughts Pinckney has on evergreens, let us *think* what evergreens suggest to us. What do you think they teach you about *death ?* They thought they rather taught them about life,

4

the soul, which lasts forever, than death. Mr. Alcott remarked, neither Mr. Pinckney or the evergreens are here; the question is, how can we get thoughts about the evergreen from his mind ? *By his words,* they said.

There was a noise. Mr. Alcott turned to the boy that made it, and said that the greatest and most powerful things made no noise. Did you ever hear the sun make a noise ? There was immediately a profound stillness.

Then the class read the lesson, each one reading the whole ; and so did Mr. Alcott. He asked which they liked best, the descriptive or the reflective part? One boy said the descriptive ; the rest, that the *reflection* at the end was most interesting. He asked if any of them in looking at outward objects, as Mr. Pinckney did in this instance, were conscious of reflections like these ? Some of them thought they were. He asked them where they lived most, in the outward world, or in the inward world of thought and feeling? Various answers were given, one thought she was growing to live in the inward world, more and more every day. Mr. Alcott asked if they knew any one who lived a great deal in the inward world? They said yes; and he said he also knew a man who lived a reflective, spiritual, inward life, more than almost any other ; and yet he seemed to enjoy the outward world more than other persons, who lived in it exclusively; and when he spoke, he gave the most beautiful descriptions of whatever was outward. How was that? It was because his mind was in harmony (and he felt its harmony,) with the outward world. They guessed he was speaking of a certain individual whom they named, which led to some anecdotes concerning him. I told them of a remark this individual once made on hearing a lady sing after the interval of a year, when he perceived that the pleasure of hearing music was increased although the acuteness of his hearing was diminished. And also an analagous remark which he made on seeing a cast of the Venus, six years after seeing the original ; both of which remarks were calculated to prove that the improvement of the mind could more than counterbalance the decay of the senses, in giving us the perception of beauty in forms and sounds.

Mr. Alcott then called on the children to paraphrase the two first verses of this poetry; and to paint out in their minds distinctly the two pictures, of summer evergreens, dark in the midst of its gorgeousness; and of autumn evergreens, bright amid the wintry landscape. He then asked them if they had ever experienced the change of the aspect of a thought under different circumstances? This question required a good deal of illustration and explanation, especially as they are hardly old enough to have experienced much of this change. He afterwards paraphrased this piece himself, but said he had not done it well. He told them they might all turn round and write a paraphrase of these three verses themselves.

Mr. Alcott then took the class in the Child's Arithmetic and asked the first boy to read the first question, and answer it, which he did. (All of them had the books, in which there were questions without answers.) And he went round the class, calling on each to read and to answer the questions one after another.

After this lesson, he told these little boys to put down their arithmetics, and take their Franks, and then he told those who had been attending to the grammar exercise to turn round in their places and take their Franks also. It was now one o'clock, and many of the children had leave from their parents to go home, and, consequently, lost this lesson.

He commenced the Frank lesson by making them analyse the first sentence, and put the words into the grammatical classes, and he put the words down on the black board as they suggested. Verbs and participles were classed together under the head of actions. Pronouns were called substitutes; nouns were called objects; prepositions were called relations; adverbs and adjectives were called qualities; adverbs of time were set aside without any name. He explained prepositions thus: He asked what relation a book that he held in his hand had to a bunch of pens on the table. They said *over*. Having asked a dozen such questions, he showed them that they gave *prepositions* for the answers every time. He then referred to their books and made them tell what relations the prepositions in the passage before them denoted. He asked them about the word *the*, and finding they did not know how to class it, it was passed over. The word cottage in cottage-garden, was placed properly among the *qualities*.

This was the same passage which the larger part of class had been arranging on their slates, while the arithmetic and the reading of poetry had been going on.

After this was over, he asked if any one in school thought he required of them too much self-control, &c. One boy held up his hand, but immediately after, he said he was not serious. Mr. Alcott said he should be obliged to have a talk with him on the sin of not being serious; he being the oldest boy in school, and often doing this foolish thing of holding up his hand when he meant nothing. He made several personal observations to individuals, to whom he had been obliged to speak, for fidgetty movements, &c.—asking them if they understood what he wished of them. His object in this was merely to bring out into their conceptions, *his wishes*, as he supposed there was no intentional, but only thoughtless irregularity.

Tuesday, January 2d.—I arrived at the school-room this morning at nine o'clock, and found some of the children at their journals, and some writing the spelling lesson as usual. But a large proportion of the pupils were tardy. This is unavoidable with such young pupils, in mid-winter; especially as the habits of Boston people are not for very early breakfasts. The children seem to come as soon as breakfast is over.

There is one study, which is pursued at home; this is Geometry. And I hear the lessons, when any are learned, as soon as I arrive in the morning; going to the seat of each one separately, and then explaining the next lesson, for them to learn at home.

One or two children, as they came in this morning, spoke; and Mr. Alcott sent them out to come in quietly. He chooses that they shall come into school in perfect silence, and take their lessons without a whisper to one another; and this is generally effected, without his being obliged to send any one out. It is very important to the quietness of a school, that the children should not begin to play in the morning. If all intercommunication is forbidden until they are fairly interested in their lessons, much trouble is prevented.

During the first hour, Mr. Alcott says as little as possible, that he may not interrupt the study and journals. A boy came in, who had been absent some days; and Mr. Alcott said his next neighbor could, without speaking, show him the place. His neighbor said, "He ha'nt got no spelling book," which of course did not pass without revision by Mr. Alcott. Mr. Alcott then stepped out, remarking before he went, that he presumed they would be equally quiet as when he was here. Some were; but about half the school whispered and made signs, or took playthings out of their pockets. One boy left his seat, and was out of it when Mr. Alcott came in, and asked him what he was up for? He acknowledged that he went to ask a question quite extraneous to the school. A little conversation ensued on faithfulness.

At quarter before ten, Mr. Alcott took the smaller division of the class, and heard them pronounce and spell their lesson. As it had some hard words in it, though they were of one syllable, he made them each spell every word. Mr. Alcott was sometimes interrupted by the boys, at their seats, drumming with their pencils; and he stopped and spoke to them. He had some difficulty, too, in hearing some of his class who spoke low, and it took a little longer than usual to hear this division.

At quarter past ten, the class turned in their seats very quietly. Two boys who are deaf were moved next to Mr. Alcott. Mr. Alcott asked them all if they were willing to bear any degree of cold they might have to bear during the next hour, as a lesson in self-control; two boys, and especially the second, seemed to doubt about cultivating the virtue of self-control. The second boy was reminded of Him who came into the world to suffer and die for the sake of others, which made so much impression on him, that when told, with a few of the older boys who had the coldest seats, to go and sit by the stove, he did not go. He had just expressed some contempt of learning self-control; but

4*

the recollection of Jesus Christ seemed instantly to change his mind. I took this occasion to observe to him that he had began to feel the *saving* power of Jesus Christ : for the way in which Christ saves the soul, is, that he saves it from self-neglect, and wrong-doing, by his noble and beautiful example ; and, therefore, a boy who changes his mind, as soon as he thinks that his opinion or feeling is contrary to Christ's character, has begun to be his disciple. Nothing is more delightful than to see a child making an effort to become a disciple ; because Christ, when he was upon earth, said children were of all human beings most fit for that conformity to him, which is the kingdom of Heaven ; and that no grown up persons could be so, till they had turned back into the state of children ; since, therefore, they are already in the state which can go to him, why should they not go ? This observation was made aside.

Mr. Alcott asked the oldest boy what word should be discussed first ; for we should not have time for all. He said " *oath.*" Each scholar gave his own definition, and seemed to confound profane swearing with oaths in a court of justice. A great deal of conversation arose upon the obligation of oaths, and the sin of profane swearing. He asked if any of the boys present ever swore ? About a dozen of them held up their hands. After a good deal of talk, and an apparently general resolution not to swear any more, there were some remarks upon " idle words." After it was over, he asked those who had been interested in this conversation, to hold up their hands ; they all agreed that it was very interesting, and that they should be influenced by it in future.

After recess I went into the anti-room to give the Latin lesson ; while Mr. Alcott gave arithmetic lessons to each of the two younger divisions of the school. After the arithmetic, they took their Franks, and when I came in, I found Mr. Alcott putting down their analysis of a passage, in the scale.

January 3rd.—As it was Saturday, the day when Mr Alcott generally reads from the Bible, the spelling lesson was put off until after recess ; and they were arranged in their chairs, in two semi-circles around him. He then commenced:

Do any look forward to the ensuing hour with pleasure? One boy said—he did not. You may go and coast,—Will any other boy go? Another boy said—he would. Mr. Alcott told them to go; but neither stirred. He told them they might go into the little anti-room, which was warm; but neither of them went. And, without farther notice of them, Mr. Alcott turned to his reading, and asked one of the youngest boys, what he was going to read? The Bible—said he. Are there any stories in the Bible? No. What is there? Plain reading. What do I mean by stories? I do not know how to express it. Well, I shall read,—and you must endeavor to see in your mind what it is—whether a story or plain reading.—" Once there was a man named Elijah "—Have any of you heard of him before? They all held up their hands. He continued :—the time came when Elijah's turn for leaving the world, was come—see in what a beautiful way the Bible expresses that; and he read,— " *And it came to pass when the Lord would take Elijah into Heaven by a whirlwind* "—he made a gesture with his hand describing a spiral ascent.

It is impossible for me to describe how this story was read. Sometimes Mr. Alcott would say over, in modern terms, what was going to be read, and afterwards read the Scripture expression ;—and sometimes he would read the Scripture expression first, and then give a paraphrase.— When he came to Elijah's saying, " Hold your peace," to those who said, " Knowest thou that the Lord will take away thy Master from thy head to day ?"—he illustrated Elijah's feeling, by supposing the sick bed of one of their brothers and sisters, where every one was feeling that there was death near, but none wished to speak of it in words. When it came to Elijah's question, " What shall I do for thee ?"—he stopped and asked them, what they thought Elisha would answer?—Would he ask for money, riches? No —he continued,—but for more love,—more wisdom,—more goodness,—more power of doing good than ever Elijah had possessed :—" Let a double portion of thy spirit be upon me."

Was that a wise wish? They all agreed it was the wisest. But what did Elijah say to it? Let us read—"Thou hast asked a *hard thing!* Nevertheless, if thou see me when I am taken from thee, it shall be so unto thee, but if not, it shall not be so." What did that mean?—did it not mean that if Elisha's mind would exert itself to keep the spirit of Elijah, when Elijah's body was not there, Elisha should have all the wisdom, love, and power of Elijah? At any rate, it was plain that Elisha was *to do* something himself, in order to get what he wanted;—it depended on himself. No person can get more spirit except they exert themselves;—"To them *that have* shall be given."

When Mr. Alcott had got thus far in the conversation, he was interrupted by seeing a boy, who was a new scholar, make a sign to another. He stopped, and said to him: Three months ago, about twenty children came into this school-room prepared to hear instruction; they were all *prepared;* so they sat down and listened, and were instructed. A few others came at the same time, who were not prepared to listen; who did not seem to understand what they came for; who were even angry and vexed at the means taken to give them some understanding and feeling of what they came for. For a time, we had a good deal of trouble with these unprepared persons. They are improved now, but are not yet quite equal to those who came prepared in the first place. Do you understand how this could be? Perhaps you can understand it, and also this sentence from the Bible,—"To him *that hath* shall be given, but from him that *hath not,* shall be taken away even that which he hath." Do you understand *that?* Almost all held up their hands. Yes, said Mr. Alcott, you can easily see, that all those who *had* attention and faith, have *received* knowledge, and much improvement;—but these benefits could not be given to those who did not have attention and faith to begin with. Do you understand that? *I* do not, Sir—said one of the little boys. Suppose you should go to your mother, said Mr. Alcott, and stop your ears, and say what, what? would you ever find out what she was saying? No. Well, some boys came here with their fingers in their ears, and how could we make them hear? They all laughed. They came with their eyes closed; I mean the eyes of the—*mind!* they all exclaimed, interrupting him. I wonder how many have their eyes open now? said Mr. Alcott, looking round. They all held up their hands, and he said just so many have their eyes and ears open, as have faith in their instructors. Have you any faith in your mother, little boy. The child hesitated— seemed not to understand. Do you believe she loves you? Yes, said he. Do you think she likes to have you happy? Yes. Do you think she is sorry to have you unhappy? Yes. Do you go to her when you are in trouble, and expect she will make you glad? Yes. Do you go to her when you are glad, and expect that she will be glad too? Yes. Do you think she is kind to you? Yes. Do you think she is *kindest* when she punishes you?—say, *all* of you—do you think your mothers are the *kindest* to you when they punish you? They all held up their hands. Then you have faith in your mothers. But are you sure you feel that they are *kindest* when they punish you?—when they give you pain? It may be pain of the mind or pain of the body. Sometimes it is necessary to give pain to the body, in order to get at the mind. Is it not better to hurt the body than to let the mind go neglected? They all said yes. And I hope, then, that when I shall give pain, whether to your mind or body, you will not lose your faith in me, and think I do not love your mind and body, for I love them both; but the mind *most*, for it is of more worth, and so I would sometimes hurt the body, rather than not reach the mind, when it is necessary to reach the mind and put thoughts into it.

During this conversation, the new scholar again played, and Mr. Alcott sent him out of the room, saying, if he had been longer in this school, he would not behave so. When he had gone out, Mr. Alcott said, that boy is not a bad one, but he has not thought; he does not know;—his fingers are in his ears, his eyes are shut;—he needs this conversation more than any person else in the room, and yet he *hath not* enough, to have that *given* him which he most needs. I have sent him out in order that he may get by thought, that which is necessary to enable him to receive what he needs.

The opportunity of learning, it has been necessary to take away from him. But let me return to a question I want to ask. Do you know what *pulp* means? Several said, Yes. Mr. Alcott continued, it is the part of the fruit round the seed; and its use is to cherish the seed, and give it life, and make it fit to become the beginning of a new tree or plant. Well, do you understand my figure when I say, that the body is a pulp, and that its use is to cherish and protect the spiritual seed? Many of them said yes. Well, suppose that we take the seed of a plant, and put it in the ground; what happens to it? They were silent, and he added: It bursts, and some parts shoot down into the earth, and some parts shoot up towards the light. Now can you understand this, —that *the soul* is a seed placed in the midst of the world, represented by the ground; and that the shoots which go down into the earth, to fasten the plant in the earth awhile, are the bodily feelings and appetites;—and that the shoots which go upward towards the light, are the affections and better feelings that seek Heaven? They said yes. Well, suppose that more of the seed shoots downward than is necessary; and that no shoots go upward; would there be any flower and fruit? No. It would all be *root ;* all would be under the earth. Well, can you understand that if the soul loves the body only, and only uses its animal appetites, and does not seek the light and Heaven, it will have no beauty nor fruit; but will be an earthly, dark thing, a root? Yes, they understood that. Well, said he, now you know why I wish to check your animal appetites; your love of the body, when that interferes with the mind's growth. It is right to love your body in a degree;—the body has its uses; but it is one thing to take care of your body, and another to indulge it. The plant must have root enough to make it stand steady in the earth; but that is enough.

And now we will go back to Elijah—perhaps we have wandered too far away from our subject.—Go, and ask that boy to come back. He came back, and Mr. Alcott went on to read about the disappearance of Elijah's body, when the chariot and horses of fire appeared. A good deal of conversation arose as to how this thing was ;—and it was suggested, that perhaps the vision of Heaven, the thoughts and feelings, the flame of love, kindled up in Elijah's mind, immediately overcame his body, perhaps annihilated it,—or made it invisible, so that his mind instantly went into Heaven, became all spirit, and was seen no more. This possibility was illustrated by a conversation, referring to that power of the mind of which all persons have enough to move their bodies, and to make their countenances look beautiful and expressive. A greater degree of this same power could be easily imagined; enough to produce the effect that is described in the story of Elijah.

He went on reading, and read the story of Elijah's sweetening the springs of water. He showed that this might teach us how to begin to change a character; you must change its sources. And he said that was the way he began to educate this school. He did not begin by teaching them to read and study;—but he went to the sources, he began by trying to make the feelings and way of thinking, right;—he put salt into the spring,—not *table salt*, but the salt of instruction. They all looked pleased.

He then read the story of the raising of the Shunamite's son, which led to a consideration of the continued life of the soul,—whether in the body or out of the body.

There was a great deal of conversation this morning, which I could not record, its changes were so abrupt. The reading and conversation took an hour and a half; and the children expressed great astonishment at finding that so much time had passed. Some said it did not seem half an hour. Recess came, and the boy who had been sent out, was kept in.

After the recess was over, many interesting words were defined and illustrated,—but I must omit this. My hand was too tired to keep pace with it.

At quarter of one, the journals of the scholars were brought up, and Mr. Alcott began to read one girl's journal, which described all she had done in school and at home this last week;—and some of her thoughts. It proved she had altered and improved a good deal since she came to school three months ago. A boy's journal was next read; it was a very pleasant account, and contained some good resolutions of conforming to the rules of the school. Then a part of another journal was read, but Mr. Alcott found a difficulty in making out the writing, it was so carelessly done. This boy was not one who had begun to learn to write in this school.

4th Monday.—Arrived at quarter past nine, and found some of the children, but many had not arrived; thermometer being below zero. They took their journals and spelling lessons.

As it was so cold, Mr. Alcott put aside the usual order of exercises, and arranged the children round the stove to read to them, saying that he had made them as comfortable as he could, and he wished them to forget their bodies.— One boy said, he could not. Mr. Alcott replied, we shall see. After I have read what I am going to, I shall ask you what I have been reading about.—I shall not *tell* you, I shall *ask* you. He then read from Thomson's Winter, the freezing Shepherd—and asked, what was that about? One said about a man freezing to death in a snow-storm. Another said, about winter. What pictures came up in your minds most vividly? A very little boy said, a man dying in the snow. Another boy said, a cottage of little children crying. And so the rest. Mr. Alcott then began to read the same story again *in a paraphrase*, as most of the children seemed not to have taken any clear ideas or pictures from the poet's own words. They *all* expressed, afterwards, how much better it was in the paraphrase. Mr. Alcott then read from a place in Thomson about coasting and skating; and talked about skating and sliding, and other winter sports.

At half past ten, I went out into the other room with my Latin class, because it was warmer, and returned after recess,—when there was a long talk about *partialities* in school, during which one of the boys expressed great dissatisfaction at the fact that there was one girl in school who was never found fault with. No boy or girl suggested that there was any fault in this girl; and many spontaneously expressed that they thought she was much better than they. This boy, however, said that Mr. Alcott thought she was

the best person in school;—and asked him if he did not?
Mr. Alcott replied that he thought she was better than the
boy, who was asking him that question. The boy replied,
that that was not right,—and another boy joined him. Mr.
Alcott asked those to hold up their hands, who thought they
were no better than this little girl. Those two boys said they
thought they were *as good*, and that Mr. Alcott ought to
think so! The rest of the school laughed at this vain glo-
rious speech.

I then asked the first boy who spoke, if he thought there
was no difference in characters; and if it was *possible* for
any person to approve equally of all?—if it was not impossible to avoid feeling differently in proportion to the degrees
of virtue which different characters exhibited? But the boy
seemed so much afraid of saying something which would
imply that he was not to be admired equally with this little
girl, that he could not reason. It was very painful to me to
see such an exhibition of vanity, jealousy, and unkindness.
He persisted to the end, in thinking that any approbation of
another scholar, beyond what was bestowed upon himself,
was *partiality*. I asked him what he meant by the word
partiality? He said it meant an instructor's liking one
scholar better than another. This he thought was the meaning of the word; and, moreover, that an instructor's having
this liberty of mind was wrong, whatever was the difference
of character in the scholars. What was most remarkable,
in all this conversation, was this boy's evident want of self-
knowledge, or even of the tendency towards self-knowledge.
It never seemed to come into his imagination that he might
be *less deserving* than the little girl, whose faultlessness ex-
empted her from Mr. Alcott's fault-finding. Indeed he re-
peatedly declared that he was quite sure he was as good as
she; implying all the time that all those things in himself,
which have obliged Mr. Alcott, *every day* since he came to
school, to speak to him more or less, were not to be considered in judging him. The only thing in all this conversation which seemed to give this boy any pleasure, was Mr.
Alcott's declaration, that he did not think the little girl the
best in the school. He said that he was contented, if Mr.

5

Alcott did not think she was the best scholar. One would have thought that this little girl was the vainest, most over-bearing, proud, arrogant person, by the feeling of dislike which this boy expressed towards her. And yet it was the general opinion, that there was not a more gentle, modest, unassuming, disinterested person in the room. What could be the feeling that made him have pleasure in having our good opinion of her pulled down? Mr. Alcott suggested that there were envious feelings in his mind; and ended with saying that although in literary acquirements this boy was superior to some of those younger than himself in school, yet in moral advancement he was behind almost every one; and especially in self-knowledge.

5th.—When I arrived in school this morning, the scholars were in their seats, as it was a few minutes after nine. The scholars were reviewing the spelling lesson that was not re-cited yesterday; and were told to draw a map that was be-fore them, if they should get through their studying before ten o'clock. The boys had no geometry lessons. These are voluntary home lessons, and they are as yet so entirely in the elements, that they have not become interested.

At ten o'clock, some change of place was made to make them more comfortable. One boy was still dissatisfied; and Mr. Alcott proposed he should arrange it. But the general impression of the scholars seemed to be, that this boy's ar-rangements were less just and generous than Mr. Alcott's arrangements. When the subject was brought up, in this way, almost all of the scholars exhibited a good deal of gen-erous feeling, and of interest that the smallest boys, and those whose seats had been the coldest, should have warm ones. I was glad to see that some, who are too often sel-fish, did on this occasion exhibit more generosity and thoughtfulness of others, than usual.

The words were spelled, and pronounced, and defined, and illustrated. The word *robe* was pursued into its figura-tive meaning, and the robe of the mind was decided to be thoughts and feelings. And the question was asked, how they would clothe their own minds? And one boy answer-ed, with an angel, which many more joined in. This was analysed to mean that good habits, good thoughts, and feelings, were the angelic robes. Mr. Alcott modified the original idea, by showing that the mind itself was the angel, and education put on the robe;—and he said that he was helping angels to enrobe themselves with an appropriate vesture of thoughts, feelings, and habits. There was a good deal of allegorical conversation on this word ; which seemed to be very pleasing and instructive to the children.

The word *safe*, led to the question whether they were *safe?* They said yes. He asked if they meant their bodies or their minds? And then the question arose what were the dangers of the mind? And Mr. Alcott said none of them were safe from these dangers.

The word *sign*, gave rise to the following questions and answers. What is a sign? A token. What is a token? Any thing that shows something else. What is the body a sign of? The mind. What is the mind a sign of? Heaven. What is Heaven? Heaven is the sign of goodness, and earth of Heaven. What is goodness a sign of? Happiness. What is happiness a sign of? Goodness. What is goodness a sign of, said Mr. Alcott again? Eternity. What is eternity the sign of? They all said they did not know. Mr. Alcott said that eternity was the sign of God's life-time, or *of God;* and that there we must stop—we could go no farther. They all acknowledged it. Mr. Alcott then quoted these lines of poetry :

> " Significant is all that meets the sense,
> One Mighty alphabet for infant minds."

and what is *significant*, said he? The answer was, *all* that meets the eyes! What does it all signify? Something *beyond the senses*. Mr. Alcott made this last answer himself.

After recess.—The first class in reading, were arranged in a semi-circle ; and all the younger scholars, (part in Child's Arithmetic, and part in Colburn's Arithmetic,) studied their lessons. The reading class turned to a piece of poetry of Mrs. Sigourney's, and Mr. Alcott proposed to analyse it in this scale on the black board :

Objects.   Actions.   Qualities.   Substitutes.   Relations:

First the word *object* was defined as the name of any thing ; but Mr. Alcott asked the next for a better definition. And it was decided that whatever was perceived by the senses, or conceived *in the mind*, were objects. *Action* was defined as any thing you do, or that was done to you. *Qualities* was defined as the words that expressed *the sorts* of actions or objects. *Substitutes* as the words which stand for other words—signs of signs. *Relations*, were illustrated, not defined.

They then proceeded to analyse the verse :

> Why gaze ye on my hoary hairs,
>   Ye children, young and gay ?
> Your locks, beneath the blast of cares,
>   Will bleach as white as they.

It was correctly analysed.   Mr. Alcott asked what the word *on* showed the relation between ?   What the word *ye* was a substitute for ?   And such questions.   Nothing very interesting transpired.

At one o'clock, the older scholars went to their journals, and he attended to the class in Child's Arithmetic.   But about half the class had leave from their mothers to go home at one o'clock, and so they lost the lesson.   Mr. Alcott demonstrated the sums with blocks,—after they had said the answers from the books.   It took a quarter of an hour to hear this lesson.   Then he heard the class in Frank read. Then Mr. Alcott asked those who had had a *tedious* day to hold up their hands.   None did so.

6th.—Thermometer at zero again.   When I arrived, only part of the scholars were present. *They* took their usual lessons ; and I heard the geometry lessons.   At ten o'clock I went into the little room, to hear the Latin lesson, and Mr. Alcott placed the children near the stove, and gave them instruction on subjects moral and intellectual, which were brought up by the words in the spelling lesson—the recitation of which had been deferred until after recess.   The

Latin class consists of fourteen children; most of whom began Latin with me. In the past three months, they have studied the verb *amo*, the *declensions of the nouns*, and a literal translation of the first sections of the Sacred History, in Walker's Latin Reader. One little girl, under seven years of age, has learned sixteen of these sections. Some of them who began later than others, or have stayed away some weeks, or are not so easy to learn, have not learned more than one or two. But all have learned thoroughly, all they have studied, having spelled and defined every word, even according to the grammatical meanings. Some of them have also written the Latin exercises in Leverett's Latin Tutor, upon the declensions and the first conjugation. To-day I made the following scale:

Nouns.	Pronouns.	Verbs.	Adjectives.	Prepositions.

and having explained this classification to make it correspond to Mr. Alcott's scale of

Objects.	Substitutes.	Actions.	Qualities.	Relations.

I told them to analyse the first paragraph, which they did, though some did it much better than others. I then made a new scale of

Nominatives.	Accusatives.	Ablatives.

For I observed that no other cases came into the paragraph; and I proposed that the nouns and adjectives should be arranged in these columns, which was done by a reference to *the meanings, not the endings,* (for with the latter they were not sufficiently familiar.) By this exercise, they came to an understanding of the relation of the nominative case, to the sentence; and of two syntactical rules for the accusative, and two rules for the ablative.

5*

At twelve o'clock, Mr. Alcott began the spelling lesson,
by asking what was the advantage of defining words ? And
then he asked what a person was like, who had words
without any ideas attached ? One said a parrot—one a
mocking bird—one an ape. He then asked what boys and
girls thought they had been too neglectful of the meanings
of words? Several held up their hands. I observed that
one boy who, in my opinion, is particularly deficient in
appreciating the force and power of words, did not hold up
his hand, but sat with a very self-satisfied air. One boy
who did not hold up his hand, was very right in not doing
so ; for he has a very admirable appreciation of words,
for his age.

The word *reel* led to a recollection of what is often seen
in the street ; and the shaping it out in words, till there was
a very sad picture on the mind. Other words were then
defined which led to the conception of some other pictures.
Mr. Alcott considers that this is a very important way of
illustrating words, when the words will allow of it; and
almost every word does.

The word *rest* was talked of in all its meanings, as *repose, leaning upon, remaining*. I suggested that *restore*
might be the origin of the word, and as *restore* came from
the latin word *resto, to stand again*, the word rest when
applied to the mind, might mean to get back to that repose
of innocence in which it was when first created ; when applied to the body, getting back to that unagitated state
which is the natural state of matter.

The word *same* seemed confounded, in most of their minds,
with the word *similar ;* one however said the very thing was
the same thing ; which was as near, perhaps, as it was possible
for such inexperienced minds to get, to the *expression* of
identity.

When these words and a few others were defined, the whole
lesson was spelled, and I was asked to read my journal;
but first Mr. Alcott asked, if any one of them thought he knew
himself. One boy held up his hand, none of the rest did.
Mr. Alcott remarked to this boy, that he thought he knew
very little of himself; and then he took down Krumma-

cher and read the whole story of Strephon's visit to the Oracle of Delphi. I then read this journal, and all the scholars said it was *just*, even those who were censured in it.

Thursday.—Still very cold, yet all but three were present and seated at their lessons by half past nine. At quarter of ten, Mr. Alcott arranged the children round the stove in a square. When the best arrangement had been made, one boy objected, and said he was cold. Mr. Alcott told him to go into the little room where there was a fire. Mr. Alcott then began to have some conversation with them on the subject of making a great noise here before he came in the morning. (It is very uncommon for Mr. Alcott not to be here *before* all the scholars.) He told them he once knew of a school of eighty scholars, between the ages of four and sixteen, which went on in perfect order for three days, although the teacher was absent, and he said all the lessons were learned as usual. Mr. Alcott then took Krummacher's fables and read the story of Lazarus licked by the dogs, and Zadoc's mercy. When he began, he said he was going to kindle a fire for the mind, which he hoped would make them forget their bodies. They listened most intensely to the story ; and when he had finished, he said, How do you like my fire ? They all burst out, I like it ! Should you like I should kindle another ? said he. And he read the story of Emily, who did not like winter, because she loved her flower garden. As he described the opening out of Emily's bulb into the flower, he made a running commentary of allegory, reminding them that they were germs. They took up this allegory with great delight. One boy said he thought the germs had already began to open. Mr. Alcott said yes, beautifully ; several pointed to one little girl and said, that one is opened out. When he had finished this beautiful story, he said how do you like that fire? I think it a *very warm* one, said several at once. They then asked him for *another fire*. And he read the story of Caroline and the canary bird. They all expressed their astonishment when he said it was eleven o'clock, and agreed with him that the fires of the mind were warmer than any other. They then spelled the lesson.

The word *rich* was the only one defined. It was decided that there were internal as well as external riches. He asked one boy if he was dying which he should prefer to have, *a whole world*, to carry with him, suppose he could carry it, or a mind full of good thoughts and feelings. The boy replied *the latter*. In speaking of expected inheritance, he referred to that common Father, who had promised a kingdom to all of them. He said they already had the kingdom in their minds, and if they would begin to rule it, and get it into order, it would be beautiful. He then quoted Christ's words, " the kingdom of heaven is within you." And asked who had the most riches of mind of any one who ever had the shape of man ? They all said Jesus Christ. He asked if these riches could be stolen ? if they could be exhausted ? if they could buy what is worth more than the world ? if they were enough to make us all rich ? All these questions were answered rightly. He then asked one boy if he knew of any person who reminded him of the rich one we had been speaking of ? (he said he need not call any names.) The boy said yes, and many others joined in saying that they had seen one or more. Mr. Alcott said, if I could take all the books, all the maps, all the pictures, all the busts there are in the world, supposing all those things were collected, being the mental riches of all men, which should you rather have, all these riches, or the riches in the mind of *that One?* They all said the latter. Recess-time had now come, and Mr. Alcott said it has been very cold indeed, and uncomfortable, but has been an interesting day, has it not ? They all agreed, by acclamation.

During the recess, Mr. Alcott prepared the slates and his own black board, with the grammatical scale, for the scholars under 8 years of age.

After they had been seated a few minutes, as there was

Objects.	Actions.	Qualities.	Substitutes.	Relations.

some buzzing, Mr. Alcott asked all those who had whispered or spoken since they came in, to rise up. Almost all did. He told them to go out, and come in again, and do as they ought. And they went out, and some of them came immediately back, others not coming immediately, Mr. Alcott went out and sent them in. When they were seated, he told those who had come in last, to go out and come immediately back. When it was all over, Mr. Alcott said ten minutes had been lost.

Mr. Alcott then told the Common Place Book class to turn round with their books. They did so. He turned to Mr. Henry Ware's "lines to a child on his voyage to France, to meet his father," on page 170th. Who wrote this? said Mr. Alcott. Mr. Henry Ware. What is it? Lines to a child going to his father. Where was the child's father? In France. What does Mr. Ware say to the child? They read the successive periods. When they had finished it, he said, is not this beautiful? They all said *yes ;* and then Mr. Alcott read it himself. Mr. Alcott asked one boy what part of this interested him the most? He said the last. So did four others. One boy said he liked best those lines " 'Tis wonderful," &c. Another boy liked the first part. What is the force of that image of the ship's being " impatient," and " eager to be free?" said Mr. Alcott. Because the ship was made to go, it was its nature to go, was the first answer to this question. Mr. Alcott asked if any matter could move itself? They said no. What moves it? It was finally answered that *spirit* moved matter. One boy said that steam moved itself. Mr. Alcott answered that if he looked deeper he would find steam did not move itself. Another boy said, I am not moving. Mr. Alcott said, your pulse is moving. And what moves the pulse of creation? said he. God. There was some conversation about growth, which I omit, as it arose entirely out of a sort of word-catching, of which one of the boys is very fond. How many of you are " eager to be free," and *of what?* One boy said he was eager to be free of the body. Mr. Alcott said he had better be willing to stay in his body till he had done all the good he could by it. Mr. Alcott then pointed

to a fine cast of Christ and said, what was *he* eager for ?
To do good, to rid people of their sins, said all. He then
pointed to a portrait in the room, and asked what he was
eager for ?   Then to the bust of Socrates, the bust of Plato,
the bust of Milton, the bust of Shakspeare.   It was unan-
imously decided that they all were eager to communicate
good in their various ways.   Do you know any who are
eager to be free from good sentiments, good laws, &c.
They said yes.   He asked from what they themselves were
eager to be freed, whether from the rules of the school and
right reason, or from bad habits.   This question seemed
to give some convictions of conscience, which Mr. Alcott
followed up, by some remarks to individuals.   He then
sent them to their seats to make their paraphrases of the
reading lesson.   The second class then came and analysed
a paragraph of Frank in the scale which is given above.

January 9th.   Friday.—The scholars were at their spelling lessons and journals this morning, when I arrived.
And at quarter of ten, Mr. Alcott took the little class of four
children, under four years of age, and who did not know
how to read, and began to read Frank.   He began the first
sentence : "there was a little boy whose name was Frank."
What was his name ?   Frank, said they.   "He loved his
father and mother," do you ?   Yes.   "He liked to be with
them," do you ?   Yes.

He went on in this manner, and read the two first sentences, which brought them to the fact that Frank was
obedient.   He here stopped and asked them questions
about being obedient, and told them how Anna Alcott (who
was one of them,) made out the night before to get up a
resolution to obey when she did not want to.   He asked
questions and described the whole process of mind.   He
personified Resolution, and then he said, well, now, you
say to Resolution—Resolution! keep me sitting still in this
chair, while Mr. Alcott is reading.   He then read the story
about the leaf of the table's falling.   And they looked very
attentive and much delighted.

In reading to little children, Mr. Alcott conveys a vast
deal of good.   In the first place, he requires from them a

distinct effort of self-control, by asking them the question, whether they will make a great effort; then he imagines and shows them how they will be tempted; and prepares them both for the temptation, and to overcome it. Without this co-operation is called for, he cannot be sure, that however interesting in his reading, any *fixed* attention will be given. *With it*, the listening becomes a moral exercise; for to govern one's self from the motive of desiring to obey and deserve instruction is a moral action. Mr. Alcott, however, lays out to aid their endeavors, by selecting an interesting story, and as he reads, he constantly asks questions to make them co-operate with him; in the manner mentioned above;—the result is active and profound attention.

These children spend their forenoons in drawing letters, of which they have a profusion at their desks, and looking at pictures. Mr. Alcott now and then goes and talks with them, concerning these. They are required to be very quiet and not interrupt the rest of the school, and this they do by means of these quiet amusements. In the meanwhile they are very much edified apparently by the discipline of the school, which constantly conveys to them the theory of quietness and self-control. They also have slates and pencils to copy the forms of the letters.

While Mr. Alcott reads to them, he sits with his back to the rest of the school, but the room echoes so that a whisper can be heard. When the lesson is over, he turns and asks, who whispered? and they stand up, and there is conversation and sometimes punishment. This has many advantages, the chief of which is the habit of ingenuousness, it ensures.

At ten o'clock the smaller division of the class of spelling, spelled their words; and Mr. Alcott told them the meanings of such words as they did not know, which took a quarter of an hour. Then the rest of the class turned round to attend to their spelling. They had had an hour and a quarter for their spelling and journals, and most of them had had some time to copy words from the copper-plate cards before them. Mr. Alcott said before he began, that he trusted the school, with its thirty voices, had made a resolution not interrupt him with unnecessary words, with improper attitudes, or with laughing. Mr. Alcott then asked if all of them were willing to be punished if they broke that resolution. After some hesitation on the part of a few, they all agreed. One little boy persisted in saying, I don't know. Mr. Alcott asked him how he was to find out? and to all his questions he answered, I don't know. As I had the Fairy Queen on my table, I carried to Mr. Alcott the passage of the Legend of St. George, which describes *Ignaro*, and Mr. Alcott read it to their great delight, and asked the little boy afterwards if *now he could tell*. The little boy replied with a smile, yes, sometimes. Mr. Alcott then turned round to the rest and said, *Ignorance*, with keys which he could not use, is that you? But if you will come here I will show you how to use your keys, some of them. I do not know how to use them *all* myself, but I know how to use *some*, and I do not intend to let any of them rust as Ignaro's did.

One boy in school, (who is a lately entered scholar,) asked if that story was true? Mr. Alcott said, there are two sorts of truth, the truth of what is *in the mind*, and the truth of what is *out of the mind*. But there are some boys who do not understand that there are realities *in* the mind; and when I shape out the realities of the mind by means of outward things that represent them, these boys say *that is not true*. They cannot believe any truth but the outward truth. Now the inward truth is the first truth; there would never have been a single outward thing, not a thing in the world, no world at all, if God had not had thoughts *in* his mind first. The world existed as *a thought* in God's mind before a single particle of it existed in such a way as to be seen, or heard, or felt. Do you believe that? He then addressed one boy eight years old; tell me, when you do any thing outside of you, any thing which others see you do, does it not exist first within your mind; do you not feel it first *really* existing within your mind? Yes. Well, can any of you tell me of a single thing that you see with your eyes, that did not first exist, *really*, within some spirit?

One boy said—did that bust of Shakspeare exist really in a
mind, before it existed out of a mind? He was soon convinced that the form of it did exist in the mind of the
moulder.

In the subsequent spelling lesson, when the word *tale*
came up, it elicited a good deal of conversation. It was
seen that *a tale, a fable,* &c. might be the medium of con-
veying *truth.* Mr. Alcott went on to show that the things
that we see tell us a tale all the time. And he asked what
the world was a tale of? After a moments reflection, several
of the children said, of God. And he asked what the things
that happen in the outward world were tales of? It was
answered that there was not a thing that happened that had
not existed in some mind, either in God's mind, or in some
man's mind. He then said the world is a tale, and life is a tale.

I here asked permission to tell the first tale that I remembered Life to have told me. I began with saying that one
reason why I told them this, was to show how a story
sometimes changed its outward *form,* when it went into a
mind; and yet carried all the most important truth into the
mind. This story, said I, had an outward truth; it was
something which happened in the outward world, and was
told to me as it happened; and this was the picture that
came into my mind.

I thought I saw a dark sea, and a cloudy, stormy, sky,
which looked gloomy. And I saw a ship on the horizon,
which came on very fast, faster and smoother than any
other ship ever sailed, in a beautiful curve line. As it
came near, there was a company of women standing on
the deck, two and two, taking hold of hands, and each
one had white robes on, which fell over her feet, and
every eye was looking up, as if she saw God sitting above
the clouds; and their faces were full of joy and love. At
last the vessel stopped by a large rock on the shore. I
did not see a single sailor, or any anchor, I never had
heard of an anchor, but it seemed to me these women
walked off the deck upon the rock; and walked over the
rock carefully, looking at their feet, and holding up their
robes; and they glided over the frozen snow into a high,

6

dark, deep, evergreen forest; and under the trees they knelt down and worshiped God, though there were no meeting-houses, and not a single dwelling house; and then they went into the bushes, and took broken pieces of trees and made little huts, like Indian wigwams, which they went into. This was the picture that rose up in my mind, as I was told.——

The story of the Pilgrim fathers! exclaimed several, interrupting me; but what made you think the Pilgrims were women? said one. It was the misunderstanding of a single word, said I; and the reason I thought they were in white robes, was because so much was said of their purity; and the reason I thought they were looking up, was because I was told that they came to the uncultivated desert to have liberty to worship God; and the reason I thought they look-ed happy, was because I was told that they loved God, and I knew God was good; and the reason that the whole thing seemed done so quick, was because I did not know about sailors, and managing a ship, and anchors, and such things; but now tell me do you think I gained most truth or false-hood from that picture? The boy to whom I asked the question, answered that I gained more truth than falsehood. Yes, said I, the truth of the mind. Had I seen the thing in my mind as it really was outwardly, (the Pilgrim fathers in seamens' clothes, and looking just like any other men,) I should not have taken the idea of how different their minds were from those of common people; for I could not have seen their thoughts. But my imagination shaped out their thoughts in such a way that I could see their very thoughts; and so the very mistakes which I made, helped me to see more of the truth, than I should have seen had my real eyes been there, looking at their real bodies. It was of great use to my character, to have this picture of true devotion, of souls full of God; so full of God as not to mind cold, nor the having no homes; and caring so much about worship-ing in the way they thought was right, that they were will-ing to live in that wilderness. Especially since I thought they were women!

Mr. Alcott said, and now see the advantage of having an

imagination which is always ready to give the most beautiful shapes to words. It makes a great deal of difference in your characters, whether there are beautiful shapes in your mind or not; and in using words, you should take great care to use such as may put shapes into people's minds, which will mould their minds right. Suppose a man says to a child: You *brat* you! get out of my sight; what an ugly picture the words make in that child's mind of himself! So that he does not feel he has an angel spirit within him.— Well, it is not true that he has an angel spirit within him, said one boy. Not true! said Mr. Alcott, indeed it *is* true, and until you feel that you have an angel spirit within you, and act according to it, you will never be free from those thoughts, and feelings, and actions, that trouble you and us so much every day. If I did not think there was something within you, much more angelic than has yet came out and made an outward truth, I should feel very despairing:—If I thought of you, as you think of yourself, I should be as discouraged as you are. You think you are as good as you can be; but I believe you can be a great deal better.

I thought an angel was a man with wings, said one boy. What do the wings mean—do'nt they mean the feelings that go upward? All men have such wings. Men are not angels, said another boy. I pointed to a picture that hung in the room, and asked if he thought much of what that person thought? He said yes. Well, said I, I heard him say once, that unless we could believe in the angels that were around us in shapes of men, it would do us no good at all to believe there were angels in another world. He seemed to be quite struck with the force of this person's authority. Mr. Alcott made some remarks upon the person referred to, and said, he had been an angel indeed, to many minds. I then asked them if they knew that in the Bible, it was said that the winds, and the flaming fires, or the lightnings, were God's angels; which showed that whatever told a story of God, could be called an angel, whether it was a man with wings, or a mere thing, or a thought within the mind. Mr. Alcott then took Krummacher's Fables, and read, by way of illustrating the subject, the story of Adam in Paradise and the Seraph; and asked them if they understood it? They all said yes.

After recess I took my Latin class into the other room, and they all had their slates given to them, and began to analyse sentences into the parts of speech, and into the variations of cases. In the mean time, those who were with Mr. Alcott had read in Frank, and Mr. Alcott had asked the children what pictures certain words brought up to their minds; and had had several interesting answers. One boy of six, said, *Try* shaped itself as a strong man. And another of five, gave quite an elaborate picture of *Day*. He said he thought of an angel sitting on the floor of Heaven, which was our sky, and letting down through an opening, a cross, in which was the Sun. When he lets down the cross, it is day, and when he draws it up, it is night. He made appropriate gestures as he described this. Where did you get that picture? It came into my mind all of itself. When? Why, now. Where did it come from? said Mr. Alcott. Oh! I know. Well? God sent it into my spirit. How does the angel look? said I to him, when I came in and Mr. Alcott had made him repeat this to me. He is the smallest of all the angels of Heaven, said he with decision. What does he do besides? Nothing but that, all the time. Does he forget this duty ever? Oh no! Did you ever think of that picture before to day? No. In regard to some other particulars which were asked in order to ascertain if it was distinct and steady before his mind, he answered without hesitation.

Another question which Mr. Alcott asked of the little boys was, how they employed rainy days? They gave various answers; and this boy said, that he sat down and thought over the stories he had heard, and acted them over in his mind, and sometimes made up new ones—Oh, very beautiful! with angels in them. This little boy afterwards added an angel of the Moon, who sat by the side of the angel of the Sun, and when the Sun was drawn up, put down the Moon in the same way. This angel also put down the stars, but not in crosses. He hung them down. But in the morning when the cross of the Sun is put down, these stars shoot back into Heaven, said he, like balloons.

On Saturday, January 10th, there was some mistake about the fire; and as the room was very cold, Mr. Alcott took all the children into the anti-room, there to spell and define the lesson, without having previously studied it. They remained with him till half past eleven, a large part of the conversation being upon the interesting subject, conscience. The question arose, whether it was seated in the head or heart; and it was remarkable that those boys, whose conscience is to them the surest guide, and the most powerful, all thought it was in their heart, while those who are not so conscientious, thought it was in their head.

After recess they all came into the school-room, and Mr. Alcott took Krummacher's Fables, and read the story of the father who gave to his three sons seeds, and sent them this way and that, to plant them. When he had finished, he asked them what this story represented? The boys severally said, the seeds were of goodness; the ground was, the heart; the father was God; the weeds were faults. Mr. Alcott asked what were the seeds of goodness? He was answered, love, truth, gentleness, &c. There was a good deal of interesting conversation; among other things, one boy said, if he had been there, he should have been better pleased to have planted his seeds at home, than to have gone away from his father's. Mr. Alcott said, who does the father represent? God. Well, have you not already *been sent forth?* Your father has already sent you forth, with your seeds. You came out of your father's heavenly house, to plant your seeds in this world.

In the grammatical analysis to day, there was some conversation about the word *object*, and it was found by its etymology, to mean what lies out of, or before the mind.—What mind laid things out of itself—laid down before it every thing? God, said a boy of seven, without an instant's hesitation. Did he put any thing into things by which they might get up? Yes, in some things he put spirit, his own spirit. And so all things that have spirit within them get up and act as much as they can? No, said he, laughing; some

6*

are sluggards.   What are you in earnest about, said Mr. Alcott, to the little boy of five, mentioned yesterday?   Not
about any thing.   What is being earnest?   Feeling that
things must be done.   And you do not feel so about any
thing?   Only about being good: Oh! Mr. Alcott, I have
thought of an angel of rain!   Well, how does he look?   He
sits by the angels of the Sun and Moon.   Do they help
him? No.   How does he know when to have it rain?   Oh,
he can see!   he knows when it is dry down here; (and he
went on to describe his operations, but I could only understand that the angel took the water in a great bubble from
the sea, went up in it, and came down with the rain.)   Cannot I see him, said Mr. Alcott?   No, not till you die.   How
came you to see him?   Oh, God sent the picture of him into my spirit.

January 12th.—Arrived at a few minutes after nine, and
found the children at their lessons. I heard the geometry
lessons immediately. At quarter of ten, Mr. Alcott took
his youngest class, and began with telling over what they
had read about Frank the last time.   Mr. Alcott asked them
if they minded as Frank did?   One held up his hand.   Mr.
Alcott said, you mind sometimes.   Well, that is better than
not at all!   But do you mind when you don't want to?   No.
Ah! but Frank did ; because he thought, and he knew that
his mother's wants were better than his own.   He then went
on and read in another place about Frank's going over the
stile, &c.; and after he had done, he said: Well, now you
have heard about meddling ; the other day you read about
minding.   Do you meddle, &c.

At ten o'clock, he took the youngest division of the spelling class as usual, and heard them spell ; and told them the
meanings of the words.   This lasted a quarter of an hour,
when the rest of the class turned.   At first, Mr. Alcott spelled the words, and called on the scholars to pronounce them.
Then he gave the definitions, and required them to tell the
words ; then he called for an illustration of each word, in
original or quoted sentences, in which the word was used.
As usual, this led to a great deal of conversation ; for the
figurative uses of the words being brought in among the

illustrations, Mr. Alcott always pursues the spiritual subjects thus introduced, thinking it the most natural way of interesting their minds in mental operations. Thus the word *steep* being illustrated by the expression, "steeped in wisdom," led to a consideration of the source of wisdom being an inexhaustible fountain. One boy said he was not yet "wet through" with wisdom.

The word *spot*, led to *unspotted*—unspotted in character—Jesus Christ—the original innocence of character in childhood—how they had become spotted—(by disobeying conscience—not obeying parents who interpret conscience, by getting into passions, loving appetite too well, &c.) These disquisitions are always conversations; the references to Jesus Christ are always by describing his character; when they say, I know who you mean, and point to the cast of Christ. There is a strong expression of reverence, and natural sensibility to excellence, whenever he is referred to.

One of the words led to a discrimination between the words *character* and *reputation;* and then to a discrimination between *the character* and *nature* of a person. In the course of the conversation, the question arose, whether Mr. Alcott understood their characters? Some of the boys said they thought he did; others thought he did not. This led to a consideration of the evil of secretiveness, and the beauty and advantage of transparency. Secretiveness, Mr. Alcott thought, was naturally connected with selfishness; and frankness with generosity.

Mr. Alcott said that none deserved to go out, at recess, because there had been so much noise. The day before, one boy said he thought the good ought not to suffer for the bad. Mr. Alcott replied, that in God's world the good always suffered for the bad; and that it was a proof of a person's being good, that he was willing to suffer for the bad. The boy replied, that he was very wicked then, for he was not willing to suffer for the bad.

Mr. Alcott illustrated the word *sure* thus: Imagine this conversation : Shall you sit still till half past eleven? Yes, sir. Are you *sure?* Yes sir, very sure. Five minutes pass —and the person is moving about. What are you doing?

The scholars all laughed.   He then said, I will tell you one
thing I am sure of: I am sure every child here has been an
angel; a pure, loving, heavenly spirit! They all smiled.
And *I am sure* that every child here can find that angel
again. I learn this in my heart. What we learn by our
hearts, we are sure of. What we learn with our heads, we
are not sure of. Which do you like best, thoughts or feelings? One boy said he liked thoughts best. Mr. Alcott said
the difference between feeling and thought, is the difference
between the Sun and the Moon; the one is the original
fountain of light and heat, the other the reflector.

After recess, having given two or three their exercise lessons in the school-room, I took the rest of my Latin class
into the other room, and gave them manuscript books, and
set them to writing down in them, the nouns of the ten first
sections. All wrote one section, and one wrote five by one
o'clock; some wrote two. At one, they took their Latin
Grammars to learn the prepositions by heart. Mr. Alcott
meanwhile gave to the rest of the scholars Arithmetic lessons, and they had a reading lesson in Frank.

13th.—I arrived at twenty minutes past ten, and heard all
four scholars say Geometry. Mr. Alcott read to his youngest class a story about a dog, which I wish I could describe,
with his conversation intermingled, but I cannot.

At ten he took the youngest division of the class as usual.
When the rest of the class turned, Mr. Alcott said: What
is a *definition?* One girl replied, it is the meaning of a
word. What is the *meaning of a word?* The explanation,
said another girl. The thought told in other words, said
one of the boys. The definition of a word is to tell all its
meanings, said another. The meaning of a word, said Mr.
Alcott, and the definition are not the same. As you have a
soul within your body, and your body *means out*, as it were,
the soul; so the word has a soul. What do you think of
such an idea as *the soul of a word?* Can you take that idea,
the spirit of a word? Yes, sir, said one little girl, very intelligently.

Now, said Mr. Alcott, let us see if we can find the spirits
of these words; if we can open the words, and bring out

the thoughts and feelings. You have seen a very little seed, a mustard seed; the meaning of that seed is not felt, till it has opened out into the branches, and leaves, and fruits.

The first illustration of the word *soar* was the figurative one. "Our minds soar when they think on some subjects." He asked if there were any who were conscious that their minds and hearts were beginning to aspire? One boy held up his hand. Two other boys expressed a wish that they had the eyes and wings of the eagle. Mr. Alcott said, you have stronger wings than the eagle, and eyes to see a brighter sun, than he has ever seen. Mr. Alcott then went very carefully over the process of an egg's being nursed into life; the warmth of the parent bird operating upon the matter around the germ of life, and making it so pliable that the germ of life, which is spirit, shapes out a form that will mean something to the observing mind. He then went over the process of a bird's learning to fly, through the encouraging love and care of the parents, animating the spirit of life, and leading it out. He then asked some questions about their minds soaring out of their bodies; and some interesting answers were given. He then brought forward a cast of a child, whose arms were stretched upwards; and asked each one of them what idea this image awakened in his mind? One boy said, of a boy stretching. But almost all the boys expressed the spiritual idea of aspiration. One boy said it was an angel, (yet there were no wings.) One girl said, it was a soul shaped out as a child ascending to a higher state. One boy said, it seemed to be a child looking up to Heaven and praying to God to send an angel down to take it up to Heaven; and that it was preparing to be received there.

One very intelligent boy, the shape of whose head seems to indicate the possession of the imaginative faculties; and who is the only one in school who has ever expressed strongly the desire of pursuing the fine arts, said he had no idea. Mr. Alcott replied, that he did not do justice to himself, in saying that. But I said, I thought that he would not take pains to clothe his thoughts and feelings in words; or that perhaps he was *proud*, and did not wish to

attempt it, lest he should fail. And yet there was no way
for him ever to learn how to express himself, except by at-
tempting it, and being helped out. I wished he would do
this, for I felt sure it would bring him a great deal of satisfaction ; and when he had once got over the difficulty, he
would not sit, his soul sending the blood out of his heart into his head, and driving it back again into his heart, while
he feels overwhelmed with feelings that he does not know
how to define. I told him he reminded me of a child that
I once knew, who carried this fault of pride so far that he
has become a very unhappy man. Mr. Alcott asked him
which he thought was most interesting, such conversation
as this, or conversation about a steam-engine or such things?
Many said, such conversation as this, though he did not re-
ply. Mr. Alcott put the question in another form ; and at
last a little boy exclaimed, I never knew I had a mind till I
came to this school! and a great many more burst out with
the same idea. I asked a very little boy, who I think has
improved in his intellect, more perhaps than any other child
in this school, if he knew that he had a mind before he came
to this school ? He said yes. I then asked him if he ever
thought before ? He said yes. If he ever thought about
his thoughts? He said, with a bright smile, No ! If he liked
to think about his thoughts ? He said yes. If he liked it
better than to think about any thing else ? He said yes. If
it entertained him ? He said yes, yes, yes. Mr. Alcott then
asked all those who liked to think about their thoughts, better than about how things were made and done, to hold up
their hands ; and almost every scholar held up his hand, for
thoughts.

One boy then said he liked things which represented
thoughts. Mr. Alcott said yes—that is beautiful—that
is a way of studying *things* which is most interesting.
But of course, no one can think about *things* as representing thoughts, until they have first thought about *thoughts* in
themselves. This boy then said he wanted to ask, if the
mind did not mean that part of us which took in learning,
as astronomy, &c.; and the soul that part of us which takes
in the thoughts of God and duty; is there not this differ-

ence, said he, for I never knew certainly? Mr. Alcott agreed
that there was this difference, and told him the word spirit
included both ; and the voice of the spirit was conscience for
both the mind and soul were necessary to inform conscience, and make it express itself perfectly and wisely.—
Mr. Alcott said that some people seemed to be all mind, and
some all soul ; but the union of the two in proper proportion, constituted the life of the spirit, and made it utter its
voice *in* conscience. I then told the history of the mind I
referred to above; and how without vanity, but through
pride, he kept himself back ; how the fear of revealing his
wants, even when he intensely felt them, deprived him of
all assistance ; how he never attempted to do any thing until he was able to do it perfectly. And how sometimes he
never attempted to do a thing at all, because he knew he
could not do it perfectly ; and how it had resulted in his
powers of action being so very much behind his conceptions of what might and could be done, that he did not have
any sense of happiness ; and was perfectly gloomy, and was
going on doing things inferior to his own capacity; and
without the means of communicating his mind to those in
whom alone he felt interest. I ended with saying there
were some persons here who had, in a degree, the pride and
the habit of that person ; and I warn such of the effect.

As I told this in a very detailed manner, it excited great
attention and interest; and several acknowledged that they
felt they had a degree of the same spirit. The individual,
I particularly thought of, was particularly conscious ; and I
had a long conversation with him in recess, upon the duty
of overcoming this pride, and not fighting against his own
mind; and I stimulated him by giving him instances of
persons very superior in the power of expression, and endeavored to show him that they never would have been able
to *sway* the minds of others with the thoughts in their own
minds, unless they had done differently from the way he
was doing; for he was repressing his mind, putting down
his thoughts into the measure of such words as he already
possessed, instead of allowing his thoughts and feelings to
go forth after words, as certain other boys (whom I named)

did, who were every day improving. He asked what he could
do, to get over his *mauvais honte.* I said, endeavor to answer every question Mr. Alcott puts out, instead of using
your mind as you do now, to evade answering the questions
at all; for this will certainly cramp, and in the end destroy
it. He seemed to understand this argument, and disposed
to follow this advice.

After recess, Mr. Alcott took the Pilgrim's Progress and
read the first description of Christian, very slowly, and all
his distress, and the want of sympathy of those around him;
and the interview with the Evangelist, and the Slough of
Despond, up to the place where the Interpreter shows Christian the picture. He had talked all along, expressing, and
in some instances applying it, to the spiritual condition of
individuals in the school; and in some instances, we had
quite a general conversation. When he came to the description of the first picture in the Interpreter's house, he
stopped, and asked why were the eyes looking upward?
One girl said, because he was endeavoring to get to Heaven.
Another said, because he was tired of earthly things. A boy
said, that the eyes looked upward because he loved God and
was thinking about him. Another boy said, because he had
a disposition to go to Heaven. The others were a repeti-
tion of these ideas. Many said they had no thoughts. Mr.
Alcott asked one, if he thought that Mr. Alcott wished his
body to be here without his mind, (i.e. without any thoughts.)
The boy blushed. Mr. Alcott asked why was it said that
truth was written on his lips? Many answered, because
he looked as if he spoke the truth. They all spoke as if
they understood truth as merely veracity. He asked why
the world was behind his back? One boy said, because he
preferred Heaven to earth. The others confined their notion to that of his being tired of the world. Why was the
crown suspended over his head? One girl said, to show
that he would be rewarded for being good. Another girl
said, rewarded for his perseverance. A boy said, rewarded
for loving Heaven better than earth. What is this way of
representing truth called? Allegory. Mr. Alcott said, I
have been reading an allegory, which pictures out truth by

—what? As they could not get the word, he said *emblems*, and that they had been interpreting the emblems. Mr. Alcott then went on and read all the things, which the Interpreter showed to Christian.

Something was said about our most imaginative boy, who was not present to-day. The scholars have great delight in hearing his ideas generally; but one who is some years older, and very fond of admiration, has expressed some feeling of jealousy. It was remarked to them that there was nothing extraordinary in itself, in any thing he said; that all children have such ideas in their souls, and more beautiful ones too; and that all the difference in the shaping power, arises from the habit of looking into himself, which this boy has, and most children have not. It is only wonderful in itself, said I, that you do not all give us as beautiful thoughts as he does. And it can only be accounted for, but by remembering that parents and school teachers have not done what they should have done to keep you from giving yourselves up to bodily pleasures and eye enjoyments, without taking the trouble to think, all the while. Play is the very time for exercising your imaginations. But you push one another about, and knock one another down, instead of playing something with a plan. I have known children play long stories, making believe a thousand things; and making believe is using your imagination. But you should never make believe bad things. Some boys in England, once killed a boy, in making believe hanging. And I knew a boy who made himself hard-hearted, by always playing Indian wars. But I have known some children cultivate their minds and hearts, without knowing it themselves, by their beautiful plays. Some anecdotes were added.

Wednesday, 14th January.—I arrived at few minutes after nine, and found the children at their lessons. Mr. Alcott read to his little class, the story of Frank's going into the garden. He read as far as why people could not take whatever they wanted; and then there was a good deal of conversation with them on meddling, and on not spoiling other people's things. At nearly ten, Mr. Alcott took the

7

smallest division of his spelling class, and began with asking
one boy, if, when he talked with his father or mother, he
ever used any of the words he found in his spelling lessons?
He said, yes. The two next boys said they never used these
words. Then Mr. Alcott said, suppose I should put a box
at your seat with six words in it, which were names of your
thoughts, and different names from any you had ever heard
of, and you opened your box and said: well, I do not know
what thoughts these words are names of, but Mr. Alcott will
tell us ;—and so Mr. Alcott comes and tells you, and you go
home and talk out your thoughts with these new words;
you would learn six new words every day. Well, let us
look into your spelling lesson, and see if we can find some
new names to your thoughts. When he had told them the
meanings of the words, he illustrated them by sentences, in
which they were used figuratively.

During this lesson, he was obliged to speak to two girls
for whispering ; and Mr. Alcott said this was the first whisper he had heard since school began ; it was the first time
he had had to speak to any scholar for any thing : the little
girls looked quite ashamed.

At ten minutes past ten, Mr. Alcott asked the rest to turn
in their seats, and expressed his approbation of their stillness, which he thought had been remarkable. He then
placed two boys, who were apt to be fidgetty, at a distance
from the rest, and proceeded to the lesson, saying this exercise which we call spelling and defining, leads to a great
deal; it not only teaches to spell the words, but to see how
thoughts and feelings are expressed by words; it gives
names to thoughts and feelings that you may acquire.—
Now, tell me, what advantages this lesson leads to ? One of
the boys repeated his remark. Mr. Alcott then said, we
learn the pronunciation of words also. One of the boys
here began to say, that he thought he knew the meaning of
words before he came to this school; and he seemed to
think that he knew so much of words before, that he was
not very much benefitted by this exercise, since only a few
words were defined each day, and the illustrations took so
long a time.

After satisfying this boy of his error, Mr. Alcott continued his remarks on the spelling lesson ; saying, that there
were nine thousand words in this spelling book, and that
they touched almost every subject of thought and feeling,
religion, philosophy, and conduct; and in going over them,
some important ideas on all these subjects might be attained, and they would have acquired the very soul of the language.

The words were all spelled rightly, and as the boys all
sat perfectly still, Mr. Alcott said, referring to the circumstance of having appointed a superintendent during this
hour, what effect a thought has, the thought of keeping one's
name off a slate !   A thought, with a little *will* in it, keeps
all these bodies still.   What power a thought has—it is very
real, and quite as real as the body it keeps still.

Took was illustrated thus : it took an hour to say the lesson ; he was *taken ;* and a story was told that had the word
in it several times, and which also had the advantage of in-
culcating a moral lesson.   A good deal was said of its various meanings ; and its grammatical distinction from take,
was mentioned.

Tool was illustrated by a wood-saw, a plane, a trowel, &c.
One person makes a tool of another, introduced a consideration of the depravity which led one person to make a tool
of another; the want of comprehension of the sacredness
of the human mind, which could allow any one to make it
a *tool.*   He illustrated this by stories.   He ended with saying, no mind is to be made a tool of—no, not even by one's
self.   I know some boys who make their minds the tools of
their bodies, and that is very bad.

Among his illustrations of tool, he spoke of school-mas-
ters, who made tools of their scholars, wherewith to build
up their own fortunes ; and he spoke of one school-master
who had this plan, and who wanted him to assist him ! And
he related their conversation, and thus had an opportunity
of giving the scholars an idea of his own principles and
views, in pursuing this vocation.   They seemed deeply interested, and I thought it very happy that he had an opportunity of bringing them to understand what his views were ;

for it gave them an opportunity of appreciating and co-operating with him ; and nothing is more important than for children to have a perception of a sacred sense of duty inspiring the instructer; for reverence is the baptism of soul which is necessary to prepare for "the mysterious communion of ignorance with wisdom."

Parents do not always understand the indispensibleness of this baptism, and often do their children a moral injury which is utterly irreparable during the whole period of youth, by putting them under the care of persons, whom they cannot, or do not, treat with reverence themselves.— There is not a procedure more profligate towards the child, to say nothing of the instructer, than for a parent to do this. There is no intellectual advantage, (I should not hesitate to say,) which can compensate for this moral disadvantage. And the intellectual disadvantage, in a majority of instances, is only second to the moral; for real intellectual action is intimately connected with the proper state of the soul. It can only be continuous, persevering, and honest, when its motive is moral. There must be a perfect *self-surrender*, for the time being, in order that the intellect may see what is before it. Reservation throws a cloud over that which should be presented to the mind ; for to childhood, reservation is always an effort ; and it is an effort in exactly the contrary direction from the effort of taking in ideas. But there will be reservation, there can be no self-surrender, when there is want of faith in the instructer; and this faith is to be inspired by sympathy from parents.

The word *vine* was illustrated by the expression in the New Testament, "I am the true vine." And the meaning of Christ was made obvious thus : Christ, when he said *I*, meant the views and feelings which constituted, made up the life of his spirit; and as these were right, he was the true vine. Those who make the same views and feelings the life of their spirits, are branches of the vine : and God the Father, is the husbandman of all. He then asked several questions, such as does the vine naturally rise or fall ; run along the ground; or twine round elevated objects; which had it better do ? Many other illustrations, literal and figurative, were given; and then he proceeded to the word *type*. What is a *type?* said he. One boy said, a type is a metal letter which is used to stamp a sign upon paper. What is a word the sign or type of? said Mr. Alcott. They severally said, of a thought; of an idea; of a feeling; of an object; of an action; of a quality. Language, said Mr. Alcott, is typical of whatever goes on within us, or is shaped out of us. What is the body a type of? Of the mind. What is the earth a type of? Of God; mind; heaven; were the several answers. I would go on much farther, said Mr. Alcott, if there was time. There are people who think and say, that the world and outward things are all; because they do not know what they are typical of. I could show you that all outward things are produced out of those spiritual realities, of which they are types. But the clock now typifies the hour of recess: and you may go out.

The Latin lesson came after recess; and I took the class into the other room, while Mr. Alcott heard the rest read, and afterwards parse in Frank: doing the latter by means of the scale mentioned above.

At the hour of dismissal, the whole school was brought together. One or two boys had been punished on their hands during the school hours, and one of the larger boys remarked that a certain gentleman (naming him) had expressed that he was sorry Mr. Alcott had found it necessary to use the ferule. Mr. Alcott said, such of you as have been punished with the ferule, may rise. Several did so. He then said, such of you as have been made better, have been assisted in self-control, and in your memory, by being so punished, may sit down. All sat down but one. Mr. Alcott then remarked that he was sorry thoughts were not realized as they might be, to govern their actions. But as sometimes they were not, and many boys deemed thoughts to be unreal, it was necessary, for outward things which they did believe real, to take the side of conscience, and help to make them seem real and visible; and he believed not one boy had been punished, without acknowledging before-hand that he felt it would do him good, and that it was Mr. Alcott's duty to give him that help. There was much conversation, which

7*

seemed quite satisfactory all round. Mr. Alcott then said, that the gentleman referred to, was very wise in his judgment on a case that he knew; but that it was not every boy who knew how to state a case truly, since in order to state any case truly, it must be seen truly; and it required self-knowledge and self-surrender to see truth in all cases. Was this boy capable of such self-knowledge and self-surrender, as to state a case whose circumstances condemned himself? We saw every day that here he could never even *see* any circumstances just as they were, when they condemned himself; and how could he represent them? Whoever thought that this boy could speak of the subject of punishment in this school justly, might hold up his hand. Not a single hand was held up.

January 15th. I arrived at five minutes past nine, and found many of the children. All who were present, were in their seats, attending to their lessons; and there were no words. Those who had learned Geometry lessons at home, said them to me. At quarter of ten, Mr Alcott began to read to the little children in Frank, and talked with them concerning the rights of private property.

He then, with her consent, told the rest how one of them had been tempted to take something which did not belong to her, and at first even took it, but bye and bye her conscience made her confess that she had it, and she gave it up. This was the story. This little girl went to a physician's house, with a lame foot, and she found a very nice bandage on the floor, and she asked her father whose it was; and her father told her he supposed it was some lame person's bandage, or it belonged to the physician. The little girl kept un-rolling and rolling-up the bandage, and wanted to have it very much. At last she put it under her cloak, so that nobody might see, and soon slipped it into her pocket very cunningly. She thought her father did not see. So she sat there a little while to see how it would seem. She found it was very unpleasant. She thought the bandage did not belong to her; it belonged to somebody else. Her eyes looked strange. Her father did not say anything. He thought her conscience would soon speak. She did not know that he had seen her put the bandage into her pocket. At last she felt she must say something. Father! said she, I am going to do something. Yes, said her father, I know it; and you had better do it now: so she took the bandage out, and said she did not want it for it did not belong to her. And when she went home, she told her mother she had come very near *stealing*. Mr. Alcott after telling the story, asked the others if they ever took any thing, and they, and several more of the other class, acknowledged that they had sometimes. The lesson seemed to make a very serious impression.

At twenty minutes past ten the whole class turned for recitation. Mr. Alcott then began. Is it right for scholars to sit idle three minutes, when they have time given them to study a particular lesson? No sir; said several.

Mr. Alcott went to several children separately, and gave them certain directions, about sitting right, not whispering, nor speaking loud, &c. and severally told them, if they were not obedient, that they should lose the recess. He told them he threatened this punishment, because there was weakness in all the individuals to whom he had spoken, and they needed this help to their inward strength. He then appointed a superintendent; for he said, though each one ought to be a superintendent of himself, the idea of a name's being written down on a slate, had a wonderful influence, as we saw yesterday. The best children did not act differently, but many weak ones did; they needed this assistance which answered a present good end.

A little boy turned round while the children were spelling and did not attend to Mr. Alcott. Mr. Alcott called to him and asked him where the words came from; if they did not come out of Mr. Alcott's mouth; and why he did not look at him? Then several words were defined and illustrated. *Trap* was illustrated figuratively in one instance; and Mr. Alcott said he hoped that the boy who was speaking, had too much respect for his own mind ever to set *traps* for human minds. They all illustrated the word literally, by telling of the traps they set for each other in play. Mr. Alcott asked if they could tell why there

was so much fun in setting traps? They did not explain
it; and Mr. Alcott undertook to do so, by showing that it was
the exercise of the understanding merely. But, he asked,
why they thought of the pleasure of ingenuity, rather than
sympathised with the boy caught, who was very often hurt
or angry? They did not seem to know. The subject
went farther, into the morality of sporting. The wickedness of cheating in school, and in other cases, was also discussed. At last it branched off into begging pardons,
acknowledging faults, &c. and the conversation extended
to twelve o'clock, without the children's making any reference to the time of recess having come.

When speaking of traps, one boy said he heard of a trap
Mr. Alcott had set. Mr. Alcott induced him to tell him.
It was a story of something which happened in another
school of Mr. Alcott's, and which one of the scholars had
told to another boy, who had told it to a boy in this school.
When it was finished, Mr. Alcott told the thing as it was,
and it seemed that the principal point of the story, which
consisted of the trap, was made up, that is, was a lie. Mr.
Alcott said the boy referred to, was a very bad one, and
was at the school so short a time he had not become better.
Mr. Alcott then told several stories of boys in that town,
who were taken away from his school, because they were
punished; and sometimes just at the moment that the punishment had began to alter their characters. He told one,
where the punishment was for a boy to kneel to his companions, and acknowledge a fault. He asked what they
thought of that punishment? One or two said nothing would
induce them to do that. I asked, when they had acted
very wickedly and injured others deeply, if they would not
delight to do any thing to repair it, and to show that they
were sorry for it? They at first thought not. But when
they came to hear what the boy in question had done, and
what traits of character he had displayed, they all agreed
immediately, that the kneeling punishment was dignity by
the side of such wickedness and meanness.

After recess, Mr. Alcott put all but the first class in reading to their arithmetic lessons; and took the class in reading.

One girl chose a piece on the 230th page of the Common Place Book of Poetry.

Whose *recollections* are these? said Mr. Alcott. Mr. Henry Pickering's, said one. What is the meaning of the word recollect? No answer. What is the meaning of collect? To bring together, said one. What then is the meaning of re-collect? One said, to collect again. What did Mr. Pickering re-collect? said Mr. Alcott. Some things he collected in childhood, said one. Are you now collecting, or *re*-collecting the impressions of childhood? Some thought they had began to *re*-collect, as well as to collect. Shall I tell you an idea some people have of recollecting, reminiscence, remembrance? Yes; said several of them. Mr. Alcott continued, (pointing to the bust of Plato,) that man believed that all our feelings and thoughts were the remembrances of another state of existence, before we came into the world in our present bodies. And *he*, (pointing to the cast of Jesus Christ,) used to say of himself, that *he* came forth from God; that *he* had lived before. In the gospel of St. John there are many passages in which he refers to his pre-existent state.

Mr. Alcott then began and read, " I thought it slept." One of the boys said, that he did not think it was right to say to the child that " he would never awake." Mr. Alcott said that the same thought had occurred to him, as he was reading; that it was the moment when it would have been well to have told the child of the spiritual waking, and not to have let it stop with the idea of bodily death. The mother, however, only intended to say that the bodily eyes would never awake.

One boy said that he thought it impious to say, " And tears that angels might have shed my heart dissolved." Mr. Alcott asked why? He said, because the tears of a child are not good enough to be called angels' tears. Mr. Alcott said, it merely means they are innocent tears.

Another boy said, that angels would not have wept; because they would have known about the life of the other world. Mr. Alcott asked, why the infant was called a cherub? They said because it was good; because it was beautiful; &c. Mr. Alcott asked what idea they had of a cherub, and each answered, according to his own ideas.

What is this piece of poetry about? said Mr. Alcott. Death; said one. Yes; the appearances to the senses when a spirit departs from the body of an infant. What were the appearances? The boy read the words; " the cradle," "the flowers," "the still body." What else is described? said Mr. Alcott. The feelings and sentiments these appearances produced, said one. Did these appearances produce the sentiments in the mind, or wake up sentiments which were already there? There was no answer to this question. Do the appearances carry the sentiments into the mind, or bring them out? One girl said, carry them in; a boy at the same moment said, bring them out. Mr. Alcott agreed with the boy, and said, he did not think there were any sentiments in the outward world. The girl immediately changed her mind.

Why did Mr. Pickering "gaze the more?" One said, because he "thought it slept." What did he observe as he gazed the more? That "its bosom did not move." What did he then do? He tried to look into the eyes. How were they? "Closed." What did he do next? He "took his hand." What did he seem to expect? That it would "clasp his," but it did not. What was his feeling then? He did not know what to do, and he addressed the body impatiently. And what then took place? The baby "would not hear his voice." Why did Mr. Pickering think he would not; where did he get that thought? He thought the spirit was still there. Yes, said Mr. Alcott. It is the spirit that wills; and to whom did his mind then turn? To his mother. How did she look? "Pale and weeping." And it seemed to typify what it was not possible to voice out, said Mr. Alcott: but do you think there are any unutterable things in your spirit? A little girl said, after a long pause, *yes*. Mr. Alcott said yes, there are some unutterable things in every mind—feelings, not thoughts; so feeling is better and deeper than thought. Were all the deepest feelings bodied forth in sculpture, or painting, or in things, or voiced out in words, what would it all be. After a pause two spoke at once, and said, *God*.

What else does Mr. Pickering say of the mother?
"tears." What are tears? Expressions of unutterable
things. All tears? No, some are on trifling occasions.
Are you ashamed of your tears? Sometimes. "Jesus
wept," said Mr. Alcott, and it was on a similar occasion,
when there was death. What else did the mother do?
She "clasped him." Why? Because she was glad that
he was alive. What else did she do? "She sighed." Yes,
another emblem of an agitated spirit.

In this way, Mr. Alcott went on over every particular of
the description, and the lesson continued for an hour and a
half, of which I have given above not the most interesting,
or the largest part, as I forgot I was writing, many times.

When I arrived at quarter past nine, January 16th, I found
the children quietly seated at their lessons. One of the
girls handed me a note, in answer to one I had written to
her, expressing my pleasure in her moral progress, after
having had occasion to blame her a good deal. It expressed
gratitude to Mr. Alcott and me for not sparing her faults.
Such demonstrations are the instructer's true reward.

At half past nine Mr. Alcott took his little class. They
looked very animated. Mr. Alcott said, you seem to look
very much pleased when I come to read to you. They all
smiled. He began, "A few days after." What is *a few*?
Two or three. "His mother called Frank!" you know
Frank always looked when his mother said Frank; *do you*
always look, when your father and mother say your name?
Sometimes, said they. She said, get your hat. What do
you think Frank did? He got his hat instantly, and he
went along jumping and singing. What did he jump and
sing for? Because he was glad, &c. &c.

It is impossible to follow these reading lessons. To hear
Mr. Alcott read at least once, would give a better idea of it
than pages of description. Every sentence is addressed to
the children, and required back from them; and there is
no point of morality or conduct touched on, which is not
taken up and applied, and wandering eyes are steadied, as
an exercise in self-control. After this lesson is read, the
little children turn round to their desks, and are encour-

aged to make letters on their tablets, from the models which are scattered over their desks in profusion. Books of pictures are also there, and they are led in this way to exercise their eyes upon forms to their great advantage, it being the most excellent preparation for all their future studies. Mr. Alcott requires them to be so still as not to interrupt or disturb the school; but that is all. They are constantly amused and engaged, and seem perfectly happy. They often turn round to hear what Mr. Alcott tells or reads to the other children; especially if they are stories.

Mr. Alcott then took the smaller division of the class and spelled and defined the words, and talked to them a good deal on the subjects brought up by the lesson. Thus: *wise* means to have good feelings and good thoughts, and to act them out. If you have no good feelings or good thoughts, you are not wise; and even if you have good feelings and good thoughts, and you do not act them out, you are not wise. *Wisp* was one of the words, and to illustrate it he read that passage of the Story without an End, where the child sees the Will-o'-the-Wisp.

At ten minutes past ten, the spelling lesson began, after he had placed the chairs of the smaller division very far apart from each other, so that they should not be tempted to whisper. One boy was made the superintendent; and Mr. Alcott said to him, you know you cannot put down a name because you wish to, nor refrain from putting it down because you do not wish to. Conscience must write down the names, not inclination. There is the responsibility of each boys' pleasure for half an hour resting on you; do you understand? Yes.

Now please all define or illustrate silence by action, or rather by no action. There was a pause. We are going to name thoughts, feelings, and actions, or to word them. Is *tree* the wording of a thing, person, action, feeling or thing? Is *trim* the wording of a thing, person, action, or feeling? An action. And all the words were thus half defined. Then the words were spelled, and what is very uncommon, three words were spelled wrong. The words were afterwards defined and illustrated.

When the word *vast* was defined, Mr. Alcott asked if that idea of vastness was within or without? Several answered, both. Some said within. One hesitated, and Mr. Alcott asked what was vast. He said the ocean. Mr. Alcott asked if the ocean did not wake up the idea of vast in his mind? He replied, yes; and so vastness is in the mind. What then is the ocean? said Mr. Alcott. An emblem of vastness, said the boy. Mr. Alcott continued, the ocean then is the external, visible, material sign, type, or emblem of the internal, invisible, spiritual idea of vastness. What is it? This definition was repeated in nearly the same words by two of the class.

The word *veil* led to a consideration of the body as the veil of the spirit, and of the earth as the veil of many of the ideas of God. When was the veil of sense wrapped round our souls? said Mr. Alcott. When we were born, said one. When will it be taken away? When we die, said several. Cannot the veil be raised till we die? After a while it was seen, and said that the veil could be raised by exercising our spirits into perfection; by being born again out of sense into thoughts or spirit; by insight. Mr. Alcott then repeated the passage from St. Paul, about being caught up to the third heaven, and asked them whether the veil was raised for that man? They said yes. He then said that the object of this school was to unveil the soul; and he was glad to hear that one of the scholars had said out of school, that it was impossible to remain in Mr. Alcott's school and not learn to know one's self.

It was now recess, and I went to prepare my class in Latin; and while I was in the other room, Mr. Alcott heard the younger class read, and parse on the scale.

I did not arrive, Monday 19th, till ten o'clock, when I found Mr. Alcott had gone through the usual exercises for the first hour, and the scholars were arranged for their spelling.

He began: Such of you as feel an interest in this lesson, hold up your hands. And all did. Why? One boy said, because it teaches us to spell, and gives us meanings of words. Another said, because of the conversations that

8

arise. Why are these conversations interesting? said Mr. Alcott. Because they give us new ideas, replied the boy. Many others said they liked them for the same reason. Mr. Alcott then said, conversations are the most perfect transcript of mind. Could all the conversations of great men be recorded, it would give us a better idea of them than the history of their lives. Why is the New Testament so interesting? because it is full of the conversations of Jesus. And the conversations of Socrates, recorded by Plato, make probably the next most interesting book in the world. *Conversation* is full of *life*; there is more of life in conversation than in other modes of life; the spirit's workings come out in conversation, fresh and vivid.

He now appointed a superintendent; and seeing a boy smile without any apparent reason, he said he might write down all *smiles* that did not arise out of the subject of the lesson; for smiles indicate a state of mind, and when something is in the mind which has no relation to the subject, it is wrong. Besides several take up the smile, and attention is diverted. It is true that smiles may arise out of the subject, and then they are not wrong. One boy said, if we had *longer words* we should have more interesting conversations. Mr. Alcott said, oh no! the short words have the most meaning in them, and he illustrated this by a great many instances.

He then took the spelling lesson and began to talk, and make observations upon the scholars, illustrating the first word *work* in every variety of application, literal and figurative; and he went on in this *talk*, bringing in every word of the lesson, and each in various meanings; the children soon caught the idea and joined in, and made sentences also, as they arose in their minds, in which the words were applied figuratively, according to their fancies. Lines of poetry were also quoted.—It would not be possible to follow this desultory conversation, although it was conducted with perfect order. At one point of it, (the word *yean*,) Mr. Alcott took down Wordsworth, and read Barbara Leithwaite, in which this word occurred. When he had read half through, he laid down the book, but they begged him to finish it, and he took it up again, and read the story through.

Yelk, he said, was the food by which the germ of life was nourished into the power of forming a body that might individualise it; and he said the earth (perhaps) was *the yelk* by which souls were nourished or born into a consciousness of the spiritual life. He explained this a little. All eyes were fixed upon him almost constantly. Neither a sense of duty alone, or the attraction of the speaker alone, could explain the profound attention of these children. But the combination of the two causes is irresistible. Also, Mr. Alcott requires them to seem attentive as well as to be attentive. He often talks to them on the possibility and the duty of making every part of their body express the thought of their minds; and that they must not accuse people of injustice who interpret even their automatic movements, and especially their careless habits.

The word *yawn* led to some amusing anecdotes about yawning; but he soon arrested them and said that was enough. He added, however, that he liked amusing stories; and he thought there was no harm in them if there were also serious stories in right proportion; but stories of one kind made the mind one-sided.

After Mr. Alcott had illustrated all the words of the lesson by this conversation, he took the dictionary and read Johnson's definitions, to see how much resemblance there was, and this led to further remarks on the words. He then heard the words spelled, and asked each one to give a short definition.

Every day he varies the mode of this lesson, in order that it may not sink into a routine. There was a hesitation at the word *yean*. Mr. Alcott said the earth *yeans* its millions of productions. To *give birth to*, was immediately responded. Mr. Alcott said *yeanling* meant a young one until it was weaned.

Zeal was defined by one of the boys, as to feel so much as to set the will a-going.—A recent scholar, a little boy, whispered once in the course of the hour and a half, and Mr. Alcott said, little boy, do you know that in this school when any boy whispers he is punished? He then remarked that to want to do any thing, was no reason at all for doing it; the question was, does God want it to be done?—While I was attending to the Latin, after recess, Mr. Alcott gave lessons in Arithmetic and English Grammar.

I arrived before nine on Saturday, and found some of the scholars at their seats, and also heard some Geometry lessons. I then looked over, in order to read my journal of the last week, while the class were spelling their lesson, omitting the defining of the words. As soon as the spelling was done, I read the journal of the week past; and they were very attentive indeed. The idea of having this journal read, seems to create a happy influence on the school. No one defends his faults when he sees himself in the journal. It is evidently a great aid to self-knowledge.*

Mr. Alcott then prepared to read in the Bible. He appointed a superintendent, and made some remarks on the assistance a superintendent gave to the weak. I am going to read about *one*, said he, of whose thoughts, and actions, and feelings, you always delight to hear; whom you are reminded of by that cast, (pointing to it); for that is a representation of the body, out of which he looked. All spirits, in this world, are in bodies; his was just as your spirits are in your bodies. Well, this one said, " *I and my Father are one;* " he did not mean one body, but one spirit; that they had the same thoughts and feelings; all pure spirits, all real spirits, must have the same thoughts and feelings; must be one with God; all that is truly spiritual in your souls, is *one* with God. But the Jews did not understand him when he said that he and his father were one; the people around him did not think about spirits, they thought about bodies, so they did not understand him, (perhaps they did not try, said he, very expressively, addressing one boy of an inactive mind.) And they replied, you do not speak truly in saying that you, that is *your body*, is God! Now he did not mean his body, but they did not attend to see what he meant. They misunderstood, as some thoughtless boys do here, when I speak in pictures. And they took up stones to stone him; but he said, remember what works you have seen me do, I have done a great many good works among

---

* Of course, in publishing the Journal, the names have been omitted.

you, such as God would do; and I did them to show you
what works God does; I have done many compassionate,
kind works; for which one of these works are you going
to stone me? They said, we do not stone you for your
good works, but for saying you are God. Jesus said, well!
in your own books, that you believe in, it is said, " *Ye* are
gods." I say nothing new when I say that my spirit is one
with God's. All spirits are of God, as you already ought
to know; and why do you say I do not speak true, when
I say I am the Son of God; especially since my works are
such works as He would do? If I do not do such works
as God does, I do not want you to believe me; but the
works! believe the works; attend to the works; think
about them, and they will convince you that I am *in the
Father*, and *the Father in me*. Then they sought to take
him, but he walked away.

They sought to take him, and why? They did not like
to hear that the spirit in them was of God; they did not
want to feel obliged to look into themselves; they preferred
to attend to their bodies. Perhaps they did not understand
him; but it was only because they did not *try;* it is our
duty to *try.*—Jesus went away to the wilderness, where
John used to put water on the bodies of such as intended
to be good; for as water purifies the body, so they were to
purify their minds, and they had their bodies washed as an
emblem.

Jesus, soon after this, had an opportunity to prove that
what he said that day about the spirit's being one with
God was true. A friend of his died; it was the brother of
Mary and Martha. That was the Mary who had anointed
the Lord with ointment, and wiped his feet with her hair.
A messenger came to Jesus and said " he whom you love *is
sick.*" Jesus said to those about him, I am glad of it, for by
this sickness of Lazarus, I shall be able to show you that
the spirit is *one* with God, that it cannot die; and I am glad
that God may be brought out to your eyes, by this display
of his power. But he stayed two days where he was, and
then he said, let us go into Judea again. Now his friends
remembered the stoning, and they said, what! will you go

8*

where you will be killed; where your body will be hurt; will be stoned? Yes; he said, he should go. Our friend Lazarus sleeps, said he; I go that I may wake him out of his sleep. His disciples said, " if he sleep, he shall do well;" they meant, if he only sleeps, for they did not understand that Jesus meant the sleep of death. Then Jesus said, (for he saw they did not understand him,) *he is dead. And I am glad of it, for your sake ; for now I shall be able to make you understand about life, the spirit's life ;. that part of us which is one with God, and that cannot die.*—Mr. Alcott went on and paraphrased the whole story thus; but I could not keep up with my pen. The children were profoundly attentive, and deeply impressed.

On Tuesday, January 20th, I was not well, and did not come; and for this I was very sorry, for Mr. Alcott review-ed all the spelling lessons of the last six weeks, and it was very interesting, he said, to see how the words brought up, by association, the past illustrations and conversations. Mr. Alcott said he was delighted to find how the little ones had been benefited by the ideas; and how they recalled the most important of them, as soon as they looked at the words. He had had every reason to believe that these con-versations were useful to them from their expression of at-tention at the moment; but it was an additional gratifica-tion to see, that the most general and ideal conversations were remembered so distinctly. For it was most worthy of remark in the review, that the most enlarged and gen-eral views, and the most ideal pictures, were those which had seized most strongly on the minds of the younger chil-dren.

On Wednesday 21st, I arrived at little after nine, and all were in school.

Mr. Alcott showed me Peale's Graphics ; which he said had brought out beautifully a part of the theory of chirog-raphy, which he had long attempted to put in practice; and had connected it with drawing. I looked over it, and found that it was the very thing for this school.

Mr. Alcott then read to the little class of four; and then took the younger division of the spelling class. One of the boys said, "Mr. Alcott I have learnt my lesson;" on which Mr. Alcott entered into that subject, and taking up a book, he imitated the manner in which a child tried to study with the lips, without the mind. They all laughed; and he then explained study, as thinking about words until pictures were formed in their minds, and ridiculed the humming, buzzing, whispering over the words, moving the body, &c. by imitating it himself; and when he asked the questions;— if they understood him; if they agreed with his views; if they had had such habits; if they had any of these still; if they saw their folly; if they would give them all up, &c. they all confessed, and seemed disposed to reform. He then described how this lesson should be studied; how they could think beforehand of illustrating the words in sentences, &c. and he convinced them that to learn the spelling lesson thoroughly, would require the whole hour assigned to it. He said that a great variety of exercises on words were coming. Next week he should vary the mode of considering words; for it was necessary to apply the mind in new ways to this subject; in order that they should not forget to think.

Mr. Alcott then said, that if any were inattentive during the lesson, and if they did not sit erect, or if they did not do, in all respects, exactly as they knew was right; he should deprive them of instruction after recess. He then spoke of the importance of looking at him, in order to catch *all* the meanings that went from him.

A girl then said, Mr. Alcott, I wonder how it is that we sit here over the spelling lesson, as long as we are in church, and yet I am never the least fatigued; and in church I am so tired, and yet we have to sit as still here as there. The rest agreed with her in wondering how it was. Mr. Alcott said it was because their own minds were active here, and activity of mind made the blood circulate, and the whole body feel vigorous. He said it was one of his great objects to call forth the soul in action to govern the body. He spoke of manners; and said that to make spontaneous good manners, there must be both refined minds, and the early acquired habit of self-control, i. e. of letting the mind govern the body.

The words were spelled first; they were of five letters. Every word was spelled right. The little boys were then told to take their spelling books, and hold their fingers on each word, while they were illustrated.

The most interesting word was *black*, in its figurative meanings, as *wicked, sad*. It was spoken of as the color for mourning, and Mr. Alcott expressed his opinion that it was unfortunate that this color should be used when people's friends departed to heaven. He spoke of the custom of burning the dead, and keeping the dust; and of other methods of removing the sad ideas of decay which it is best to separate from death. We observed that the children had no sad ideas of death at all, and that they generally thought it was more a subject of joy than of grief, could we but divest ourselves of circumstances.

There was a talk with one boy who made objection to the encroachment upon the recess; and Mr. Alcott said that this boy thought it was wrong to lose one moment's play, but he did not think it wrong to occupy ever so much time in school hours with unnecessary opposition. He said, were it not for his health, he should deprive him entirely of recess, on account of his encroachments upon school hours; he should, if necessary, however, give him another punishment after recess, to-day.

After recess. The very youngest scholars were employed, some in drawing, and some in arithmetic. And the rest were formed into a large semi-circle, with Frank; for an analysis of the passage, " Stay thy soft murmuring waters, gentle rill ; " &c.

The scale was made, and Mr. Alcott asked them if they thought *objects* was the best name for such words as were generally put in that column. Some thought that the word *things* would be better; but on further reflection perceived it would not be so general as the word *objects*. He then asked what they thought about that word, *actions ?* Some said *movements ;* one, *stirrings ; changes* was suggested ; *acts* was decided upon.

After the analysis was finished, he asked them whether the objects in this passage, were external or internal ? External. What sort of poetry is this? External; worldly; material; were the various answers. He at last led them to say descriptive.

When pointing out questions, they always told what object or action was qualified. When they noted a substitute, they told what word it was substituted for; and the relations were explained.

After it was over, Mr. Alcott explained to them that this was *grammar*, and every thing in language could be learned without the words, verbs, nouns, tenses, &c. One of the children asked why then they should ever learn those words? Mr. Alcott told them, for the convenience of learning other languages. They then retired to their seats, and some remarks were made on order. Mr. Alcott said there are two persons here who are always very orderly indeed. Several children immediately named two of the scholars.

On the 22nd, I arrived late.—When the little class was arranged, Mr. Alcott said he should read a short lesson. One said he wanted a long one. Mr. Alcott said that might be, if their minds did not wander away. The reading and the moral lesson therein contained, then went on.

The younger division of the spelling lesson, then spelled the lesson, after having read it over aloud. He then told them to take their books, and keep their fingers on the words, as the rest of the class spelled and talked about them. The class turned and arranged themselves very quietly.

What ideas does the word *blade* bring into your mind? said Mr. Alcott. A spire of grass, and the part of the knife that cuts; said one. The next added, a gay young man; the next, a sword. The next, a scythe. Another boy said, a blade may be a figurative expression for the mind when it is sharpened by wisdom. Another said, the shoulder blade. The next said, a pair of scissors. Mr. Alcott then read Johnson's definition; and spoke of the blades of corn, and quoted the expression in the Bible, " first the blade, then the ear; then the full corn in the ear."

What ideas do you connect with the word *blame?* To reproach, said one. What is reproach? Find fault with, said the next. Blame is speaking ill of, said the next; and the next said, to accuse one of being the means of something wrong being done. One little boy said to blame was to punish; another said it was to scold. Mr. Alcott then read Johnson's definition, and the definitions of all the derivatives. He then asked those who thought they were *blameless* to hold up their hands. No one held up his hand, but one boy said his minister was blameless. Mr. Alcott said he was glad he had so high an idea of him. The next boy pointed to the cast of Christ, as the " only blameless one." Mr. Alcott said to a boy who did not like to be blamed, that it was a great character which could receive blame without resentment. Another boy said that he could never be blamed without being angry. Mr. Alcott said that was just his fault. A good deal was said of bearing blame meekly, even when deserved.

After a while Mr. Alcott asked two of the scholars if they did not think that a few months before, they were too apt to be angry when they were blamed; and to defend themselves when they were really in the wrong? They both confessed. Mr. Alcott said then they had entered the Wicket gate, and the Burden had loosened from their backs; for that he never saw any children who were such extraordinary instances of the determination not to be found fault with; and that if they had got over that, they had accomplished more than if they had learned a whole science. He was glad that they had made progress, especially one, who had made the most decided progress.

Bliss was defined as the highest degree of pleasure. One boy remarked that pleasure had once before been defined, as the enjoyment of the body ;* and happiness as the enjoyment of the mind; and that it was then said, that *bliss* was happiness. Another boy said *bliss* was the pleasure of the body and mind ; indeed, he thought pleasure and happiness were the same. Mr. Alcott said he did not like to have these things confounded, and that he thought it was only when all the pleasures of the body were defined and lost in the happiness of the mind, that there was *bliss*. He

* See Journal for January 1st.

spoke of the pleasures of the body as interfering with those of the mind by overtasking the body. He asked those who thought they knew what bliss was, to hold up their hands. Some did. He then asked why we were so made as to delight in pleasure? As no one replied, he answered, that he thought that by the disappointment which it involved, it led us to seek for real happiness. He spoke of Hercules' choice. He then asked those who thought they had ever mistaken pleasure for happiness, to hold up their hands. Some did. Mr. Alcott said, pleasure is the divinity of earth, and bliss descends from heaven. He allowed, however, that pleasure may typify bliss.

Bloat, he said was a good word to follow this conversation, for pleasure sometimes bloats. It was defined as swelling out. An intoxicated man was bloated. By pleasure, said Mr. Alcott, or by happiness? By pleasure, said several at once. Mr. Alcott said that some nations, who gave themselves up to the appetites, had a tendency to bloating, inherited from each other.—*Brace* was defined, and carried into its figurative meanings, of strengthening the mind, &c. And virtue was said to brace body and mind. These were the most interesting words.

Saturday, 24th.—I arrived a few minutes after nine, and found them in their seats writing, as a writing lesson ; and Mr. Alcott went round and round looking at their writing, till quarter of ten. When he had read to the little class as usual, he asked those of the other class who had not whispered at all, to turn round. Only ten turned, and none of the older scholars had been silent. Mr. Alcott then asked some of the scholars, calling them by name, for what they came up to the Temple to day? One boy did not answer. Another said, to come to school. Mr. Alcott asked why he came to school? As there was no answer, he said, that the object for which boys generally went to school was to learn the sciences, but he hoped that all who came here knew that they came here not only for science, but to learn *themselves.* He then asked a very good boy what he thought he came to school for? He said, to improve his mind and heart. (A little boy then began to move about, and Mr.

Alcott told him he had troubled him for several days, and now he should take him out of the room and punish him by hurting his body, in order to save the necessity of harder punishment bye and bye, which he did.)

When he came back, a little girl was asked what she came for ; if she came merely for the lessons ? She said no. Mr. Alcott said, you come to learn how to behave at home ; I do not mean to learn how to make bows and curtsies, but to feel and think better. And then he said if any had begun to be conscious that they treated their parents at home with more feeling, from having more feeling, than they used to do, they might hold up their hands. Many held up their hands. Some thought they could not care more for their parents than they did now. To one boy who thought so, Mr. Alcott said that when he never disobeyed them, when he cared as much for their wishes as his own, he might say he could not love them any better ; but not till then.

I then read my journal, and they all agreed that no injustice had been done to them in the journal ; though one boy said that two things seeméd to him to have been stated differently from the fact ; he could not remember what they were, however.

Mr. Alcott then proposed to read, and gave five minutes grace, during which several children went out. Then he began, and having read a story of jealousy and malignity on the one side ; and of generosity and long suffering on the other, he asked those who thought they knew what this spirit of generosity and long suffering was, to hold up their hands. Several did. Who among you has exercised it? said he. One boy alone held up his hand, at which the rest smiled. Mr. Alcott thought that all present might find scope for the exercise of this feeling every day, at home and in school. Mr. Alcott then asked, what is forbearance ? One boy answered, bearing things for others ; another said, patiently bearing other people's malice, and doing good to them. Mr. Alcott then said, does bearing and forbearing come from the body or the mind? From the mind. Which is uppermost when you bear or forbear ? The heart. Mr. Alcott then said to a little boy, did you ever give up one of your body's wants, because it was right? Yes, said he.

Mr. Alcott then said that the measure of goodness might be taken, in any person, by seeing how much they sacrificed their body's wants to those of the mind. No person was good who found that he could not sacrifice his body's wants to those of the mind. Every boy might judge himself by reflecting how much and how easily he sacrificed his body's wants to those of the mind. He wished they would all think in their own minds, how much goodness they had, according to this test.

After recess, the children came in and took their seats, from the anti-room, and from the Common. A boy brought up his journal which he has just begun ; and Mr. Alcott remarked, that he was one who had begun to learn to write by printing, and therefore, though his hand was not yet strong enough to make his writing graceful, yet the distinctness of the writing showed that the idea of every letter was right in his mind. Mr. Alcott said he always found this distinctness in the writing of those who began with printing.

He then read this journal to himself, at the boy's request ; and afterwards, the other journals, aloud. He told one journalist that he wished he would put more of himself into the journal ; the boy of that journal was a mere automaton ; he came in, and went out, and did things, but he never felt or thought. He took up another boy's journal next ; because the boy seemed to be very anxious to have his journal read ; Mr. Alcott found great difficulty in reading his hand-writing, however, and at last he had to give it up ; and it was recommended to him to print for a month, all the time, in order to give some clearness to his hand-writing. When the next boy's journal was taken up, he wished it should not be read, and Mr. Alcott looked over it, and seemed to agree that there was nothing worth reading in it. Mr. Alcott then said that four of them must either give up writing the journal, and write printed letters,

(the best way to learn to write,) or they must write the
script hand better, and more clearly.

A great deal of movement, unnecessary speaking, &c.
interrupted Mr. Alcott in all his conversations this morning. So he stopped reading the journals, and went round
and told what boys and girls he had faith in, and what
boys and girls he had not faith in. There seemed to be
a general sense of justice in his classification. He said
that he had been so much interrupted to day, that he
should retain some of the scholars after school. This produced a perfect silence, during which time he told a story
to illustrate the grounds of having faith in others.

Mr. Alcott praised the writing of one of the girls in her
journal, and said that the journal gave something of her
mind. One of the four boys whose writing had been blamed,
did not seem to like it that she should be praised ; and to
fear that Mr. Alcott omitted mentioning all her bad spelling. Mr. Alcott said two words were spelled wrong, but
there were a great many words wrong in his journal, which
he had omitted to mention, because he thought it would
make him angry, for that he had said, a day or two before,
he could not have his faults pointed out without being
angry. Another girl's journal was full of her thoughts and
feelings, very much superior to any journal we have had ;
and Mr. Alcott praised it, but she was not present to-day.
He expressed that he had not time to read two of the journals, and that he had not been satisfied with either of them
the last week.

On Monday, January 26th, at about ten o'clock, Mr.
Alcott called on the class of spelling to rise, and fix their
black boards, and write the spelling lesson to his dictation
with their chalk pencils. This afforded occasion for remarks on their writing. It takes two things, said he, to
make a good writer ; one is a clear conception of beautiful
forms in the mind, and another is the skill to guide the
hand. Some persons have one of these qualities without
the other. He recommended a careful study of the forms
in Peale's Graphics ; and a great deal of practice, telling

them how, when he was a child, he was fond of printing on the snow, in the dust, &c.

When they came to the word *brain*, Mr. Alcott asked what was the difference between the brain and the mind? One boy said the brain, when not used figuratively, means a part of the head, and the mind means the seat of learning and thought. Another said the brain is the soft part of the head, the inside; and the mind is the hard part of the head. Mr. Alcott asked him if he thought that matter could think. He said no. Mr. Alcott said, but you think the mind is matter, if you think it is the hard part of the head. A small boy here said, is not the brain the case of the mind? and another boy answered him, the brain is the seed of the mind. Two other little boys said, the brain is the sense, and one girl said it was the understanding. Mr. Alcott said, I should say the brain is the instrument by which the spirit acts; from which remark ensued a long conversation, to meet the difficulties of the older children, who had confounded the mind with its organs; and the subject not being exhausted at half past eleven, was left to be resumed another day, as the recess hour was come, and the time after recess was devoted to Latin and arithmetic.

On Tuesday, the 27th, the subject was resumed, and the materialist of yesterday was brought to discriminate the mind from its organs, by the question, whether he thought that when the soul went to heaven, the brain went with it. The truth was, that it was only a disputatious spirit, which had made him fight off the right idea so long. Mr. Alcott closed by asking those who thought the mind and the brain were not the same thing, to hold up their hands; and all held up their hands.

On Wednesday, the 28th, when the school turned at ten o'clock to face Mr. Alcott, he said, all who have whispered this morning may turn back. All the girls, and some of the boys, turned back. All who asked unnecessary questions may turn back; he continued. Several more turned. He then said, now those who have not whispered, who consulted their own memories about their places, and depended on Mr. Alcott to supply them with all that they wanted, without any questions, may rise. They did so. And he said, these are my scholars; the rest keep schools of their own. After some little talk, all agreed to give up their schools, and go to Mr. Alcott's. He explained the bearing of all his rules on their habits of mind and character; and they all acknowledged their propriety.

He then said he was going to read some pictures of what goes on in the mind during the period of its development on earth, by means of the duties of life; but if one boy or girl interrupts me, said he, I shall stop; and that boy or girl will bring a deprivation upon the whole school; those who are innocent being obliged to suffer, as the good are always willing to do, for the instruction of the guilty. This remark elicited some doubts, which were settled, by reference to Christ, and all martyrs, and self-sacrificing philanthropists, who make it their vocation on earth, to seek and to save that which was lost, to suffer and die to bring life and immortality to light.

At last, the Fairy Queen was opened, and Mr. Alcott began,—Goodness may be said to be at war with Wickedness; and Spencer has pictured out Goodness as a knight who goes forth into the world to combat with enemies. When I read about St. George, you must understand that he represents Goodness; his enemies are the enemies of Goodness. I shall first read about St. George combating with Error, which is the first enemy that Goodness meets in the world.

He then read, or rather paraphrased the description of Una, and told them that she represented Truth. She " inly mourned" because Wickedness and Error existed; she was " in white," because truth is pure, bright, and innocent. He then read the account of the Wood of Error and the adventure in it, in a very free paraphrase, interweaving the explanation of the allegory. They listened with the most intense interest, and could not help exclaiming, as they sympathized in the various turns of the battle. At the end of the battle he stopped, and asked them if he should go on; and they all exclaimed, go on, go on. He went on, and read of the meeting with Hypocrisy, up to the scene in the House of Sleep. When he had finished, he asked: what has this taught you? One boy said, to resist evil. Mr. Alcott then went on to speak of the conduct of good and evil within themselves; and made individual applications which brought the subject home to each one's own experience.

On January 29th, at the usual hour for spelling, he called on those to turn round, that had not broken one rule about whispering, &c. All turned but five. He commended the conscientiousness of these five in not turning round; but said that they were wrong in breaking the rules. He then said to the rest, that if any of them had turned without examining themselves, they had deceived, had told a lie; that they had injured their souls, had commenced the career of falsehood. He enlarged upon falsehood and its consequences, and at last, two girls turned back. The rest remained firm; and Mr. Alcott said he considered these as his scholars; for they obeyed his rules. The rest kept their own schools, and had their own rules; at least for to-day, and might keep their faces turned from him. He told the class to take their spelling books; and he called on several scholars, to pronounce the words they had been studying, and they did so. He then spoke of pronunciation; its importance.

A long conversation ensued on the word *blush*, which the children illustrated by sentences all round; and it was at length decided that the comparison which the soul makes of its own ideal with the actual, naturally produces an excitement in the mind, which the body expresses with a blush.

The word *brass* being illustrated by the sentence, " an impudent person is said to have *brass*," led to a still further illustration of the material signs of mental delicacy.

The word *brave* led to a long disquisition upon true and false courage.

After recess, there was a reading in Frank, and a lesson in grammatical analysis, with one part of the school, while the rest drew the map of Boston on their black tablets.

On Friday, January 30th, Mr. Alcott read "The birth-day
9*

Blessing," from the Boston Observer. He began, after the
writing lesson was over, and they were all turned to listen,
with remarks on the duty of forming the habit of attention ;
and its usefulness in fitting them to be benefited by lectures,
of which there were so many, and which were of so little
use to most who heard them, on account of their want of
power to attend. Then he begged them to think, as he
asked a few questions, preparatory to the subject of the
reading.

What do you mean by *birth-day?* said he.

The day on which you are born, said one. What do you
mean by being born ? Coming into the world. What comes
into the world ? A person. What is a person ? The body
and mind of a child. Which comes into the world, body
or mind ? Body.

Birth-day is the day on which the spirit is put into the
body, said another boy. Did you get that idea in this
school, said Mr. Alcott ? I never thought of such subjects
before I came to this school, said he.

Birth-day is the day when the soul and body meet together the first time, said another boy. It is the day when
the soul takes the body and comes into the world, said a
very small boy. Do you mean that the soul brings the body,
or the body brings the soul ? The soul brings the body.

Another little boy said, the soul comes from Heaven ; the
day it comes is its birth-day. Another little boy said, babies are not born for a week. What does *born* mean, said
Mr. Alcott to him ? It means when a child is very young ;
first, there are bodies, and in about a week souls go into
the bodies and make them live. Where do you think the
bodies are ? Oh, lying all about, on the ground, on the top
of the ground.

A little girl here said, she thought soul and body began on
the same day. One of the boys added, that he had always
had an indistinct idea that the soul lived before the body,
that there was a transmigration of souls. The little boy
who thought babies were not born for a week, said, God
makes the body and soul separate at the same time and puts
them together afterwards. Mr. Alcott heard them all, and

then said : Those who believe the soul lives before the body, hold up your hands. All did, except a few ; but some did not. Mr. Alcott asked those who did not, if they thought soul and body were made at the same minute? One said, yes. The rest said, they thought soul was made first. Then, said Mr. Alcott, but one thinks the soul lives before the body. Now, as many of you as think that the soul comes out of God, is of God, more godlike than any thing, hold up your hands. All held up their hands.

Now go forth into the *external world*, said Mr. Alcott, and find some fact, or appearance, in the external world, with which to picture out and typify birth. They were quite animated by this, and the following were the most striking analogies. One said, the seed sown, and springing up. Which do you mean by the seed, body or soul? Both. Another said, the branches from the trunk. The soul is the trunk, and the branches the body. Another said, I should think the trunk was God, and the branches were the soul. Another said, the soul is a rose-bud putting forth leaves. Another said, God is a rock, and we are pieces broken off. Violently? said Mr. Alcott. No, not violently. The next said, God is the water, and our souls are drops : he afterwards added, that God was the only real person, and we were pictures of him. God is the ocean, and we are the rivers, said the next. Another said, God is a sower, and we are the seeds which he sows. Mr. Alcott said, I have had that image myself; listen to these lines :

> Man is a seed sown in the soil of Time,
> And God the sower—life the allotted field :
> And Education is the husbandman,
> That, skilled in Culture's art divine, culls out
> The obstructing weeds, the generous mould incites,
> Imparts the quickening ray, the vital warmth ;
> And, nurturing still by Nature's influences,
> Brings forth the opening blossom, and matures
> Its promised fruit, in Piety and Truth.

Another boy said, the seed is God, and we are the fruit that springs out of it. Another said, God is the earth, and we are the productions. Another said, God is the shepherd, and

we are the sheep.   Mr. Alcott said, that is Scripture phrase-
ology; but Jesus is generally called the shepherd.   One of
the little girls said, God is the Sun, and Jesus Christ is the
Moon, and we are stars.   You mean, said Mr. Alcott, that
Jesus is superior to us, and God is superior to all, and gives
his light to Jesus?   Yes.   That is the best one of all, said
the rest.   I then remarked, that I had lately heard our soul
compared to a river of thoughts and feelings, pouring through
us from God, the eternal fountain, and augmented in the
course of our mortal life, by other rivers from the same
source.

Mr. Alcott allowed these analogies to run on, that they all
might clearly understand the principle of metaphor; for
this is a preparation for analysis of the language of imagination, so as to use it consciously.   At last he said, these
are analogies, and many of them are good, but none are perfect; for there is nothing in the vegetable or animal world,
which is quite adequate to typify the great fact of birth, the
incarnation, or embodying of spirit.   The internal eye sees
this fact; the external eye cannot see it.   You have expressed by your analogies that the soul comes from God;
do you think that when it first appears in the human form
it is God-like, pure, innocent?   All held up their hands.—
Well, do you think that those who have lived in the world
awhile, that you, any of you, are as good as you were when
you were infants?   None thought so.   Why is it, that you
universally grow worse as you live on?   They generally
thought, that they saw vice and tried it to see how it would
seem.   One girl said, when we are babies we do not know.
Mr. Alcott said, is knowledge the cause of evil?   Do you
remember the beautiful illustration of the beginning of sin
in the Old Testament, the tree of knowledge and the tree of
life; or the fruits of the head, and the fruits of the heart?
One boy said, we are brought up to think the old do right,
and when we see them do wrong, we think it is right, and
imitate them.   Is it irresistible to imitate the old? said Mr.
Alcott.   They all said no.   He then read the lines called
" A birth-day Blessing," which they listened to, and talked
about with great intelligence.   When he came to the lines:

And doth the Eternal Beauty, Truth and Good,
Thus o'er the fountain head of soul forever brood:

he stopped and asked, if they knew what that meant ? They
said yes, it means God, and because the soul comes from
him. Mr. Alcott then repeated Jesus Christ's remarks about
his own origin, and about childhood ; and closed with reading the lines from Wordsworth :

Our birth is but a sleep, and a forgetting, &c.

After recess, I took my class in Latin ; and Mr. Alcott
heard the rest analyse sentences grammatically.

The next day was January 31st, and Saturday ; and Mr.
Alcott chose for his readings from the Bible, such passages
as would bring up again and again, the idea that Jesus considered childhood innocent ; and that innocence is a positive condition ; that it comprehends all the instincts and
feelings which naturally tend to good, such as humility, self-
forgetfulness, love, trust, &c. ; and that the only method of
self-cultivation is to retain, or return to the childish state and
re-produce these feelings. He began,

" And they brought to Jesus little children." This, said
Mr. Alcott, was when Jesus was on earth ; but Jesus now
lives, as much as he did then ; he lives in Eternity, not in
time. He then went on to the expression, " of such is the
kingdom of Heaven ;" and through the story of the young
man who " lacked ;" and the parable of the laborers who
all had a penny. He made some applications of this parable to those present. He then passed over to the question
of which was the first in the kingdom of Heaven, applying
it to a disposition he had seen in this school ; then he read
the parables illustrating forgiveness, and he asked how many
had this spirit of forgiveness ? Some held up their hands.
Mr. Alcott went on to speak of forgiveness ; and said, when
they yielded in a quarrel, and forebore, they were not yielding to this or that boy, but they were yielding to God. And
when they fought with a fellow-being, they were fighting
against God. As this seemed to strike the children with astonishment, Mr. Alcott referred to Jesus Christ's expression,
" Inasmuch as ye do it unto the least of these little ones, ye

do it unto me." He then read the account of Christ's en-
trance into Jerusalem, and the expression, " Out of the
mouths of babes and sucklings, God hath perfected praise,"
which he explained to mean the innocent expressions of
pure childhood, in word and deed.

Now, said he, I am going to read what will show how a
child may be perverted ; and he read the story of the Phari-
see and Publican, (in paraphrase as usual,) up to the place
where Jesus said that, " whosoever will not receive the kingdom of Heaven as a little child, shall not enter it." He then
read the conversation with Nicodemus.

After recess, the children were arranged to hear the journals read. A small boy sat near me ; and while we were
waiting, I called him to me, and asked him if he thought
he had improved since he came here ? He said, yes. What,
said I, do you think any more ? Why, said he, I did not
know I could think, before I came here ! What did you do
before, all the time, said I ? I am sure I don't know, said
he. Mr. Alcott talked a little with one of the girls, on her
thoughtlessness, and on the duty of trying. After waiting
nearly quarter of an hour, for the boys, who seemed not to
have heard the clock strike, Mr. Alcott began to read without them. He said he did not read one journal, because it
was not written well enough. He began another, during
which time the absent boys came in, having stayed out
twenty minutes too long. Such a case never occurred before.

At the commencement of the school, Mr. Alcott appointed the recess at half past eleven, that the clock striking
twelve, might be the signal for return ; and this he distinctly said to each scholar, as they were sent out, one by one,
for their first recess. A lady, who came to place her son at
school, that day, expressed her astonishment at Mr. Alcott's
confidence in such little boys' obedience ; and said she was
very sure her boy would not come in, if he were among
them. When her boy came to school some weeks after, it
is true that he did play truant, frequently ; not only at recess-time, but before school ; and, in one or two instances,
did not come to school at all. But none of the other schol-

ars ever remained out five minutes after the clock struck, excepting in one instance, of a very imaginative boy from the country, who had just entered the school, and who wandered to the other side of the Common, with a little fellow of five years, that was very much a creature of instinct at that time ; and in this instance of to-day, when the boys declared that they did not hear the clock strike, being in Temple Court, instead of on the Mall. And Mr. Alcott, having entire confidence in their word, merely told them not to play in the Court another day, at least without a sentinel to watch the clock.

Monday, February 2nd.—I arrived at nine o'clock. Mr. Alcott did not talk much, except to make remarks upon journal writing, to the older boys ; and upon the desirableness of high education, to those who were to wield the interests of the world by commerce. He came then to a little boy, and said, Oh I am very much encouraged about you ; you have written a whole column of words ; you begin to know what you are in school for. He then took Krummacher, to read a parable to the little class. He read the story of the Canary-bird, talking with them in his indescribable way, all the while. He then took the younger division of the spelling class, and heard them pronounce their lessons in spelling, and told them the meanings of the words.

He told the rest of the class who had not broken any rule to turn round. All turned but two. Do any of you remember those words of Scripture, " Set a watch upon thy heart ?" Yes, said they. It does not mean to put a timepiece on your bodily heart, but to superintend your minds : have you put a sentinel over yourself to-day ? What is the sentinel of the soul ? Conscience. If the sentinel sleeps, what becomes of the city ? The enemies get in, said a little boy. What is the enemy ? said Mr. Alcott. Error, said one ; Doubt, said another ; Passion, said a third ; Revenge, said another ; Self-will, said several. In one word, Wickedness, said Mr. Alcott. Now all those who do not set a watch on themselves, I shall consider as not desiring to be better. Do you remember these words in the Bible : " By

patient continuance in well-doing, seek" (for what?) I
don't remember said the boy addressed. "Seek for glory
honor, and immortality"—how many of you have this patient continuance? None spoke.

Mr. Alcott remarked, that one boy of this school had said,
when asked, why he did not answer Mr. Alcott's questions,
"do you think I am going to speak before thirty children?"
As many of you, said he, as have this feeling of embarrass-
men may hold up their hands. Several held up their hands.
And he then spoke of the duty of making an effort to conquer this feeling, since it was impossible for him to assist
them in cultivating their minds, unless they would show him
the state of them. He then asked them to spell the words,
which they did; and I was obliged to leave the room for an
hour.

When I came back, they were speaking of the word *birch*,
which had led them to the consideration of school discipline. And they all spontaneously said, that they had never
been in a school where there was so much order, and so little punishment, as in this. Mr. Alcott asked them how they
felt when he punished them; and they expressed that they
always felt he punished them for their own good, and not
from anger.

Something was said of hurting the body as a means of
reaching the mind; he said, that in some instances, boys
needed bodily punishment to rouse their sluggishness of
mind, because they would not attend to the meanings of
words; and could not be reached by words that were intended to revive the conscience. Other boys needed it on
account of their obstinacy and opposition. There were
rivers which were very strong, but would not go in the
channel made for them by God; but wanted to make new
channels; and there were some which were stagnant. And
there were some shallow rivers which babbled. As he described these various rivers, the boys appropriated to themselves, and one another, these various types; and Mr. Alcott
confirmed some of these, as very just applications.

On Tuesday, February 3d, I did not come to school; but
when a little boy, who lived in the house with me, came
home, he told me they wrote, for a writing lesson, till ten

clock. And then Mr. Alcott read about Christian—how he came to the Cross and his Burden fell off into the sepulchre ; and he said Mr. Alcott told of a procession, and proposed that they should all go in it, and bury their bad habits—the bundles on their backs. (Mr. Alcott told me, this morning, that the subject of *self-sacrifice* was discussed, when he brought Christian to the foot of the cross ; and it was under this principle of self-surrender, that the procession was formed.)

The little boy also told me, that after recess Mr. Alcott described two worlds ; and that the boys said one was *heaven,* and one was *hell.* (Mr. Alcott said that he described the world of spirit, and the world of flesh ; and the issues of these different principles, in an allegory ; and that the children themselves came to the conclusions, and alone used those words.) This little boy also told me, that Mr. Alcott said, he could tell what *shapes* their minds would come forth in, if they could take shape ; and, said he, mine came out in the very thing that I have always wanted more than any thing else ; and he screamed with laughter, as he spoke— the *very, very thing,* said he. Well, what was it ? said his mother and I, at the same moment. A sword, said he, a sword to prick all the boys with ! Well, can you remember the shape that any other soul came forth in, said I. He said two of the boys were to come forth as *whispers ;* but he did not remember the rest.

Wednesday, 4th.—I arrived at quarter past nine, and found them all writing their journals, or their spelling lessons. At quarter of ten, Mr. Alcott began to read to the youngest division of the spelling class, and those of the youngest class who were present. He read a parable of Krummacher to illustrate *indolence,* which not only awakened their attention very strongly, but attracted the notice of many of the rest ; and he talked a little with a boy of the larger class, to enforce the lesson upon him.

At ten o'clock, the class turned to spell. They all spelled well, until it came to one little boy, who missed. Mr. Alcott said, do you know why you do not spell the words right ? The child looked enquiringly. It is because you do

10

not use your eyes, to see how the letters are placed; and so you have no picture of the word in your mind. And he went on describing how he should look at the letters, picture them out, lay up the picture in his mind; and when he heard the word, should think how one letter came after the other. He talked a great while; and not only the one addressed, but all the little boys, seemed much interested and edified. The words were defined to these children, and then Mr. Alcott called the rest of the class to turn and spell.

Birth was the first word. Mr. Alcott remarked that we had once before talked of birth, and their ideas had been brought out. Now I am going to speak of it again, and we shall read Mr. Wordsworth's Ode. He then asked the youngest child present, how old he was, and found he was four. He then asked the oldest, and she was twelve years old. He said, that little boy, in four years, has not had time to make much comparison of thoughts and feelings; this comparison makes up *conscious life*. He asked those who understood him, to hold up their hands. Several held up their hands. Those who do not understand these words, may hold up their hands. A great many of the younger ones held up their hands.

Mr. Alcott said he was not surprised that they did not understand; but perhaps they would understand some things he was going to say. Life is a kind of memory—conscious life is *memory*. Now, said he to the oldest, do you feel that any change has taken place in you, in twelve years; do things seem the same to you as they did six years ago? She recognised a change. A boy of ten, also said, that he did also. Mr. Alcott said, that Mr. Wordsworth had lived, when he wrote this ode, about thirty years, and consequently he had felt changes, and he had expressed this in the lines he was about to read. He then began and read the first stanza of the Ode to Immortality, up to the line: "The things which I have seen, I now can see no more." He here stopped, and asked why Mr. Wordsworth could not see the things which he had seen before; had they changed, or had he changed? He had changed, said a boy of ten. Have you had any degree of this change? Yes, and more in this last year, than in all my life before. Mr. Alcott said he thought that there were periods in life, when great changes took place : he had experienced it himself.

He then said : but let us all look back six months ; how many of you look at things, and feel about them differently from what you did six months ago ? How many of you feel that this school-room is a different place from what it was the first week you were here ? Almost every one, immediately, with great animation, held up his hand. He then asked those who knew why this was, to hold up their hands. Many did. And when called on to answer, they severally said, because we know more ; because we think more ; because we understand you ; because you know us ; because you have looked inside of us. Mr. Alcott said, the place is very different to me ; and why ? They gave similar answers ; but he said they had not hit it. At last one said : because we behave better. Yes, said he, you have it now ; knowledge is chaff of itself ; but you have taken the knowledge and used it to govern yourselves, and to make yourselves better. Why, if I thought I only gave you knowledge, and could not lead you to use it to make yourselves better, I would never enter this school-room again !

He then went on and read the next stanzas of the Ode ; stopping to ask them about the effects of the rainbow, the rose, the waters on a starry night, on themselves. He then stopped and said, there are some minds which live in the world, and yet are insensible ; which do not see any beauty in the rainbow, the moon, the waters on a starry night. As he went on through the next stanza, so descriptive of the animation and beauty of spring, he paused on every line, and asked questions. Why are " the cataracts said to blow their trumpets ? " A little girl said, because the waters dash against the rocks. " The echoes thronging through the woods," led out to recollections of the sound in the woods in spring ; to echoes which they had severally heard. As the animating pictures of " children pulling flowers on May day ; " the " child springing up on the mother's arm," &c. came up, every countenance expressed the most vivid delight ; and one girl exclaimed, what a succession of beautiful pic-

tures! All full of life, said Mr. Alcott; and he went on to
the lines, "but there's a tree;" and when he had read these
lines, he said: was that a thought of life? No, a thought
of death, said several. Yes, said Mr. Alcott, Mr. Wordsworth had lived long enough to feel changes; he had
known death, as well as life.

When he came to the line: " Our birth is but a sleep, and
a forgetting," he stopped and asked how that was? After a
pause, one of the most intelligent boys, eight years old, said,
he could not imagine. The two oldest girls said, they understood it, but could not explain it in words. Mr. Alcott
then observed that the little boy whose attention to the spelling, and reading, and arithmetic, he is so often obliged to
spur up, was holding up his hand. Do you understand it?
said Mr. Alcott. Yes. Well, what does it mean? Why,
you know, said he very deliberately, that, for all that our life
seems so long to us, it is a very short time to God; and so
when we die it seems all a sleep to God. He repeated this,
at Mr. Alcott's request; and I said to him: so Mr. Wordsworth was thinking of God; and how God felt on seeing
that a child was born into the world? He paused, looked a
little distressed, and repeated the word forgetting. I said,
wait and tell me your thought. Why, you know, said he,
God knows us, but we don't. He looked at me with a look
of doubt whether I should understand him. And our knowledge of ourselves, in comparison with what God knows
about us, said I, seems like *forgetfulness* itself? Yes, said
he, that is it, (with a cleared up countenance.) All the rest
listened with interest and an expression of great pleasure;
and then one girl said, the soul comes from heaven ; it goes
to sleep in that world, and wakes up in this.

Mr. Alcott then read on to the line: "Heaven lies about
us in our infancy ;" when he shut up the book, and asked
every child separately, what he understood by birth. They
all answered, and many repeated the definitions which they
gave the other day.

Mr. Alcott said, that he observed one striking difference
in their answers; some expressed the idea that the soul
shaped and made the body ; others that the body was made

and the soul put into it. Which is right? said one boy.
That is more than I can tell, but I incline to the first opinion; that is my opinion. You are all nearly right, however; you all have the important ideas, birth is not the
beginning of the spirit; life is the memory, or a waking
up of spirit. All the life of knowledge is the remembrance,
or waking up of what is already within; "the rising of
life's star, that hath elsewhere its setting." What is life's
star? The soul, said they. But birth is sometimes the
prelude to the death of the soul, said Mr. Alcott. How?
said one boy. Because the soul becomes the slave of the
body; is governed, darkened, shut up and buried in it;
and it is necessary that it should be born again, born out
of the body, do you understand that? Yes. Some of you
have needed to be born again; and have begun your new
life, said Mr. Alcott.

After recess I took my class into the other room to attend to Latin, and Mr. Alcott attended to Arithmetic and
English Grammar.

February 5th. I arrived at half past nine and found the
children in their seats. Mr. Alcott talked a little with the
little commentator of yesterday, commending him for his
writing, and especially because he had been rather indo-
cile, not through opposition, but from a sort of obstinate
clinging to his own inward thoughts, which are probably
clearer than those of most children of his age.

Mr. Alcott read from Northcotes' Fables, to the little
class; and had a long talk with them on punishment, to
make them comprehend its theory, the hurting of the body
for the benefit of the mind, and their faces looked all, "like
fires new stirred," as they listened. I thought I should like
to have some of those sceptics who do not believe children
can comprehend the sacrifice of the body to the mind, to
have seen these little things, under four years of age, listen
to and apprehend the philosophy of pain.

At ten the whole school turned to face Mr. Alcott; and
he then arranged some restless boys in situations where he
thought they would not be tempted. A great deal of talk
was made about these arrangements, in order to impress

10*

them with the great importance of complete self-control. Mr. Alcott said, that if interrupted to-day, he should discontinue his readings.

He then read the first stanzas of the Castle of Indolence, without letting them know what it was, and asked each to write on his slate what he or she thought it represented. They several'y wrote: sluggishness, calm pleasures, sleep, ease, heaven, doubt, death, earth, the world, and deception. Mr. Alcott having gone round and looked at each, told them each to keep their own secret, and he read it again; and said those who changed their opinions to go and tell Miss Peabody. Several changed; and there were added new answers, as idleness, pleasures, sleepiness, solitude, laziness, silence, deceit, misers, slumber, hell, doubting castle, and several said indolence.

Mr. Alcott then read the song of the Wizard, and asked, who believed, with the wizard, that hard work makes all the vice in the world. A large lazy boy held up his hand; but a little boy of six made a gesture of astonishment at his doings. When Mr. Alcott read the Invitation, he asked who would accept it? Some smiled and held up their hands. He continued to read through the Proclamation, the description of the interior of the castle, and the Mirror of Vanity; when he stopped, and said, as many of you as think you ever visit this castle hold up your hands? Thirteen held up their hands. How many of you delight to rise at break of day, cold mornings? Almost all held up their hands. This room, he continued, is often the Castle of Indolence, and he pointed to several chairs, saying of each that is the Castle of Indolence.

After recess, the twenty younger boys and two younger girls of the class, found their arithmetic all prepared for them. The rest found their Common Place Books in their places and Mr. Alcott after giving them the directions about the lesson, called out the class in A. C. P. B. of Poetry. The American Flag was selected by one of the boys for the lesson. Mr. Alcott asked him to read the part he liked best, and he read the stanzas, *Flag of the Brave*, and *Flag of the Seas*. Mr. Alcott asked another boy why he thought that boy liked it so much? He said it was because he had such a temper, he liked to have things in his own way. Another said, because he liked battling and violence. The boy himself said it was because he liked his country; and he read over again the most thundering lines of the piece. The girls all laughed as he read the words "War and Vengeance," with so much gusto. Mr. Alcott said, well; he is very ingenuous, he turns out himself before us; he loves vengeance, war, slaughter, don't he? Yes, said he. Do you ever think of the sufferers? Sometimes I think of the widows. Which do you think of most, the soldiers or the widows? About the same. I am sorry; but I hope you will think of the widows most, bye and bye. Mr. Alcott then read the same stanzas very slowly, and stopped and asked questions about every line. What is the image here? What feeling does it gratify? One boy said, did you hear Dr. Channing's sermon,* Sir. No; but I know what he thinks, I am glad you remember it. A little girl said, I did not hear it! (very despondingly.) Mr. Alcott then spoke of the right of self-defence, and of defensive war, and there was quite a discussion; which resulked I thought in very just views all round. One boy, on being asked, said there was nothing in the piece which pictured out any of his thoughts and feelings. But at last he read the last stanza, as the one he liked best, on the whole.

Mr. Alcott then asked, what is freedom, does it give us the right to do as we please? No. What is it? the opportunity for what? He did not know. Is it the right to do right, or to do either right or wrong? To do right. The boy who had selected the piece said it was, besides, the right to speak one's own mind. Mr. Alcott said, what, carelessly, whether it will do good or harm? At first he said Yes, then No. Another boy said, we have no right to do as we please, unless we please to do right. The girls agreed with him. Mr. Alcott then told the boy who had selected the piece, that all his difficulties at home and at school arose from his confounding the ideas of *Freedom*

* Sermon on War.

and *Indulgence.* He then spoke of *Law* as the guardian of Freedom, and the laws of this school as emanating from conscience.

One boy, on being asked which stanza he liked best, said he saw very little in the whole thing, he said he never wanted to be a soldier. The boy who had selected the piece said he wanted to be a soldier; he wanted to ride on horseback; and be dressed up in uniform. It would not be so pleasant to ride unless he could be dressed up in uniform. Another boy wanted to be a king. As this ode hardly admitted of a paraphrase, (having no ideas in it, or the little claim they had being in the words;) Mr. Alcott said they might go and write their journals, while he heard the Arithmetic lessons.

February 6th.—I arrived at half past nine and found them at their spelling lessons as usual. Immediately Mr. Alcott commenced with the youngest class; and read about Frank's breaking the window, and made a very animated lesson on ingenuousness by a conversation with them, intermingled with the reading; which, as usual, led them to the conclusion that they should prefer punishment to going on in wrong doing.

This is the great principle which Mr. Alcott labors to bring out in the young consciousness, to be willing to be punished, to accept, nay to *seek* punishment, in order that they may not indulge themselves in wrong doing, and to look upon pain as the blessed instrument of producing good character. His own little girl is led to tell him of all the naughty things she does, and the telling does not save her from punishment, but often only ensures it. Even the scholars here often tell him what will produce punishment, knowing that their ingenuousness does not save them from the penalty, so successful has he been in making them feel that spiritual good is worth deprivation, or bodily pain, or whatever the punishment may be.

Mr. Alcott then took the youngest class but one, and heard them spell their lesson, giving a great deal of time to that little boy whose deep interest in the general, makes it a peculiar effort for him to enter into the details of the particular. It is really very curious to see on the one hand how difficult it is for this child to receive a strong impression from any outward arbitrary thing like a letter, or the arrangement of letters; and on the other hand, how rapidly and completely his mind discovers the idea conveyed by a poetical image, or a natural fact. Nature seems transparent to his eye; but it is for him an effort of obstruction to see the outward and arbitrary.

The lesson was spelled at quarter past ten o'clock. He asked the younger division if they received new ideas while we talked about the words. After a while, one after another held up their hands. One little boy said he understood Mr. Alcott when he spoke to himself, but not always when he talked to others. Mr. Alcott then asked whose words he understood best? he said mother's and father's and Mr. Alcott's. Mr. Alcott said, do I talk about the same things. No, said he. Mother talks about things *out*, and you about things *inside*, and he knocked on his head to express the inside.

Mr. Alcott then asked them if he should not make a tremendous law! If every boy present who got into a lazy position, or got things into their hands, were inattentive, &c. should not receive a blow upon their hand? A large boy said that would not be *just*. Mr. Alcott asked him if it was not just that he should punish a certain boy (naming him) if he did what would interfere with his own attention, and the attention of others. He said yes, *but not so*. Mr. Alcott then asked if he had not a right to choose his own modes of reaching the mind, and if words did not do, and a slight pain on the body did do, if he had not a right, and if it was not his duty, to take that means? The boy thought any other way but that. Mr. Alcott asked the rest if they thought it would be just to punish them as he proposed, if they did what he had spoken of, if they indulged themselves in these habits often, so much instruction as they had had. Every one held up his hand. Still this boy, who has a horror of physical pain which is peculiar, persisted. I said to him, I cannot conceive why you should think that it is so dreadful to have a touch of pain on your body, that you can one moment weigh with it your improvement of mind; I should prefer to be beaten like a West Indian slave, to resting in a bad habit. One of the girls said, I should be very glad to be whipped, if it would cure me of my bad habits. Mr. Alcott asked all present who would willingly receive a good deal of bodily pain from him, if it would rid them of these habits of in-attention, self-indulgence, &c. which interfere with us every day, to hold up their hands. All did but one little boy, and the great boy spoken of before.

The uses of pain in developing the mind and awaken-ing sympathy, were considered; and a comparison of the external and internal world was made. And Mr. Alcott told how his little girl came to him the other day and said that her sister had pulled her hair and pinched her cheek, for her sister was a boisterous child who inflicted pain thoughtlessly. And he said that he called the little girl (knowing that it was as her sister had said,) and said, sister says you pulled her hair so, (he gave it a hard pull;) she looked at him and almost cried. And that you pinched her cheek so, (and he gave her a hard pinch;) but he did not look at her any differently from usual, merely seri-ously. He said that she immediately understood how her sister had been hurt; and *sympathy* arose in her mind, and she immediately went and kissed her. Do you think it was worth while that I should give her pain to bring out that sympathy; or let her mind go uncultivated because I was afraid of hurting her body? The result of the conver-sation seemed to be a universal agreement with Mr. Alcott.

The first interesting word that was illustrated to-day, was *bleed*. One said, the heart bleeds when it has suffer-ing. Mr. Alcott said that these figurative, or rather he would say spiritual meanings, were the most real; the lit-eral meaning was the real meaning in things, but nothing happened in things which did not image forth some move-ment of spiritual life.

The word *blend* was variously illustrated and defined. One little boy of five years old said, when a thing is made of one substance, and when we want it to be of a different

color, some other substance is put over, and then the two
are said to be blended. Mr. Alcott said, this boy's definitions are from his own mint; and then he explained this
figure, by describing a mint.

Blind led to the idea of spiritual blindness. Mr. Alcott
said, some of you, when you first came to this school, were
spiritually blind; some are here now, who are spiritually
blind; their outward eye is a very good one; but they do
not seem to look inward. The spiritual eye is the soul itself; and he quoted Byron's words: " A thing of eyes, &c."
He spoke of the causes of spiritual blindness. He said the
reason that boy, with whom he had just been talking, could
not understand the theory of punishment, was because his
soul was blinded by the predominance of bodily fear, and
outward things in his thoughts.

A great deal was said about the uses of the bodily eye;
the cultivation of it connected with a parallel advancement
of spiritual vision; and then the reciprocal influences of
bodily and spiritual vision on each other, and on the advancement of the mind and soul.

At last he called for the slates of the superintendents, for
there had been two. On one there was only the superintendent's own name; the other had several names, which
were explained; and the boy had evidently been very careful to do justice. None thought he had been unjust. Mr.
Alcott said what was set down did not warrant any punishment; they had all tried and had succeeded in being self-
controlled and attentive. Before he said this, however, and
while they were expecting punishment, a little boy said : I
spoke, but he has not written me down. Mr. Alcott said,
you are right to tell me.

After recess I took my scholars into the other room.—
When they came back, Mr. Alcott asked who had been
faulty; and several held up their hands. Mr. Alcott asked
one of these what he did ? He said, played. Why? He
did not know. At last he said, he was thoughtless. Why?
He did not know.

Mr. Alcott took him and brought him to the little boy,
who gives such spiritual answers, and said : ask that little

boy how you can learn to think? The little boy said, he must employ all his thoughts. Well, said Mr. Alcott, that is very good advice. But I don't know how, said the boy. Well, ask him how. The little boy said, with a great effort to get out the words: Why, he must set his heart to work. Very well, said Mr. Alcott, you must set your heart to work, and employ all your thoughts ; and then you will not play, when you ought to be doing something else.

I found Mr. Alcott had given a writing lesson on the black tablets to the rest of the school, while I had had my Latin class in the other room.

February 7th.—I came and looked over my journal during the hour before the reading commenced, as it is to be read after recess.

At about ten o'clock, Mr. Alcott began to read the story of Abraham's sacrifice of Isaac. After he had finished it, he asked those who had any ideas about it, to hold up their hands. Two boys thought there was nothing mysterious about the story. It was very natural that so good a man as Abraham, should instantly do what God commanded him. Almost all agreed with them. Then one boy said, it was very mysterious to him that Abraham could have consented to the killing of his son. Mr. Alcott asked him if he doubted whether Abraham did right. He said, No—he knew that Abraham was good, and that made it mysterious.

Now, said Mr. Alcott, I am going to ask all a question of which you must think before you answer. What do you love best? God, said the first one addressed, without any hesitation. Mr. Alcott said, I should like a more deliberate and particular answer, and I will put the question in another form. Do you love any being or thing, as well as yourself? Yes, said he. Do you love any being or thing better than yourself? I do not know. The next said, he thought he loved God best—better than his mother—better than himself. All the most thoughtless boys were very sure they loved God best ; and also one or two of the most thoughtful. One little boy at first could not tell. At last, he said he thought it was his mother. Mr. Alcott asked if he loved her better than God? He said, No—but as well.

Another little boy said, he loved his uncle Charles best. Why? He did not want to tell. Do you love him because he is good, or because he loves you; or because he has given you any thing? Because he is good. Did he ever give you any thing? Yes. Has he given you any thing lately? No, he is in England. The next little boy said, he loved God best, Jesus Christ next, and his mother next. Why do you love your mother? Because she takes care of me. Why do you love Jesus Christ? Because he is holy; (Mr. Alcott did not hear, and the second time he said, because he is good.) Why do you love God? Because he is good. Why do you love God better than Jesus Christ? Because he has more goodness. Do you love yourself? *Not one grain.* Don't you love your mind? That is not myself. What is yourself? My body. Don't you love it? No. Don't you love to feed it? *Yes!* said he, slowly, with surprise at this home question. Don't you love to feed it more than you ought to do? Yes, said he, with a sigh and a look of deep reflection.

There were no more new ideas given. I intimated that I thought many had answered as if the question was, What ought you to love best? which produced a few remarks from Mr. Alcott. Some however had evidently given their own minds.

Here the continuous journal of six weeks closes. Its details are very imperfect, because it was impossible for the pen to follow all the transitions, which the different associations of thought in so large a company produced. It will be observed, that although the journal almost exclusively records the conversations upon words learned in the spelling lessons, and on the readings; yet grammar, geography, arithmetic, and Latin lessons, were given every day. It is important to notice this, as some persons have the impression, that no lessons of the latter kind are given in school. The grammar was taught by parsing in the manner which has been frequently touched upon; arithmetic was taught upon Colburn's system, with a slight intermixture of cyphering exercises; and the Latin on the system of Locke.

11

The geography was at first taught on Mr. Carter's plan, although we did not quite approve it for our pupils; and as it succeeded less in interesting these children than the other lessons, we soon laid it aside, determined to think out another plan which might combine more advantages. A few words will be given to this subject here, as the method adopted seems to be working well, notwithstanding we are at some disadvantage on account of the difficulty of collecting books and pictures for our purpose.

The whole school being resolved into one class, they receive three conversation lectures a week on Geography.— The first three lectures consisted of a description of the solar system; addressed to the picturesque imagination. They were called on to imagine themselves placed in the centre of the sun; and to picture out the scene presented to the eye, supposing that organ strong enough to look through and beyond Herschel. The discipline of Mr. Alcott's readings, and their good habits of attention, rendered these conversations very successful, as was found when they were called on to describe the scene themselves. The forces that produce circular motion, were illustrated; and thus, all the astronomy which such children could well comprehend, was set forth. At the third lecture, Bryant's " Song of the Stars," was read, which very much interested them, as they were called to form out in their minds all the imagery.

Having given an idea of the solar system, the earth was approached more nearly, and its atmosphere considered. They were led to imagine the clouds which hang in the atmosphere as they would appear to a person coming to our earth from another planet. And to illustrate this, extracts were read from books describing the clouds as they appear from mountains, when they hang below the summits. Descending upon the surface of the earth, we observed on what principle it was divided into zones. And the characteristic vegetation, &c., of each zone was dwelt upon, in a lecture devoted to the purpose. The mountain scenery of the various parts of the globe was next considered; and descriptions of remarkable scenes among mountains, were selected from such books of travels as we could procure;

among which, Humboldt's was found most interesting.—
Having proceeded thus far, the pupils were set to drawing
the outlines of the four quarters of the globe, being only required to indicate where about the mountainous parts were.

As it is very difficult to draw these outlines, on account
of their irregularity, it required repeated trials, which occupied them day after day. But it is obvious that in constantly looking upon the maps in order to draw these outlines, a great deal could be learned from them. But a great
deal of warning was constantly given, lest the impressions
on the imagination, left by the descriptions that were read,
should be lost by dwelling on such an inadequate representation of the green and flowery valleys, the snow-clad, and
forest-cinctured mountains, and the rock-bound coasts of
the magnificent ocean, as a mere map must necessarily be.

Lakes and rivers naturally come next to mountains, as
striking features of the earth's surface. These also afford
scope for picturesque description and illustration. The waters of our own country are so magnificent, that they have
attracted much attention. Flint's Valley of the Mississippi,
Irving's Tour in the Prairies, occasional passages in Audu-
bon's Ornithological Biography, &c., afford much aid to
this portion of the course. Engravings and paintings too,
of the river and lake scenery of many parts of the world,
can be procured. When the children come to draw these
lakes and rivers, of which they have seen pictures, or with
which they associate scenes of human life from the journals
of travellers and naturalists, they will find it much more
easy to remember their names, than if they had no other
idea than a mere black line may convey. It is not impossible,
also, for the instructer to assist the young imagination to
take birds'-eye views of the rivers and lakes of a continent,
by suggesting to them to look down as from a balloon upon
the earth, and see how these rivers flow from the mountains, mingle together, and find the sea.

The ocean then becomes the object of study; its propor-
tion to the land, and its general characteristics. Parts of
Mr. Greenwood's article on the Sea, were read from the
Token; and striking sea scenes from various books, espe-

cially beautiful scenes of the tropical seas. Here some account would be naturally given of the first attempts to explore the ocean; of the voyages of Columbus, and other discoverers. The boys were recommended to read Cook's voyages at home. The more a human interest is thrown over external objects, the more easily they can be remembered; and therefore, the narratives of voyagers are so important. Descriptions of whale-catching, seal-catching, pearl-diving, &c., are therefore very useful when brought into these lessons upon the ocean.

Columbus' journal of his first voyage, gives us beautiful descriptions of the West India Islands, and Irving adds much in his two works. And the intention is to give a very complete idea of all the shores of the sea. There is much difficulty, however, in finding information for this part of the course. It would be very convenient if a book were to be made containing a description of the coasts and harbors all over the world; and of the sea-ports, with their commercial relations. And would not this be the best practical geography for boys?

During the whole of the course, the drawing of maps should be continued, and all the natural features of the earth should be indicated. The last part of geography studied, should be the arbitrary divisions made by human politics. By associating this, however, with the history of nations, as the other parts of geography were associated with natural history and biography, it will be more easily remembered, and those parts of the world will be best known, which it is the most important to know accurately. When these political divisions are considered, the children can draw them on their maps, and indicate the places of the towns.

Is it not obvious, that geography, studied in this way, might put into the mind some adequate conception of the face of the earth? while the common plan fails to touch the imagination, and terminates in nothing but a knowledge of maps, which is not sufficiently interesting to be retained in the memory. For it is a fact, which every thoughtful teacher must have observed, that nothing is permanently remem-

bered, which does not touch the heart, or interest the imagination. Years are given by children to the study of geography, and yet scarcely any person retains an accurate
recollection of the relations of places to each other beyond
their school days, so as to dispense with the constant use of
a map. It would not be so, if the thoughts wandered over
the real earth, with all its pomp and garniture, instead of
being fastened to that linear hieroglyphic, the much lauded
map, which is perhaps a necessary evil, but certainly is an
evil, when it precludes the mind from forming within itself
a real picture of the original. For beauty and magnifi-
cence are inspirations, and secure the constant recur-
rence of the mind, and lingering of the thoughts, over
whatever fact they associate themselves with; and enable
us to *learn it by heart,* — which very phrase, like most of our
idioms, is full of the spiritual philosophy.

Before quite dismissing the Journal, however, I must
give some farther extracts, illustrating a weekly exercise,
which has now become the appropriate business of Wednesday; and is likely to continue so. It was suggested by a
conversation, which took place on the 9th of February, the
whole of which is worth giving.

The word *bless* came up among the words of the spelling lesson. It was defined as wishing well to others; wishing God's blessing; making happy. Mr. Alcott asked, if
any one felt he comprehended all its meaning? No hands
were held up, and a small boy said: Mr. Alcott I do not
believe you comprehend all its meaning. Mr. Alcott asked
what blessings God gives? They answered severally, food;
sun; air; clothing; dwellings; flowers; wisdom; our
souls; parents. Do we have blessings whether we deserve
them or not? Some said yes; some said no. But there is
one blessing greater than all you have mentioned. They
severally answered, after some consideration, Spirit; God's
Spirit; the Bible.

The Bible, said Mr. Alcott, is God in words. But the
Bible is not the only Revelation of God. There are many
Bibles to those who think. Nature, the outward world, is
a Bible. Its objects typify God's thoughts. The soul is a
11*

Bible. What do we read in the passions? I will tell you: God's punishments; for the passions are the overmastering effects of indulgence. What tremendous pains they involve, by necessity!

But what blessings have you had? He addressed a boy who thinks little, but who catches the habit of answering. He replied, the Bible. How is that a blessing? said Mr. Alcott. The Lord blesses us with it, said he. In what way? He makes us happy. With the Bible? He makes us good. Your answers do not sound as if they were your own reflections, but like parrotry. Tell me what blessings you have been blessed with to-day? With a mind. Are you thoughtless? said I, (referring to a confession or excuse he always makes, when he has done wrong.) Yes. But does not thoughtless mean without thoughts? Yes. Can there be a mind without thoughts? No. Then how can you say your mind is a blessing to you? I have been baptized, said he. How is that a blessing? said Mr. Alcott. It purified me. Are you pure, purified? I was, for a little while after I was baptized. Was your soul or your body baptized? My body. Does not purity belong to the mind? Yes. Do truth and love keep the mind pure? Yes. Do you understand what I mean, when I say, the soul is baptized with truth and love? Yes. Was your soul ever baptized so? Yes. How often? Every day. How long does it last? A little while.

All these answers seemed given without thought; and Mr. Alcott pursued it still farther, his object being to show this fancifully worded boy, that he had no self-knowledge; and that his ideas were not representations of his own thoughts and feelings, but mere verbal associations, and meaningless images. This boy's memory of words and images, which has been over-cultivated, is great; and he seems to have been led into a shallow activity of mind and tongue, that deceives himself. I thought he was enlightened a little to-day; and the rest of the scholars, who were very attentive, and occasionally joined in the conversation, with much intelligence, evidently understood his mind very well; and were guarded against the same fallacy.

Mr. Alcott here opened the Bible, and read the beatitudes in paraphrase, thus:

Blessed, inconceivably happy, are those who feel as if they were without any thing; for such are prepared to receive heaven.

Blessed are they that mourn; for comfort comes to the mourner that others cannot understand.

Blessed are they that desire goodness more than any thing else; for they shall be filled with it.

Blessed are they that are kind and merciful; for they will not be in danger of being cruelly treated.

Blessed are those who are pure, have no wrong affections or false thoughts; for they see God, his goodness, excellence, love, and truth.

Blessed are they who suffer in order to do right; for they already have heaven.

We began with our own definitions of bless, said he; and now you have heard Jesus Christ's definitions: do you understand, now, what *bless, blessed* means? They all held up their hands.

When they returned to the school-room after recess, Mr. Alcott said : such of you, as gained some clearer ideas than you had before, of one boy's mind this morning, hold up your hands. The older ones all did. Mr. Alcott here explained the difference between fancy and imagination, and asked which principle was in greatest activity in the mind of that boy? They replied, fancy. What boy has an opposite kind of mind? Several were named. One of them, Mr. Alcott said, was literal. Two of them, he said, had a high degree of imagination. One had fancy and imagination also. Some farther questions were asked, which proved how truly children analyze each others minds, when brought to attend to them.

The next day, when I arrived, all the children were writing on the black tablets; an exercise which occupies, excepting on the days of the spelling lesson, the first hour of school time; and Mr. Alcott had divided his black-board thus:

Spirit.	Soul.	Mind.
Love.	Faith.	Conscience.	Appetite.	Affection.	Aspiration.	Imagination.	Judgment.	Insight.
Good.	Happiness.	Truth.

He asked the children what they thought he was going to do? They did not know. He asked who among them would be willing to be analyzed, and tell all their faults and all their virtues, for the benefit of themselves and the rest in self-knowledge? All held up their hands but one.

He then selected one little girl, who is remarkably simple and truth loving, and asked if she was willing to answer all his questions truly, whether they laid open her faults or her virtues? She replied, yes.

Having drawn them into two concentric arcs of circles round his table, over which the black-board hangs, Mr. Alcott began to speak of Love: Do you think you love? Yes. Whom? My mother. What do you love in your mother? She was silent. Her voice, her manners, her appearance, her spirit? Yes, all. Suppose she lost her voice; and her appearance changed; should you still love her? Yes. You think that, independently of all that pleases your eye and mind, and of the good she does you; even if she were to die, and you should see, hear, be taken care of no longer by her, you should love her? Yes. What do the rest think? (these questions are not half as many as were asked, however; and the answers were very deliberate.) They all said: Yes, she does love, it is real love.

Mr. Alcott then said: if your mother were going to die, and the physicians said, that if you would die, your mother's life could be saved; would you die for your mother? She was silent. Mr. Alcott then went on to speak of the importance of her mother's life, to her father, her brothers, and sisters. She was still silent. How would it be with the rest? said he. One boy said, I should not hesitate one moment. Mr. Alcott enquired into this, and he said: Because his mother's life was more valuable to her friends than his was; because she was important to his younger brother; and because he should not be very happy in life if his mother were dead. There was some conversation with some other boys; and one said, that he was sure he could not die for his mother, though he cared more for her than for any one else. Mr. Alcott said, why, what do you think you should lose, if you died? He replied, I do not know. You would lose your body, said Mr. Alcott; and. then, turning to the little girl, he asked her if she had concluded whether she could die for her mother? Yes, said she, very quietly; and after this long deliberation, in which it had been evident, she was determined not to deceive herself. Do the rest think she could? said Mr. Alcott. Yes, said all; I do not doubt she could. Well, said Mr. Alcott, do you think, if by suffering a great deal of pain, you could make your father and mother happy all their lives, you could suffer it for that? She was silent. Others called out: Oh yes! I know she could, and professed that they could. Mr. Alcott turned to the cast of Christ, and spoke of his life; his sacrifice of enjoyment; his acceptance of suffering; his objects; his love. Questions were asked whose answers brought out a strong view of his spiritual, unselfish love of the spirits of men: and it was asked if her love had any of this deep character. She was silent; and even the rest were here awed into some self-distrust. But few thought their love had any of the characteristics of Christ's love.

Mr. Alcott then asked her if she could bear the faults of others, and love them still? Sometimes. Can you bear with the impatience of your sisters and brothers at home? She smiled and said, she never had any occasion. Have you ever had any occasion for forbearance and patience any where else? She did not remember, she said. Never in any instance; not in this school, or any where? Yes, she recollected once, but not in this school. Well, did you forbear? Yes. Does any one else think this little girl has had any occasion for forbearance in this school? Several said, yes. How many think she acted with forbearance then and now? All held up their hands. Who think they were the ones who required her forbearance ? Two held up their hands; and Mr. Alcott congratulated them on their acquisition of a better spirit, than they had shown once.

Do you still think, said Mr. Alcott, that you really love,— love enough to sacrifice, and to forbear? Yes, said she. Nothing you have heard, has led you to doubt this? No What do the rest think? That she loves, she sacrifices, she forbears, that it is real love. Well, look at the scale. You see the first division is Spirit. The Spirit comes from God ; it loves, believes, obeys. We obey what we have faith in ; we have faith in what we love ; love is pure spiritual action. The Spirit loves. The spirit, with its love, faith, and obedience, sanctifies or makes holy the soul, in its appetites, affections, and aspirations, so that it gets happiness. And it clears and purifies the mind, in its faculties of sense, judgment, and imagination, so that it discovers truth.

A week after, February 17th, this analysis was renewed. Mr. Alcott said : we discovered, last Wednesday, that love sacrifices and forbears. We might say a great deal more about love, but now we will go on to *Faith*. First, all of you think, what is faith? Soon, all the hands went up.

He began with the youngest, who said, faith is spirit. Did you ever have any? Yes. The next said, faith is not to doubt goodness in the spirits of people. Another said, faith is a thought and feeling. When did you have faith? Yesterday. What was it about? I thought school kept yesterday afternoon,—mother thought it did not,—I was sure it did. Another said, faith is only a feeling. Another said, faith is love. There is faith in love, said Mr. Alcott. Another said, faith is liking people from their looks. Who have you faith in? I have faith in my mother. Why? Because I like her looks, and love her soul. All the children who answered above, were under six years old. One of seven years old, said, faith is confidence in another. In another's what? In another's spirit; that people will do what they promise. A boy, who is always doing wrong, and failing in duty, said, faith was obedience. Have you much faith? No. You have come pretty near losing your faith? Yes. You have more now than you have had?

Yes. How will you get more faith? By doing as I am told. He looked very serious, and somewhat distressed; and Mr. Alcott said : Well, go on and be obedient, and you will find you have faith. Another boy said, faith is confidence. Who have you confidence in? In you. Why? I don't know. A little girl said, faith is to believe. Do you believe or doubt the most? I think I have more faith than doubt, said she. A boy said, faith is to trust and believe. Is trust in the heart or head? said Mr. Alcott. In the heart. And belief? In the head. Another boy said, to confide in the souls and promises of others. Another said, to confide in one you love. You must love? Yes. Faith then comes out of love? Yes, I think so.

One deaf boy, who sat near Mr. Alcott, but could not hear the rest speak, said : I don't know any thing about faith, but I guess I shall learn now. Then you already have some faith, said Mr. Alcott. Do you think faith is a thought or a feeling? They all decided that it was a feeling. Such of you as think this little girl has this feeling, may hold up your hands. All did so. Such of you as have faith in her, faith that she will do as she promises, that she will never disappoint any just expectations, may hold up your hands. They all did so. Does any one doubt her? No one. Well! this is a matter of opinion ; it is the head's faith. How many of you have the feeling ; the faith that grows out of love to her? Several. Do you think you have faith? said he, addressing her. Yes, I think I have. Can you remember any instance when you proved it? No. Do you generally think people are good, when you see them first? Yes, generally, not always. In some particular instance that you have not had faith, can you tell what was the reason? I don't remember. Do you have faith in people's good intentions, even when you see they do wrong? Yes, generally. Can you think of any persons in whom you have no faith ; in whom you do not have confidence? A very few. Do you think, as you grow older, that you have more or less faith in others? More in some people. Suppose you make a distinction between people in whose

intentions you confide, and those in whose characters
and actions you confide, — have you been disappointed
much? No.

How is it with the rest of you; does any one of you
doubt, more than confide and love? One boy held up his
hand. Do you want to doubt? I cannot help it, in many
instances. Does the doubt come from your heart or head?
I don't know. Several more doubters held up their
hands; and were conversed with. Who of you think you
believe more, and doubt less, than you did six months ago?
Most held up their hands.

Mr. Alcott then turned to the little girl. In whom have
you faith? In my father and mother. Has your faith
more feeling than thought in it; or more thought than feeling? More feeling than thought. Do you think you get
thoughts, at this school, which explain your feelings more
and more? Yes, I think the mind explains the heart, said
she. Knowledge explains faith? Yes. Does faith begin
in feeling or thought? In feeling. Has a little infant any
faith? Yes, a great deal.

A boy here said, that he thought an infant brought faith
into the world with it; for when it did mischief, it always
thought that its mother could mend it all, and perhaps that
was the reason it was so apt to do mischief. (There was
great profoundness in this observation. The unity of children's spiritual being is so deep and interior, that it is long
before division, a break, or destruction, even in the outward
world, can be apprehended. The natural condition of
things to their apprehension, is unity and perfection. In
apparently disturbing this, they feel their own power. To
reconstruct the unity by art, is man's highest action, a dim
image of the creation of God.) Mr. Alcott went on: If
you all come into the world with faith in your hearts,
what do you suppose the object of living here is? All
listen and hear, what this little girl says. She said: to try
to keep it. Yes, said Mr. Alcott, that is a great truth; you
must try to keep it, by feeling it out, thinking it out, acting
it out.

What is the first object, out of itself, on which the faith of an infant rests? On its mother. What brings faith out? The mother's love. Does it stop in the mother? No, it goes to the father, to the brothers and sisters. Does it stop there? No, it goes to God. Does it go immediately to God? Not till it hears about him, said she. Have you faith in any thing but persons? After a while she said she had faith in nature. Have you faith in yourself? Yes. Your faith begins in yourself and goes all round among your friends, and into nature, till it finds God? Yes. Who gave you faith? God. God then is the source and supreme object of faith. Did you ever hear these words, " In him we live, and move, and have our being?" Yes, it is in the Bible. When did God give you faith? When he made my soul — it is my spirit. Yes, said Mr. Alcott, as a tree without sap would be no tree, but a dead thing, so a soul without faith would be no spirit. This little girl has faith in herself, that is, in her soul, in her father, mother, sisters, friends, teachers; in nature, and in God. One of the boys said, God should have come first. Mr. Alcott said, she means that she has found out her faith, and her knowledge of God has explained the feeling of faith entirely.

What is likely to carry faith away, or deaden it? There was no answer. He continued, all the other parts of our nature, especially the body, that is the appetites, may carry faith away, may quench the spirit. What tries your faith most? My impatience. All the rest seemed surprised and laughed ; and declared she never was impatient. Mr. Alcott said, if she calls herself impatient, what do you think of yourselves, the rest of you? This involved a long talk, in which the most impatient boy in school expressed his opinion that he was very patient. He only made out to prove that he was not utterly destitute of patience, that he was not always infinitely impatient. But like most persons who think a great deal more about themselves than other people, he takes the germ that really exists, for the cultivated plant which might but does not come from it. Mr. Alcott now turned to the little girl. Have you ever been impatient in this room? Yes. About your lessons? About my Latin lesson. (Her teacher can truly say it never was
12

perceptible.) Have you ever felt impatient with any of the scholars? No, they treat me very kindly. Such as think they have ever treated this little girl ungenerously, unkindly, may hold up their hands, said Mr. Alcott. Four or five did. Did you know that? said he to her. No, said she.

Suppose some one should say about you, (and he particularized many slanders,) could you preserve your faith in people's good intentions, and in yourself, and in God? After a long silence, she said, I should know my sisters would not believe it. You have too much faith to imagine such slanders? said Mr. Alcott. Another girl said, a good person could not be slandered so. Socrates was slandered so, said Mr. Alcott, he lost his life on the absurd accusation of having corrupted the youth of Athens. The martyrs were accused of bad intentions towards society. Jesus was accused of deceiving the people, on the one hand; and of wishing to dethrone Cæsar Augustus and become Emperor, on the other. There was never a great benefactor to man, who was not accused of being opposed to the very objects he had at heart. And it is so in common life most frequently. The noble-souled are misunderstood. The generous are misrepresented. Martyrs, and even discoverers of science, have been uniformly traduced by people around them. The greatest benefactors of the present age, are all of them slandered grossly. The best people I know are the most slandered. Have you faith enough to bear slander then? for if you have not, you will not keep your faith. She thought she had.

Feb. 24th. A week after, and this analysis was renewed. Mr. Alcott began: we have found that this little girl's love is so spiritual that it has in it self-sacrifice and forbearance; and that she has faith enough in herself, her friends, in nature, and in God, to give her courage and fortitude. You see by the scale, that the Spirit not only loves, and trusts, but obeys. Do you know what it is to obey? To follow. How? With actions. Must there be any feeling in the action? Yes—a willing feeling. What should we obey? Reason and conscience, said a large boy. Is not reason always in conscience? No. What is there in conscience, when there is no reason? I cannot express it. Another boy said, we should obey the Bible and conscience. What is it within you to which the Bible speaks? The conscience, said he, at last. Some of the little ones said, we must obey the ten commandments; fathers and mothers; the Lord; and one said, our own spirit. How do you find out, said Mr. Alcott to him, when you want to know what is right and what is wrong? I ask conscience. Another boy said, I ask my parents. A case was stated in which the parents could not be near; how should you do then? I don't know. Would not conscience tell you? If I knew which was right, conscience would tell me to do it. You must know first, before conscience would speak? Yes. (This boy was seven years old.)

Another boy then said, if one's parents should tell him to kill somebody, would it be right to do it? What do you think, said Mr. Alcott. I think it would not be right, said he. Why? Because God commands us not to do wrong. You would know it was wrong then, even if your parents did not tell you so? Yes. Then you do not depend on your parents to know right from wrong? We know God's commandments, said he. Suppose you were in a country where the true God's commands were not known; but the laws of an imagined wicked god were the law of the land, as in some heathen countries; should you know it was wrong to murder? I think I should. Then conscience is not made up of what has been told you is right and wrong? Yes it is. How then would it be made up, in a country where the true God is not known? It would not be a good conscience; but there is some of the true God in every body's conscience. (This boy was nine years old.) I hoped Mr. Alcott would tell him that this vision of the true God, which is in every conscience, more or less, is the spontaneous reason; and that the feeling of conscience which gives it authority, is the Absolute being which we share with all spirits, even God. But he turned now to the little girl.

Do you think you have always obeyed? No Sir. What oftenest tempts you to disobey? As she did not immediately answer, he turned to the rest and asked each one what tempted them most, which led to some observations to each. At last he said to her, do you often feel inclined to disobey your mother? Not often. Your father? No, never. Did you ever disobey your conscience with respect to your brothers and sisters? Yes, once. How long ago? About a year. Will you tell it? My brother was sick, and worried, and troubled me, and I was impatient to him, and hurt his feelings. Shall you ever forget this? I don't know. Who else here have been as bad as this little girl was, in this? Most held up hands. Do you remember any particular instances? Several did, and one told that once when his brother was sick, he was cross, and said, Before I would make believe being sick! — Did you ever, said Mr. Alcott to the little girl, disobey your conscience with respect to people out of the house? Yes, sometimes. And did they know it? Yes, I suppose they did. Do you think you love to obey your father and mother, and teachers, and conscience? Yes. And generally find yourself ready to do so? Yes. Do the rest of you? Some said yes, some said no. How many wish you did love to obey more than you do; and were more ready to? Many did. Have any of you failed, to-day? Several. What do you call people that readily obey? They answered severally, good; obedient; kind; honest; obliging; generous; charitable; liberal; self-denying; good-natured.

Do you know what the word docility, docile means? Tame, said one. He explained that he had heard it applied to animals. Mild and gentle; submissive; easily governed; were some other answers. Do you think this little girl is docile? All held up their hands. Do you think so yourself? After a pause she said, generally. What does docile mean in the dictionary? They took their dictionaries, and found that Johnson said teachable. He told them to put them up. Some did not obey. Are you docile? said he. Instantly every book was put up.

On the next day for analysis, March 4th, the little girl who was generally questioned, was not present, and a little boy of five years old was taken. Mr. Alcott said that we had learned that spirit loved, trusted, was docile, or obedient. But there was much more to say about obedience. Little boy, he continued, we are going to find out, not whether you have good health, or have knowledge, or enjoy yourself ; but whether you are good. What makes us good? Conscience. What is conscience? It is the spirit speaking. Have you any conscience? Yes. How do you know? My mother told me so. When? Why once she was washing my face and hands, and I did not want to have her ; and she told me that people would think my conscience was dirty, if my body was dirty; and so I asked her what my conscience was, and she said it was what told us right and wrong. Well, did you look in then, and find there was conscience? Yes. Such of you as think you were told of conscience, before you found it out, hold up your hands. Most of them did. How many of you think your conscience began to be, when you were told of it? Some did ; and the little boy added, there was a spirit before. Well, said Mr. Alcott, was not this the way ; there was a feeling before, and your mother made a thought of the feeling? Oh yes. Some, however, thought there was a time when there was neither a feeling or a thought. Can you conceive that the spirit lived before your bodies were made? Most of them said yes. About half a dozen including the older ones, thought it was not possible.

Mr. Alcott then said, I observe that those who cannot conceive of spirit without body, existing in God before it comes out upon the earth, are the very ones who have required the most discipline and punishment, and have the least love of obedience. The rest are those who exercise most self-control, and seem to have the most conscience. You all have conscience? Yes. How did you get it? No one knew. At last a boy of seven, (mentioned once before) said, God gives us our conscience. When? Why, when we have learned right and wrong, God sends us conscience to make us do right. So I think, said the oldest boy in school. Is it born out of the soul, said Mr. Alcott, or does God add it to the soul? He adds it. Is it some-

12*

thing new ? Yes. Do the rest think so ? No one agreed.
And the oldest boy said, it is in the soul but it does not act,
till there is knowledge. Does it ever act, then, fully ? No.
True ; there is much in the spirit that can never be represented in thought probably, nor acted out, at least on earth.
And so, little boy, when you went to be washed, you did
not ask of conscience whether you were going to act right
or wrong, while you were being washed ? No ; I was a
very little boy, and I used to think if I did not do what was
right, my mother would punish me. Was that all you
thought about right and wrong; being punished and not
being punished ? Yes, that was all. Well, what do you
think now ? Now I think of Pilgrim. What part of Pilgrim's Progress ? Fighting Apollyon. Do you think you
should be better if you never were punished ? No, for I
should wish to do wrong, and it would be very wrong to
wish to do wrong.

How many of you think your wishes are almost always
good ? Two boys held up their hands. How many think
their wishes are too often bad ? Two ; and the little boy
questioned was one. When you wish to do wrong, what
stops you ? My conscience ; when I want to hug very
little children so hard that it would hurt them, and I very
often do, my conscience stops me. Does your conscience
go into your mind and find out a reason for not hugging
these little children. Yes ; the reason is, it would hurt
them to be hugged so hard. Did you ever wish to strike ?
No, never in my life. How far does your desire to hurt by
hugging carry you ? Why as far as my conscience lets
me go.

How many of you keep all your feelings within the
limit which conscience says is right ? Not a single one
held up his hands. When conscience does limit your feelings within the bounds of right, what spiritual action do
you perform ? Obedience, said several. Mr. Alcott again
turned to the little boy and said, supposing you should say
when you wanted to do some particular thing, Oh I must
do it, (though conscience says no.) And so you do a little
worse than conscience would allow to-day; and to-morrow
you go a little farther ; and to-morrow a little farther.

What sort of a boy should you be at last? Just such a boy as —— he named one of the scholars who is undoubtedly the worst boy in school. Can you do wrong, and escape punishment in your mind? No, never; it always makes me worse. Suppose a boy is angry, what is the punishment in his mind? Why, he feels as if he could take the world and break it into two pieces, tear it in halves. And Mr. Alcott will you let me tell you what part of Pilgrim's Progress I like best? Yes, said Mr. Alcott. It is where Mr. Greatheart is killing the Giant Despair. Is there any Mr. Greatheart in you? Yes, and he is just killing the Giant Despair; for once I thought I should never be good. Why not? Why, I would get tired sitting, and so leave off doing something, and look around. Should you like to be very good? Oh yes. How good? Good as I can be.

Who was the best man in the world? Lafayette. Was he the very best? Oh no, it was Jesus Christ; I am surprised I could forget that! How many of you think, said Mr. Alcott, that you can be as good as Jesus Christ, at least in another world? Several held up their hands. Do any of you feel in despair, as if you never could be what you want to be? Several held up their hands. One said he was in despair of doing what he wanted to do with his mind. What do you want to do with it? He could not explain. Several said they wanted to be good. One said he would go through fire for it. Another said he wanted to have a strong mind. Strong thoughts or feelings? Strong thoughts. Another wanted to be good, and to do good. Yes, said Mr. Alcott, part of being good is doing good. I cannot conceive of being good without the goodness shaping itself out in actions. Several wanted to have self-knowledge. One wanted self-control. Another wanted to be generous. Such of you, said Mr. Alcott, as think you came into the world to do all these things you have spoken of, hold up your hands. All held up their hands. Do you know recess-time is passed, half an hour? No, said all, with great surprise, looking at the clock. Well, there is half an hour. You may take half of it for recess; or I will read you a parable from Krummacher, illustrating our subject of to-day, conscience. They all decided to hear the parable, and Mr. Alcott read Chryses and the Widow. What have you heard about obedience to-day? That we must obey conscience, was the final answer.

Mr. Alcott began the next analysis, March 11th, by first asking questions to define the word *power*. Is power in you, or out of you? One said, out of you; that is, out of your soul; but it is in the body. The rest simply agreed that power was in us. On being asked what one word included all the powers of the human being, one said Will. Mr. Alcott asked if these powers were always in action? Yes, was the answer; which was afterwards modified, on their being led to see, that we felt more and thought more, at some times, than others.

He then asked questions to define the word *quicken*. It was decided that to quicken a thought or feeling, was to call it forth into action. He asked such as thought that they had been quickened since they came to this school, to hold up their hands. Many did so. What has quickened you? They severally and simultaneously replied, *your* spirit; *your* conscience; your *life*.

He then asked questions to define the word *tempt*. He described a temptation, without using the word, and they recognized it. What is the object of temptation? said he. To quicken the powers, was the final answer. He asked several of them what tempted them most? A little boy answered, I cannot tell yet, I have not done — (thinking, he meant.) Many answered, play; pleasure; appetites. Some did not know. The thinker at last said he wanted to pull people about more than any other wrong thing. Who says they were never tempted? No one. He described a temptation, and a resistance to it, and asked what would be the effect upon their spirits, of going through such exercises? They answered that they should grow stronger in spirit. Such of you as think you grow stronger in spirit, by resisting temptation, hold up your hands; do you understand how it is? They all thought they did. Such of you as think you have already weakened your spirits by yielding to temptation; I mean those who eat too much, drink too much, play too much, may hold up your hands. All the hands went up.

When he had asked many questions to define the word *discipline*, he said, who have been disciplined in this school? Many. Who feel they have needed discipline? The same. Who think Mr. Alcott disciplines your minds? All. Who think they are in a better state of discipline than they were? All.

Who has often said, *I will?* All. Who has had the feeling that leads to saying, *I will not?* All held up their hands. You all have a will? Yes. Do you expect to have your will brought out in this school? Yes. How? By its being tempted, said one. And disciplined, said Mr. Alcott; but where does the will act? Within. In your hands, feet, &c.? Yes. How many think you have understood all that has been said pretty well? All.

He then asked questions to define the words *sense* and *flesh;* and then to define the word *obedience;* and then discriminated obedience to conscience, from obedience to flesh and sense. Can any one obey their conscience unless they have confidence in it? No. Who has no confidence in his conscience, that is, does not believe in it? None. If you do believe in your conscience, and have confidence in its teachings, what spiritual principle have you? Faith. How many mind me, because they would be punished if they did not? None would admit that they obeyed him from any other principle than faith in him. Some, however, confessed to particular instances of obeying him from fear of punishment.

There was recess ten minutes; and Mr. Alcott said that whoever was not in at half past eleven, would be obliged to punish him.* They were all in. Such of you; Mr. Alcott began, as would like to go on with this exercise may hold up your hands. They all did, excepting three who were very frivolous. And Mr. Alcott, remarking that these three persons did not like the trouble of thinking,

* For an explanation of this see N. B. on page 143.

asked the rest where we left off, when they went out?
Several could not remember. Some said we were talking of obedience and faith. Such of you as do things
without thinking, hold up your hands. Many did. Such
as never do things without thinking. None. Such of you
as think this recess has quickened the spiritual principles of
thought and will, hold up your hands. Many did.

What is that within you, which sometimes carries you
on as if you could not help it, and against your thoughts;
urging you on, you do not know why and how? Some
said the soul. He then referred to the birds' building their
nests; and several said, instinct; but others seemed to think
that human beings could not have instinct. Mr. Alcott
then spoke of the motions, &c. of a very young infant; and
some said they were instinctive. One boy said they were
imitation. Another asked if imitation was not instinct?
Mr. Alcott then spoke of the instincts of the various scholars, which accounted for their characteristic movements,
&c. much to the amusement of all; and seemed also to
define the word. He ended with asking if all understood
instinct now? All said yes. Is it in the mind, or soul,
or body? said Mr. Alcott; that is, is it in what thinks,
or what feels, or in the body? It is in what feels, in the
soul, said one. But it acts in the body said another. Do
you all think so? Yes.

How many of you know that you live? All. How did
you find it out? They did not know. Does a little infant
know it lives? Some said yes; some, no. Do you remember the time when you did not know you lived? No.
How many think you felt before you knew it? How
many think you knew it first? None. Does a little infant feel the air when it is fanned? Yes, and it wants to
take hold of the fan said one; it wants to eat the fan, said
another. If a person could not feel the air, or pain, what
would he be? One said, I should say he was *a thing*.
Another said, he would be a body. Another said, I should
say he had no soul. How many of you have heard the
word *susceptible*? Many hands went up, and it was ex-

plained to the rest. What are you susceptible of? Bodily
pain ; mental pain ; pleasure ; love ; truth ; were the various
answers.

Do you know you are in this room ? Yes. How many
have heard the word *conscious* ? Is it the mind or the soul
which is susceptible ? The soul. Is it the mind or the
soul which is conscious ? The mind. Consciousness is in
the mind, said Mr. Alcott; and instinct is in the soul; is that
it ? Yes. Where is imagination ? In the mind. Where
is love ? In the soul. Reason ? In the mind. Knowledge ? In the mind. Affection and passion ? Instincts of
the soul. Imagination, reason, and knowledge, are the
consciousness of the mind, said Mr. Alcott; and instinct
and affection, and reason, are in the feelings, the soul ?
Yes.

[N.B. In explanation of the threat on page 141, it may
be necessary to explain Mr. Alcott's ideas upon punishment,
rather more at large, than by the occasional hints on the
subject, scattered up and down this Journal; and especially since there are some mistakes prevalent concerning
his views. When he first began to teach school, he thought
no punishment was desirable, and spent an immense deal of
time in reasoning. But besides that this consumed a great
deal of time that might have been better spent, he was
convinced, in the course of his observations, that the passions of the soul could not in all cases be met by an address
to the understanding, and only were diverted, not conquer-
ed, by being reasoned with. What would excite feeling was
to be brought to bear upon wrong feeling, when that actually existed ; and to rouse sensibility, when there was a de-
ficiency.

More deep observation of life and human nature, convinced him that the ministry of pain, was God's great means
of developing strength and elevation of character; and that
children should early understand this, that they might accept it as a moral blessing. He, therefore, introduced punishment by name ; and found that in theorising on the subject with his scholars, there was a general feeling of its
desirableness and necessity ; and he never failed in obtain-

ing their consent to it as a general principle. On some
occasions, there was to be corporeal punishment, *which
always consists* of one blow with the ferule upon the palm
of the hand ; more or less severe according to the age and
necessities of the pupil. When this punishment was administered, it was always accompanied with conversation ;
and was always given in the ante-room, excepting in one
instance, when one of the oldest boys wantonly disobeyed
for the purpose of displaying to his companions, his daring
spirit, and needed the mortification of seeing himself punished before the rest. To the credit of the children, it must
be granted, that they received this kind of punishment without deserting the general principle which they acknowledged at the beginning ; and with constant acknowledgment
of Mr. Alcott's justice and good will towards them. They
considered it much less severe than to be sent into the ante-
room when he was reading.

One morning when he was opening Pilgrim's Progress
to read, he said, that those who had whispered, or broken
any rule since they came into school, might rise to be punished. They expected the punishment with the ferule.
About a dozen rose. He told them to go into the ante-room,
and stay there while he was reading. They did so. The
reading was very interesting ; for though it had been read
before, every new reading brings new associations, and peculiar conversation. Those in the ante-room, could hear
the occasional bursts of feeling which the reading and conversation elicited. A lady visiter, who was present, went
out just before the reading closed, and found those who had
been sent out, sitting in the ante-room, and looking very dis-
consolate ; and perfectly quiet, though no directions had
been given to them. She expressed her regret at their
losing the interesting reading. Oh yes, we know! said
they. We have heard them shout. Nothing is so interesting as Pilgrim's Progress, and the conversations, said one.
We had rather have been punished any other way, said another.—When they were called in, they said the same thing
to Mr. Alcott. He asked why ? Because it would have
been over in a minute, said one boy ; but this conversation
can never be another time, said another.

Having brought the whole school to this point, Mr. Alcott introduced a new mode. He talked with them, on the Monday before this last analysis; and having again adverted to the necessity of pain and punishment, in a general point of view, and brought them to acknowledge the uses of this *hurting of the body*, as he always phrased it, in concentrating attention, &c., he said, that he now intended to have it administered upon his own hand, instead of theirs; but that the guilty person must do it. They declared that they would never do it. But he soon made them understand that he was serious. They said they preferred being punished themselves. But he was determined that they should not escape the pain and the shame of themselves administering the stroke upon him, except by being themselves blameless.

The effect was a profound and deep stillness. Boys who had never been affected before, and to whom bodily punishment was a very small affair, as far as its pain was concerned, were completely sobered. There was a more complete silence, and attention, and obedience, than there had ever been. And the only exceptions, which were experiments, were rigidly noticed. Mr. Alcott, in two instances, took boys out in the course of the forenoon, and made them give it to him. They were very unwilling, and when they did it first, they did it very lightly. He then asked them, if they thought they deserved no more punishment than that? And so they were obliged to give it hard :—but it was not without tears, which they had never shed when punished themselves. This is the most complete punishment that a master ever invented,—was the observation of one of the boys, at home; Mr. Alcott has secured obedience now,—there is not a boy in school, but what would a great deal rather be punished himself, than punish him.

It must be observed, however, that the point of view in which this vicarious punishment is presented to the minds of children, is not that in which vicarious punishment is generally placed. It is not to satisfy the claims of any inexorable law; but to give a pain which may awaken a solemn attention, and touch the heart to love and generosity.

13

The children do not feel that they escape punishment; for it is taken for granted that they feel a greater pain, in seeing others suffer, than they would in suffering themselves. But its great object is to display to them that Mr. Alcott's infliction of punishment, is not want of feeling for their bodies, but a deeper and intense interest in their souls. And this was completely effected. A new sense of the worth and importance of that for which he was willing to suffer pain, seemed to spring up all round. While the unquestionable generosity of it, was not only understood, but felt to be contagious. One boy, of nine years of age, who was superintendent one day, and obliged in the discharge of his duty, to put on his slate the names of several boys, some of whom seemed to look forward to their punishment as a frolic, and one of whom cried for fear, having remained with them after the rest had gone, begged so hard to be allowed to receive the strokes himself, that he was allowed to do so ; and it had the most gracious effect, both on himself and the rest. The real exercise of magnanimity necessarily elevates the one who rises to it, and who is by nature incapable of vanity, (the weakness of the selfish,) while the spectacle of it, works on the dullest and the coldest. Of course such scenes must be rare ; but their occurrence even once, is enough to spiritualise all the punishments of the school, in which such a circumstance happened.]

March 18th, was the next day for analysis. Mr. Alcott began by speaking of the scale. Look at this scale. You see the spirit, which manifests itself in search after good ; loves, trusts, obeys ; and what is its law ? Conscience, said they. Is not the spirit, power ? Yes. Suppose a being does not love, and trust, and obey Good, according to conscience, has he any spirit ? No. Has he no power ? Yes. Suppose a person's action begins at the second division, what is the object ? Happiness ; pleasure ; enjoyment. The object of the soul then, is pleasure ? Yes. And what is the law ? They did not know. Is it not desire ? Yes. Is enjoyment the same as goodness ? Not always. Good is to be attained at the expense of enjoyment, sometimes ? Yes. Is there any one word, which includes the two meanings of enjoyment and good? After a while, one girl said, happiness. The soul does not mean the same as spirit then? I thought it did, said one. When the soul loves, trusts, and obeys, then it is spirit.

Where does the spirit come from? From God. Yes, said Mr. Alcott, when the soul looks towards God, it is spirit. Spirit is life. Life comes from God. Spirit comes from God into the soul, and is tempted to become appetite, affection, passion. What does *tempted* mean? It means tried. Can perfectly good spirit be tried, tempted? There was no answer to this question; and he opened the Bible and read the temptation of Christ, paraphrasing the word *devil*, as appetites, passions, false ideas; in short, whatever feeling or thought may lead away from virtue. By the first temptation, was shown the principle on which the appetites were to be resisted. Jesus said, said Mr. Alcott, that man does not live by bread alone. It is his body only that lives by bread; but there is something more than body in a man; something which lives upon what comes from God. "Every word," means every manifestation of God in things and beings. By the second temptation, he showed on what principle the passion of ambition, or of working by splendid self-displaying prodigies, was to be resisted. We should put our trust in general principles, and not in the expectation of extraordinary interpositions; for to trust in the power of goodness and truth, shows the highest kind of faith. By the third temptation, he showed the principle on which the desire to use pious frauds, and the plans of a narrow expediency are to be resisted; sincerity being the true worship of God.

All this was brought out, not without a great deal of talk, which I could not seize for the Record. Thus, in the beginning, one of the boys laughed, as soon as Mr. Alcott said the word devil, having a ludicrous association with it. Mr. Alcott said, what does devil mean? An evil spirit. An evil spirit within you, or out of you? Out of me. How many of the rest think the word devil represents a shape out of your mind? About half held up their hands. How many think the word devil represents all that tends to wrong doing within you? All held up their hands but two, who persisted in saying that they thought the devil had a shape out of the mind.

As the little girl, who was generally questioned on this day of analysis, was not present, a boy of ten years of age took her place. Mr. Alcott began with asking, when a soul resisted temptation? When it does not give up to the body, said the boy. Is the law of the flesh the same as the law of the spirit? No. What is the law of the flesh? Desire. What is the law of the spirit? Conscience. If a boy gives up his conscience to his desire, he subjects the law of the spirit to the law of the flesh? Yes, he yields to temptation. Suppose you sit down at a table where there is every' thing good to eat and drink, (he went on and described a great many luxuries,) what part of your nature is tempted? Appetites. How many of you seek to gratify your appetites? [He enlarged, and made graphic descriptions of common temptations to the appetites, which elicited a good deal of confession from all the boys.]

He then read from Spencer the description of Gluttony in the train of Lucifera. Do you think, said he to the boy who was especially questioned, to-day, that you obey the law of the flesh, or the law of the spirit, on this subject? He said, the law of the spirit. Always? Always. Do you never desire any gratification for your body, to a degree that wars against the law of the spirit? No. All the boys smiled at his self-complacency, which they seemed to think might proceed from self-ignorance. Mr. Alcott reminded him how impatient he was of cold last winter, much more impatient than many others. Some anecdotes were then told of fortitude and self-denial in children, by way of awakening a higher sense of spirituality in him than he seemed to have; for it was the want of an adequate sense of the law of the spirit, which made him feel that he obeyed it, when in truth he is a good deal controled by the law of the flesh.

Mr. Alcott then asked all the school such questions as these: How many of you are apt to trouble your parents about your dress, because you cannot bear any little annoyance, or it does not gratify the appetite of the eye ? How many give way to anger ? How many can bear an insult ? Not one boy thought he could bear an insult without revenging ; and some expressed, that they ought not. Did Jesus Christ bear any insults ? Yes. Did he return them with injury ? No. But if you are insulted, you ought to return it with injury—so great a wrong is done you ! They were silent. Is it the law of the spirit, or of the flesh, which makes you want to strike ? Of the flesh. Which law is it that makes you want to speak harshly, when so spoken to ? The law of the flesh. Did Jesus Christ revile when he was reviled ? No. Did he strike when struck ? No. Did he let his disciples fight for him ? No. Why not ? There was silence. What was there in his spirit that prevented it ? Love, said a little girl. How many of you desire to obey the law of the spirit, instead of the law of the flesh upon this subject ? Many held up their hands, and the boy questioned, among the number ; but he said that he could not help revenging an insult. You acknowledge your weakness on this point ? Yes.—Mr. Alcott and I both agreed, that this weakness which he was willing to confess, was not so great in his case, as the other weakness, which he would not confess. However, we said nothing. In one point he was true to himself; he was true to his own want of moral courage. No one who compared his answers, during this analysis, with those of the two former children, could fail to see the difference between their absolute simplicity, and his non-committal spirit.

Well, some of you desire to obey the law of the spirit; what is the difference between desire and resolution? Resolution has will in it; resolution has thought in it; resolution has self-denial in it; resolution is spirit;—were the various answers. How many of you have seen people in the world, who can refrain from revenge? Many thought they had. How many respect yourselves the more, when you have given up to your passions? None. Do you know revenge is the first principle of murder: how many have felt this murderous principle? Several. How many think you have power within you, if you will use it, to mas-

13*

ter all the desires of the body? Many did. Three boys
thought they had not. How do you expect the power will
come? said he to one. I do not expect it will come.
What! God has sent you into the world—and told you to
seek good—and you never expect to feel the power—have
you no spirit? He was silent. Oh, you have a giant spirit within you—stronger than all the earth—it will remove
mountains if you will call upon it.

One of the boys here said, It is twelve o'clock. Who
think it a punishment to be here? said Mr. Alcott. None.
Who think it a reward to come to school? All. Who
think there would be no punishment here if the law of the
spirit was obeyed? All. How many of you think that all
my punishments are to bring you back to the law of the
spirit? All. Why do you not come under the law of the
spirit of yourselves? There was no answer. I kept a
school once, in which there was no punishment; but the
reward was, to come and see me twice a week in the evening, or to stay with me half an hour after school. How
many would like it if I had this reward now? Several
held up their hands. Why? One said, I should like the
instruction; another, I should be benefitted; &c. Well, said
Mr. Alcott to the boy analysed, you have been weighed in
the balance to-day, and even according to your own opinion,
have been found wanting in one respect: perhaps you have
felt yourself wanting on both points, on which we have
conversed. You may go.

The analysis was renewed on March 25th, Mr. Alcott
said, Shall any of you want any thing, during our lesson?
Seven or eight boys asked for water, and Mr. Alcott took
the pitcher and a cup, and went to each, and gratified the
want. He remarked that this was a practical illustration of
the subject of the day—the appetites. One boy who had
asked, said he would wait till recess; but Mr. Alcott insisted
on his drinking.

Having done this, he said, the soul wants to satisfy itself
in its search after pleasure. This want is called desire.
Desire is the law of the soul. What is a law? A command, said one. Something that must be done, said an-

other. Is there desire in appetite? Yes. What is appetite? It is a part of the soul, said a boy of five. Several said, No; appetite grows out of the body. Suppose a body dead, said Mr. Alcott, is there appetite in it? No. Why not? Because it is not alive. What made it alive? The spirit, the soul. Then appetite is in the soul, and operates through the body; is not that it? There was a doubt.

It is common to confound the organs of appetite with the appetites; but can you not conceive there could be appetite without a body? They could not conceive of this. Does the eye see? A boy of five said, When we look on any picture, there is a picture reflected into the inside of our eyes, and the mind sees it. But you know, said Mr. Alcott, that there are some pictures which we see in our imaginations? Well, said the child, the way that is, I will tell you: The pictures we look at out of us, go into our minds, and change, and mix up, and come before our minds in new forms. Do these pictures come into our outward eyes? said Mr. Alcott. Oh, no! our mind looks into itself, and sees them. As many of you as think the soul sees by the eyes, and that the eyes would not see, if it were not for the soul, hold up your hands. They all did. As many of you as think the appetites are the soul seeking for pleasure, by organs, as the soul looks out by an organ of vision, hold up your hands. Only a part did; and one boy, who did not, said, people do not always have appetite, though they all have bodies. The sick have no appetite. Mr. Alcott replied, that appetite was not merely after food, but for any bodily gratification or easement. He then asked if they thought the desire of sleep an appetite? the desire of motion? the desire of sweet sounds? the desire of seeing beauty? the desire of smelling sweet odours, and of touching delicate things? Most of them agreed, that these seemed to them appetites. Well, said he, do not all these desires display themselves in the body? Yes. Yet they are soul? Yes. What do the appetites want? Food, said one. All outward things, said another. Are outward things adapted to the soul's appetites? Yes. Do you think there is enough in the world to satisfy the appetites? Yes. Is there enough outward to satisfy the soul's spiritual wants—its love, faith, power? None held up their hands.

How do you know when the appetites have obtained enough? We are satisfied, said the little girl, analysed. What is the law? Satisfaction. Is not temperance a better word? said Mr. Alcott. And are you temperate in your desire for these gratifications we have mentioned? Generally. In what do you find yourself most liable to fail? She did not know. Have you an inordinate desire for food? No. Do you eat to gratify your taste, or to gratify your hunger? For the last. Do you drink any thing to please your taste? No. Do you pursue amusement beyond the rule of temperance? Sometimes; but not without thinking of conscience, said she, adding the last part of the sentence as an after thought. A boy here said there was no use in carrying conscience into play. She said she could not conceive how we could help carrying conscience into all we do. Mr. Alcott said, every thing, even amusement, has a tendency to good or evil, and conscience always speaks on that question.

This gave rise to conversation on the subject of amusements, and the character of plays, and their effects on the habits of the mind and heart, and the duty of having plays that will cultivate the imagination in the right way. Some anecdotes were told to illustrate the evil of playing with no plan, and of playing like brutes; and the good effects of playing beautiful imaginative plays. Mr. Alcott described a place of amusement, which should be fitted up with every embellishment that art could afford; and in which there should be every assistance that sympathy with youthful joyance could give. They were very much delighted; and he asked if such a place on Boston common would not change the character of Boston boys? They thought it certainly would.

Then he said, what do you think you should be, if the restraining power of conscience was taken off? The various answers were: bad; just like satan; a fool; a monkey; a donkey; a snake; a slave; a liar; an idiot; a toad. (I could not help telling Mr. Alcott afterwards, that I was struck with the names of these animals; for every one seemed to hit upon the very animal he would in reality resemble.) One girl said, I should do a great many bad things; another said, I should do all the wicked things that can be thought of; and a little boy said, I should not know anything, I should be a kind of a drunken person.

Now, as many as disobey their conscience, hold up their hands. They all did. Well, you become, in the same degree as you disobey, just what you would become if you had no conscience. Who has done wrong to-day? Many held up their hands, and then confessed the particulars. What is the result of our analysis to-day? That this little girl is temperate in seeking gratifications of her appetites.

N. B. At two different times, there was reading during the last winter, with especial reference to the subject of temptation; one was the account of the temptation in Paradise Lost; and one was from Genesis; and when Mr. Alcott had finished reading, he asked all round, what new idea had been gained. Some said they had learned that they had gardens to superintend. Mr. Alcott asked what was the tree of temptation to them, and each answered, which involved a good deal of particular confession. One small boy said, he thought the tree of life was God; that God formed himself out into a tree. Did you ever see the tree of life? said Mr. Alcott. I suppose I did when I was born, said he; but I don't remember how it looked, for now I only see God with my mind. And what is the tree of temptation? Indolence, and error, and anger, and passion, said he. Perhaps the whole world is a temptation? said Mr. Alcott; every thing which you see? No, I do not think that; I think part of the world is the garden of God, and part of the world is the garden of naughtiness. God is on our right hand, and the garden of naughtiness is on our left. I asked him if the spirit might not be considered the garden of God, and the body the garden of naughtiness? He smiled, and said yes. And when you let your body govern you, you are in the garden of naughtiness; and when you let your mind govern you, you are in the garden of God? Yes, said he.

If any one should ask about the previous culture of this child, it may be said that he had one great advantage over common children; viz. that almost the only book he had ever read with great interest, was Gallaudet's book of the Soul, a book which has been the means of bringing forward the finest children I have seen; and which does the greatest credit to their author's genius.

The affections were the subject of analysis on April 1st. Mr. Alcott took the Bible to read from it. He then asked some questions to bring their minds into attention. One was, do you know what the meaning of the word love is? They all held up their hands. Then we are not going to speak of a subject, of which you know nothing. How many think it is an interesting subject to talk about? Several. How many think it is interesting to feel love? All. Who, of all persons that ever lived, knew the most about love? was it Jesus Christ? Yes. I am going to read this morning what he says about love.

He began, They were at supper, Jesus and his friends, it was their last supper together. He was going very soon to do something which would show what love was; but first he was going to talk about it. Shall you be interested to hear what he said? Many held up their hands. If there are any who wish rather to go into the ante-room than to hear this, reading, they may go, he, said. There was considerable demur, when about eight concluded to go; he stopped them and asked them if they thought it right to go? And having called up many reasons why they should not, by asking them questions, so that some concluded they would prefer to stay, he let the rest go. When they were gone, some remarks were made, and soon he went out and called them all in.

He then asked some more questions, and proceeded to read. The paraphrase was very beautiful. It took up almost all the conversation at the supper. He then laid aside the Bible, and arranged the school for the analysis.

Is there any conscience in love? Yes. Could there be any love without conscience? Silence. Can you like another without conscience? Here was a difference of opinion. Do you like any body whom you do not love? Yes. Do you love any body whom you do not like? No. Do any of you think the body loves? No. Do the appetites love? They love good eating. Do you love to eat, or like to eat? Some said they loved, and some said that they liked the object of appetite. Loving, said Mr. Alcott, is all it seems, and much more; liking seems more than it is. Who think it is wrong to like to eat, like to play, &c.? One said, it is sometimes right and sometimes wrong. Liking is not wrong, said Mr. Alcott; but who think it is wrong to *like* these things better than our spirits? Most held up their hands. That is the very mistake that the drunkard, the sluggard, the glutton, and all who love their appetites, make. You have all of you been drunk, not with rum, or wine, but with amusement, with pleasure. There was a good deal of answer to this remark, which was completely understood. Who think it is wrong to have pleasure? Some held up their hands. Do you think so? I do not; but how are we going to find out when you have pleasure enough? By conscience, said one. Yes, the bowl is at our lips; but conscience says, that's enough; conscience takes care even of our bodies. He made some personal applications, and then went on; you know it is the spirit that sees, the spirit that feels, that touches, &c. Suppose God had so made our bodies, that every time the spirit wanted to see, hear, taste, touch, smell, eat, drink, or move, it must be accompanied with some pain of the body, would life be as it is now? No, said they. No, continued he; God has accompanied all these things with pleasure; and so we abuse his goodness, and act for bodily pleasure itself. Is not that ungrateful and foolish? But the drunkard, because when he drinks, it gives him pleasure, thinks that he will drink; does conscience rule over your pleasures? said he to the little girl, analysed? Yes. When you sit down to table with your father and mother, and brothers, and sisters, do you carry your conscience with you? Yes. Some people only carry their bodies to the table, and they talk all the time about what they are eating, how good it is. He pursued the questions, do you carry your conscience to play ; to church ; to bed ; every where ; and under all circumstances? (particular-zing;) Yes. The others also answered, and thought they carried it, especially to church. I said, I know some children in the room, who do not carry their conscience to church. Mr. Alcott said, your conscience goes with you, at any rate, but I asked if you carried it, if you tried to be conscious of it ! They seemed to doubt. How many of you ever think there is a right and a wrong way to play ? Many did. Do you always carry your conscience with you to play ? On second thoughts, she thought she did not. Probably none, said Mr. Alcott, always feel conscious of their conscience ; sometimes their likes, their appetites, *their flesh* (as the scripture calls it, because their appetites express themselves in the flesh,) get the mastery over the spirit. But you said there was conscience in love ; what do you mean ? Conscience makes us love good people. And keep faithful ? said I. Yes.

Who think they love the spirit better than their bodies ? Many did. Who prove it by their actions? Several. Who would like to have Mr. Alcott see all that they do; and think it would prove to him that they love their spirit better than they like their bodies ? One girl thought it would make no difference. One boy doubted. Most thought they should not like it.

Well, this little girl, said Mr. Alcott, has found something better than eating, or drinking, or seeing, or tasting, or touching, or smelling ; she has got out of her appetites and senses. He then told a story of a fowler and his net ; which illustrated the temptation of the senses ; and asked if they thought any of them were ever caught in this net ? They all confessed. Who spread this net? No answer. Which one of you is it, that when you see a person who does not look just as you would like, who does not gratify your eyes, finds it hard to like him ? Some held up their hands. Those who held up their hands, Mr. Alcott said, were caught in the net of sense. He supposed the case of a boy offered to the school, whom he should describe as full of excellence, as a beautiful boy, thinking of his mind, and the next day he should come, and his face should be plain, not so beautiful as was expected; how would it be? Some said that spiritual and material beauty were never disjoined. There was recess.

At 20 minutes after eleven the children came in. Do you think, said Mr. Alcott, the pleasure you have had during the last ten minutes is more satisfactory than that before recess? Five said yes. Is there any one who took no pleasure in the lesson this morning? Two. Does affection think as much of other people as of itself? Yes. Has it all it loves within itself? Yes. Do you think the love which this one had, (pointing to Christ) was extended to every body? Yes. Does any one think not? One. Who were those he did not love? He did not love the Jews. He loved the Jews; said Mr. Alcott. Then he did not love every body, said the child. If any think they have such love, hold up their hands. No one.

There is a boy here, who has been unfortunate in the forming of his character; there is more than one; they interrupt us, they deceive, they are not ingenuous, they require punishment. Do you love those? No answer. I will put the question differently; do you love that part of them which may become good? Yes. There are cells in this city, where are those who have robbed, and murdered; such as think that they ought to be loved, hold up their hands. None. Such as think Jesus would have said, take the life of these criminals; there is no good in them; hold up their hands. None. Such as think the reverse. All. How many think they should be content to die, had they committed murder? Several. How many think that if a pardon came, and he was freed though he deserved to die, he would sin no more, but love men more? Several. How many think the law of love is more beautiful, more powerful, than the law of strict justice? Some; and the little girl analysed said she preferred the mercy which saves, to the justice which kills.

[N. B. I generally agree with the views that Mr. Alcott brings out from his pupils; but in this instance I disagreed; and I am inclined to think that he unconsciously led them

14

into his own views; by contradistinguishing mercy and
justice. I had left the room, and left the pen in the hand
of a friend, who agrees with him on this subject; but who
admitted to me that the children did not seem to think it
wrong that capital punishment should be inflicted, until Mr.
Alcott led them to feel that he thought so. The testimony
of children, however, on a subject requiring a great deal of
understanding of society, and of the practical operation of
social circumstances, is not so important in my eyes, as is
their testimony on subjects whose ground is merely spiritual. It is not spontaneous reason, but the reflective understanding, that decides on this question, which is a question
of practice. Believing as I do, that "mercy and justice
kiss each other," or are one, and not to be discriminated;
and that the right of capital punishment, reserved to the
arm of civil government, is the only protection against
duelling and the avenging of blood; that is, that it assumes
to itself, moderates and frees from passion, the exercise
of an eternal principle of our nature, which leads us to
protect the defenceless innocent; I cannot doubt that Jesus Christ would approve of it. It is true, he would not
allow that the cause of abstract truth should be defended
by the sword; because he relied on spiritual means for a
spiritual result, as opinion must ever be. And it would
have been well if the church had always remembered this.
And it is true that he saved a criminal from being stoned,
who was doubtless less injurious to society, and less deserving of punishment, than those who were condemning
her, and tempting him; but no unanswerable argument has
yet been deduced from his words, against the occasional
propriety of civil government's taking one life, for the protection of many. This is no place, however, to bring forward the arguments on this subject. I only wish to avoid
seeming to agree with a view, which is, I think, defeating
the ends of the benevolent feeling in which it originated;
besides, that I think the opposing of mercy and justice, is
false philosophy, and false religion.]

How many think they had that feeling yesterday when a
little girl went out of the room and lost the reading for the
good of the rest? Several.

This little girl's name was on the superintendent's slate, but all thought it was not a great violation of the law, which brought it there ; but it was also thought that if she should be excused, others who were thoughtless would be careless; for the sake of the rest, she very cheerfully decided to go out and lose the reading.

How many think it did them no good? One. Those who have no sensibility cannot feel another's suffering, said Mr. Alcott. How many of you like your father and mother better, when they do not punish you, though you deserve it ? One. How many think your fathers do not love you when they punish you ! None. How many think they love you most when they punish you ? One. Little girl, said Mr. Alcott, after all this do you think you love father, mother, brothers, sisters, friends, teachers, wicked people, every body ? Yes, yes. Such as have got an idea to-day which they never had before, and which they can express, hold up their hands. Several. How many think they have certainly got one, though they cannot express it ? Several. When I see a boy disobey me, shall I think he does not love me ? Yes. Such as think they love me may go home. All ran out. Come back. Such as think they love to go home better than any thing else, may go. They all stood still, till he dismissed them.

April 8th.—We are going to talk to-day about the desire of growing better; of aiming high, and at a great deal ; what word expresses this kind of action ? They severally said, sensibility ; faith ; love ; virtue ; spirituality ; aspiration.

Aspiration, said Mr. Alcott, what does that mean ? To go up. What goes up? The spirit. For what? For goodness and truth. Who knows such a person ? Nearly all held up their hands. Are they now living in a body ? Almost all put down their hands. Name those alive ? Dr. Channing and Mr. Taylor were named. Who did the rest mean ? Jesus Christ. Mr. Alcott said, yes; and Jesus said, if any one aspires to follow me, he must give up his appetites, and false affections, and go earnestly to work to do difficult things. How many of you aspire in that way ? Several.

Who says that we should aspire after what we can see
with our eyes? One boy said he did not see why we should
not. Who says we should not? Several. Why—what
were eyes made for? To see with, said one. To help our
spirits, said another. How can they help the spirit? The
eyes can see the works of God, which show our spirits his
wisdom, and they can read the Bible. When we look at
any thing do we see it all? We do not see the happiness
it gives, but we feel it, said one. Some others thought we
saw the whole of what we looked at. Mr. Alcott called on
a boy to rise and stand in the middle of the room. Do you
see that boy? I see his body, said one. Is there any thing
which you do not see, that helps to make up the thought
of that boy? Yes, his feelings; his thoughts; his spirit;
said they severally. What is the use of seeing his body?
It is the sign of his spirit. Shut your eyes and imagine
him; can you? Yes. Who sees this piece of crayon?
Many. Professor Silliman would convince you that you
saw but little of it. One boy said, I have seen my own
spirit many a time. You are thinking of insight. Who
now think they should aspire after what we can see with
our eyes? One boy. Who think you should never seek
after *things*, except as signs of something better, more
spiritual? All, without exception. I know persons, said
Mr. Alcott, who look after beautiful things always, and for
present pleasure, without thinking whether they are signs.
One boy here has said to me, that he could not like a person who was not handsome. I did not say I could not, but
that I did not, said the boy; and I cannot help it.

Who thinks there is a beauty more beautiful, than any
thing their eyes see? Several. Who think the action of
the good Samaritan was a beautiful action? All. Is love
beautiful? Yes. Who have done a beautiful action; and
he explained, by instancing beautiful purposes, and their
enaction. A few held up their hands. Are you willing to
tell what they were? No one was. You think perhaps it
would take away its beauty to tell it? All again held up
their hands.

Now all tell me, which you think you ought to do, aspire
after beautiful thoughts, beautiful feelings, beautiful actions,

or beautiful things? All said the former, but the æsthetic added, beautiful things too. Oh yes, said Mr. Alcott, or we should have to throw away all our pictures and busts? Portrait and all, said the boys. Well, do you think I value that portrait for the form of the face, as it presents itself to the eye? No, you like him; you think he is good; you like his spirit; and so you think he is handsome; were the several answers. Yes, the expression of his spirit seems to bring beauty to my eye, said Mr. Alcott. Now look at that bust of Socrates. A lady who came in here once, said; What an ugly thing that is! I want to put it under ground! Put Socrates under ground! said several, with surprise. Yes, so she said;—but I think of the mind of Socrates; his thoughts about beauty, his beautiful life; his beautiful death; did you not think his death was beautiful, when he drank the hemlock? Yes. Perhaps there is not a bust in the world that brings to mind so many thoughts of beauty, as that does. For Socrates led people to think above beauty in itself. He was the teacher of Plato, the very philosopher of beauty. Here Mr. Alcott went towards the bust and touched the capacious cup of brain. What a brow this is! They all looked very reverent. He then went towards another cast, and said to a small boy, what does this represent? A child praying. And prayer is aspiration, said Mr. Alcott.

Now who think they have been misled by their eyes; have not looked deeper than the shape of things; have not thought enough of what things are the sign of? Many confessed. Well! it is a common fault. The scripture calls this fault, *the lust of the eye.* Mr. Alcott said he had in his youth, fallen into this snare. He had an inordinate pleasure in pretty things, even in dress. He asked what mistake a dandy made? To think too much of personal appearance. How many think so much of dress, as to trouble their fathers and mothers about it? Several held up their hands. Who are not at all particular? Several. Some of you perhaps make the opposite mistake, and are hardly tidy.

14*

He then turned to the little girl who is generally analysed and said, do you remember being deceived by your eyes? She had been, she thought; but could remember no instances.

Such of you as aspire after spiritual beauty, hold up your hands. All did. Such as aspire after natural beauty? The æsthetic held up his hand again, and said I want both. When God made the world, did he make things so beautiful to deceive us?—or to show us his own beauty, so that outward things might lead us to him? For the last. What did I say? You said God made the world beautiful, so that we might know he was kind and beautiful, said one. Can you understand, then, that the beautiful may lead us to the true? Most held up their hands. And that the beautiful and true are the sign of the good? Yes. Then when you see any thing beautiful, you should follow after, and find what true thing it leads to, and then follow on, and find what good thing it is the sign of, and then you are very near God: what did I say little boy? You said, said he, that beauty is the sign of truth, and truth is the sign of love, and God is Love. (This boy is five years old; the choice expression will be observed. Both Mr. Alcott's words and his have been carefully retained.) Do you want good, beautiful feelings? continued Mr. Alcott to him. Yes. When did you get some? To-day. When? As soon as you began to talk about the eyes.

Where did the beautiful thoughts you had this morning come from? said I to this child, at recess. Part came from the conversation, and some from God. This idea, constantly expressed by this child, that his original thoughts come from God, is his own. At least, it was not gained at school; unless indirectly. No such expression has ever been used here.

Such of you as know any person, who, instead of aspiring, seems to go down, may hold up their hands. Many did. If any of you think any one of your companions here aspires above your mark, signify it. Almost all did. Do you know of any one here, who seems never to have gone low? All did. Who is it? said Mr. Alcott to the little child of five.

He named a boy of eight. in whose thoughts he always expresses interest. The rest of the boys smiled, and wanted to tell who they thought: but Mr. Alcott would not allow it.

When they came in after recess, Mr. Alcott asked who had gained new ideas from the morning's conversation? Most held up their hands. What different classes of goods are there? He answered himself;—things—outward goods; knowledge—intellectual goods; and spiritual goods—faith, hope, charity, &c. Is knowledge a good, when is it used for our own, rather than others' good, and we are proud of it? They severally said, we should use it for others; for ourselves;—for ourselves, but some also for other people. Is it aspiration to seek knowledge for our own good alone? No. Does a lawyer, who is using his knowledge to make himself admired and powerful, aspire? No. Does a school teacher, who teaches in order to get money, aspire; even though he does by the way help his scholars? No. In looking about does it seem to you the people you see, are trying after spiritual good, generally? No. After intellectual good? Some of them. Do people generally seem to be striving after money, houses, carriages, reputation? Yes. Do many seem to try to get money to do good with? A few. Who think people seem to be striving for money for themselves only? Several; and Mr. Alcott said, when did you find that out? To-day, said a boy of ten. When I was five years old, said a reflective and conscientious boy of eight.

A gentleman visiter present, here asked a series of questions, calculated to bring out their opinion of Mr. Alcott's disinterestedness; and they signified their undoubting confidence in it, not only by holding up their hands, but by jumping into their chairs, and stretching up with both hands. So you think, was his last question, that some people aspire after something higher than physical good? Yes. Such of you as think Mr. Alcott would make as good use of his mind as he does now, if he kept his thoughts to himself, signify it. They jumped down from their chairs, and said, No. The gentleman remarked to me, Mr. Alcott has his reward.

Where do you think all truth and beauty are ? resumed
Mr. Alcott. In God; and there is some in our souls, said
a little boy of five, after a pause. How do we get it in our
souls ? We ask God for it, and he puts it in. If we do
not want it much, does he put it in ? Oh no; we must
want it very much. Did you ever hear these words, said
Mr. Alcott; ask, and ye shall receive; seek, and ye shall
find; knock, and it shall be opened unto you ? Yes, Jesus
Christ said them.

Who think that spiritual good is the best good ? All.
Who think that in aspiring after spiritual, we get all other
good ? All. Who said, seek first the kingdom of heaven,
spiritual good ; and its righteousness, act accordingly ; and
all these things shall be added unto you, for then they can
do you no harm ? Jesus Christ, said all.

Little girl, after all that has been said about aspiring, do
you think you aspire after spiritual good more than any
other? I think I do, said she. And next to that the intellectual good, which helps the soul, as the hand helps the
body ? Yes.

Who among you think that a school which does not aim
at spiritual good, has the right aim ? None. Who have
received some new thoughts to-day, which they think they
shall remember always? Many. Who know themselves
so well, that they fear they shall forget ? Several.

Who think that in play, they shall aim to be the strongest
and most cunning? None. Do you know what ambition
is? Striving to get more than you have, said one. What
is your ambition ? I don't know. To be admired? No ;
to have the best things. Who else says so ? A younger
one said, the best spiritual things ; and many joined with
him. Who has not much ambition ? Several. Who will
let things go on their own way ? One, (who is very indolent.) Who feel within, a power and will to do every thing ?
Almost all.

I know a man, said Mr. Alcott, who believes that, if
others would help him, he could make every slave-holder
in this country, free his slaves. It would be wrong for them
to do so, said one boy ; for the slaves cannot take care of

themselves. Perhaps so, said Mr. Alcott; but does that man aspire? Yes, said all. And I know a man, he continued, who believes that, if others would help him, he could make every child good? So do I, said several. And I know a lady who thinks that, if others would allow, she could make the Bible intelligible to every child: do these persons aspire? Yes, yes.

When they were dismissed, the visiter called a little boy of five to him, and said, Do you know what Jesus Christ meant by these words, "If you had faith, like a grain of mustard-seed, you could say to this mountain, &c." I have read it, said the child; but I do not remember what it represents. What does the mountain mean? said I. It is a mountain in the mind, said he, without hesitation. And the mustard-seed? A little faith, that will grow larger, said he; and he bounded away to go home with his companions.

The analysis of April 15th, began thus: Who enjoy this exercise? Several. Who have brought fresh minds this morning, ready to attend? Many. Who have dull minds this morning? None. And one boy said, his mind was fresh from the well! Fresh from what well? The well of the spirit, said he. Mr. Alcott went on: We are on imagination to-day, the power of shaping thoughts; who think they shall be highly interested in this? All held up their hands but one boy, who was out of temper.

To the question, of what do you mean by imagination? there were several answers, among which were the following: The power of conceiving thoughts in your mind, so as to see them with your eyes; the power that brings ideas out of your mind, so that others may see them; thoughts that come out of your mind; to see things in your mind; to picture forth ideas; to see thoughts and feelings; to picture forth ideas and feelings in words, which have not come out in things; to picture out things in your mind a great deal more beautiful than any in the outward world. The last was the answer of the boy, who at first was out of temper. He was interested in spite of himself.

Mr. Alcott here read *the Transfiguration;* and then asked, what does transfigure mean? To change the shape.

What does imagination mean? To make new shapes? Did any of you ever feel any thing like this: did any of you ever see shapes, beautiful shapes going out of your own minds? Many said yes. Two boys gave accounts of what they called visions. One said he often imagined Jesus Christ standing before his eyes. The other described a particular instance very minutely, of an angel coming with music, and the music's seeming to be shaped. What is that faculty which is not imagination, but something like it? Fancy. I am going to read something fanciful, now; and he read the description of Queen Mab. That is fanciful, said he. Now I am going to read something; and when I have read it, I am going to ask you whether it is imaginative or fanciful? And he began in Coleridge's Ancient Mariner, and read Parts III and IV.

Which has the most shaping power in it, said he; this last, or the description of Queen Mab. The last! was the acclamation. Such of you as think you have fancy, and not imagination, hold up your hands? Several did. Such as have the most imagination? Several.

Such of you as think you have the power of putting all you think and feel into words, hold up your hands? Several did. Who say that they never yet found words that would hold all their thoughts and feelings? Several. Can you understand this definition; imagination is the power that represents, re-presents spirit? Yes. Imagination re-presents spirit, soul, mind, the outward world and God; said Mr. Alcott. What is imagination? Imagination is the power by which you picture out thoughts, that never were realised in the world; as in Pilgrim's Progress, said a child under six. Several more repeated the idea which Mr. Alcott had expressed, more or less exactly; none of them so fully as this boy had done. Do you know any one who has no imagination? Some said, no, except an idiot. Mr. Alcott said there were many people with uncultivated imaginations, who were not idiots. Mr. Alcott asked the little boy who described the angel of day and night, where he thought he got his imagination? He said he did not know he had any imagination; he knew he had fancy. Mr. Alcott

then asked the rest if they thought he had imagination?
They all said yes; imagination and fancy too. Mr. Alcott
then asked concerning each scholar; and they discriminated very well in regard to the individuals, showing that they
had observed the operations of one another's faculties.

Mr. Alcott then described imagination, as the life and
power of the spirit, the eagle that carries us up to high
views; and said that it was the name of the mind in the
highest action. He then asked, when the imagination looks
back, what is it called? Memory, said one. When it looks
forward to the future, what is it called? One said, curiosity; another, expectation. Curiosity and expectation are in
it, said Mr. Alcott. Foresight, said one of the girls. A boy
of excellent understanding, and little imagination, said, understanding. Mr. Alcott said, oh no! Understanding is a
mole; it crawls in the ground; it sees only what is immediately around it.

The next Wednesday, April 22nd, when they were arranged for analysis, the most lawless boy in school was
made superintendent; the only employment which keeps
him from wrong doing. Mr. Alcott began with saying, that
this hour was a pleasant one to those who looked for realities within, instead of without themselves; and he asked
some questions to bring their minds steady.

At last he said, we are going to talk about judgment to-
day. What is judgment; what do you do, when you judge;
do you guess? No, said one. A little boy of five, a new
scholar, said, to judge is to know certainly. A boy of nine,
said, judgment is to discriminate between good and bad;
and see what to do. Do we judge only about actions? said
Mr. Alcott. No, about feelings, and quality, and size. A
boy of eight, said, to judge, is to think whether things are
right or wrong. Another of the same age, said, judgment
is examination. The power of judging, said Mr. Alcott, is
one of the noblest which is given to man: where does it
show itself in our nature? In the mind, said a boy of ten.
In which faculty of the mind? In the understanding, said
one; in the will, said another. It requires a great deal of
thought to judge, said a boy of eight. What do you think

of that boy who last spoke ? said Mr. Alcott, to the rest of
the school. He is a good boy. How do you know? By
his actions. How? This led to an analysis of the judgment, in this one instance. He then named several build-
ings, and asked which was the most beautiful ? They told
their opinions; and he analysed the process in this instance
again.

Who says we can get along in this world without judgment; without asking reason; without comparing? No
answer. What should you think of this: that a mind
should see all things and subjects so quickly, that it would
know immediately how things were, and not feel that it
was comparing or reasoning? It would be the judgment
of an angel, said one. This room we can all look upon,
and form a great many judgments upon, at a glance. Supposing a little fly, having all the mind that we have, were to
undertake to form these judgments; how much time it
would take; and what a quantity of geometrical and other
reasoning, it would have to go through. The universe is a
much wider space to us, than this room would be to a fly.
But this is about outward things. Which do you think
is easier to judge of, outward things, or ourselves ? There
was a difference of opinion; but the most reflective ones
said, it would be easier to judge of ourselves; of inward
things, for we could know what we were feeling and thinking, better than what is all around us, and out of our sight
also; and we could know all about our own actions better
than we could all about the actions of others.

Do we judge about every thing we do ? We ought to do
so, said one. When we look at the sun, and it dazzles us,
ought we to judge whether it is best to shut our eyelid or
not? said Mr. Alcott. Oh no! it shuts of itself, said several. Then some of our actions are not the result of judgment; and cannot be made dependant upon judgment; but
are what? They come by instinct. Can we make our
judgments instincts; that is, as quick as instinct? Sometimes, said one boy; we do things which we might judge
about, and which are wrong; but we do them by instinct;
how can we help that; what is that? It is passion; and

passion is not judgment; is it? said Mr. Alcott. No. What is it? Instinct. But is instinct wrong? When there is too much of it, said Mr. Alcott: when it is not governed; when instinct is passion, it is wrong; how can we govern instinct, so that it may not be passion? By reason and conscience, said several. Is there judgment in reason? Yes. Is there judgment in conscience? Yes. Is there will in judgment? Yes. Is the will which is in the judgment of conscience your own? It is my own, and God's also. What do you do when you judge? We think of a great many things. Do you compare? Yes.

In comparison and reasoning, do you go into yourselves? Yes. Well: in comparing the things in the universe, and reasoning geometrically, &c. as we supposed the fly to do, should we go inward? Yes. Thus you see that even in studying outward things, you are aided by something within? Yes. That which is within us must contain the idea, being of the spirit which created the outward world. And, to govern the spirit within us, and by making it strong and loving, to put it in harmony with the author, will enable the outward world to wake up within us its own image, and a sense of the beauty, and power, and goodness, that produced it in the creator. (This perhaps was said in simpler language.)

But what is a standard—a rule of judgment, respecting inward things? No answer. There was one, whose very instinct was reason and conscience, and he is a standard: who was that one? An angel, said our new scholar. Jesus Christ, said another.

Well, said Mr. Alcott, let us hear what Jesus Christ says about judging, and judgments! He read in paraphrase; Judge not without a great deal of care; for by the same standard as you judge others, you will be yourself judged. you show your own character by your judgments; if they are just, and liberal, and generous, it is because you have the sentiments of justice, liberality, and generosity within your own heart; for these are necessary in order to have any means of sympathizing with the magnanimous sentiments of others, and of so far escaping the annoy-

15

ance of their faults, coming against your self-love and interest, as to blind your eyes.

You, all of you, came to this school some months ago, with some notion in your heads about Mr. Alcott. You came day after day, and saw him do things, and heard him say words. Were you able to form a judgment of him immediately; or have you found your opinions have altered? They have altered. How many of you have misjudged me? Many. How many of you have misjudged your companions; father, mother, brothers, sisters? Many; and one mentioned a particular instance. What is the most necessary thing for us; that we may judge others correctly? *To know ourselves.* And we can judge of ourselves, —of inward things—more easily than we can of outward things? Yes. Does the mind shape itself in the outward world, or does the outward world shape itself in the mind? It is God's mind that shapes itself in the outward world. And what is our mind? It is the image of God. The human spirit is the image of the divine spirit? Yes. And is the human spirit's action, an image of the divine spirit's action? Yes, sometimes; it ought to be. Can the human spirit shape itself, then, as the divine spirit does, in the outward world? Yes—by words. Only by words? Yes, by actions. Only by words and actions? By paintings and sculpture. Heroic actions, poetry, painting and sculpture, are men's creations then? Yes. Does the hero, the poet, the painter, and the sculptor think most of the inward or outward world? The inward. And they go from the inward to the outward world? Yes. And always find something or make something to correspond with the inward? Yes. They find the inward explains the uses &c. of the outward? Yes. Then for judging of the outward world, as well as our fellow beings, we must begin with ourselves? Yes.

On Wednesday, April 29th, Mr. Alcott took the Bible, and said : There are two laws which govern all things; one is the law of necessity, or force : the other is the law of —— what? Love; good will; conscience; the spirit, were the several answers. Can any one who is governed by force have his liberty? No. What is the law of liberty? Love.

The people of this country are free, said one boy; but it is not governed by love. I am not talking of political government, said Mr. Alcott. When we love good, and are left to do what we please, do we do right or wrong? We do right, said a boy of five, if we love right. Who acted very wrong yesterday afternoon, said Mr. Alcott, when I was not well, and did not come? Many stood up. You are not moral; your goodness depends on another; you are weathercocks; you have no principle; neither the law of love, the law of liberty, good will, nor conscience, governs you; is all that true? Most thought it was. You are not trustworthy? No. Your goodness depends on the presence of Mr. Alcott? Yes. Who think the law of force should be brought to bear on you? Many did. You know a thief is shut up because he abuses liberty? Yes.

Mr. Alcott then told the youngest boy in the class, to go and touch the heads of all who, as he thought, would do right, if all punishment, all outward laws, &c. could be done away. He went and touched five heads, with excellent judgment. Mr. Alcott said, I believe all the best heads have been touched but one. He looked puzzled, and went to several who were next best. Mr. Alcott said, no, and it is no matter. He went to his seat. All the boys smiled at his unconsciousness, and one said, *that is real.*

Mr. Alcott then said, to-day we talk of Insight, what is insight? Insight is looking into ourselves said one. By what power do we look into ourselves? said Mr. Alcott. By insight, said another. What outsight have we? The senses, said one of the oldest boys. Insight, said Mr. Alcott, is the spirit seeing itself; and seeing the outward world in the spirit. Which of you have gone inward and viewed yourselves; seen with the spirit, and into spirit? None held up hands.

Who among you ever dream? All held up their hands. Are your eyes closed? Yes. Do your ears hear any sounds? No. Who has shed tears in sleep? Some. How did you hear, what did you see, when you saw and heard nothing outward, and yet shed tears in your dreams? Things seemed to happen, said one. Where do you think

your mind was, when your eyes and ears were closed, and
yet you saw, and heard, and laughed, and cried? A little
boy said, my spirit was in God; my heart, and soul, and
mind were in me,—and (he hesitated and said, oh Mr.
Alcott!) Very well, said Mr. Alcott, smiling—that's enough.
Who else can answer that question? One said, our minds
left us; and God was within us. Is he more within us
when we are asleep than when we are awake? said Mr.
Alcott. Sometimes. After some more talk, the boy illustrated, thus: I have had the nightmare, and wanted to kill
somebody—and thought it was wrong, though I was asleep.

Mr. Alcott spoke of the bad dreams of a glutton and intemperate man—and asked if they ever had bad dreams?
He then said that some people had bad dreams, because
they had sick bodies; sometimes these sick bodies were
their own fault; sometimes they were inherited from faulty
ancestors. (Some boys were sent out.) One boy's idea about
dreaming was, that bad dreams came partly from bad minds,
and partly from not having well bodies; generally the last.
Mr. Alcott said that all illness of body was always to be
ascribed to wrong doing somewhere; and sometimes it
was *ignorant* wrong doing of our own and our ancestors.
A good deal of talk arose, and some anecdotes were told.
Mr. Alcott then read a dream from the Bible; it was that
beautiful one in Job. He then read the dream of Jacob ;
and after some conversation on its meaning, he said, such
of you as think you have an outlooking power, may hold
up your hands. Several held up their hands. Who says
they have not such a power? Several. Why: don't you
see me? Yes. Who think they have such a power? All.
Who think the power that looks out, is deeper than the
eyes? Several. Who think it is no deeper than the eyes;
that only the eye looks? Several. We speak then of a
power, an inward power, that looks out of the eye;—what
is it called? Some said sight; some said the mind; some
said the understanding; some said the spirit. Mr. Alcott
said, the soul has two great faculties, insight and outsight.
Some boys in this school have insight, and some outsight;
and it would be very easy to show who have insight, and

who have outsight, in the greatest degree, by thinking on what subjects each answers most readily. But all have both classes of thoughts, in a degree, said he; there never was a child without both classes of thoughts; without the power of seeing shapes without, and seeing the feelings and ideas in their own souls also.

I am going to read what St. Paul says about these two classes of thought, said he. And he read in paraphrase the last part of the fourth chapter of 2 Corinthians and the first part of the fifth chapter.

He then addressed the little girl analysed, by name. What is there in the outward world that you like best; that you think most beautiful? After a while she said nature. What objects in particular? No answer. Do you like flowers? Yes. Do you like running brooks? Yes. Do you like the ocean? Yes. Do you like the pebbles on the shore? Yes. Can you describe the feelings that you have, when you see the ocean? imagine yourself there, how should you feel? The power, said she.

A series of questions were now asked as to the comparative effect of different scenes on the feelings of the several children; and some preferred ocean; some mountains; some rivers; some caverns in the earth; some cataracts; some shells; some stars, &c. He went on to ask questions which might show into what departments of natural history their tastes would lead them. He found some zoologists; some geologists; some botanists; some astronomers, &c. One at last remarked that he liked machines, engines, &c. Many other boys agreed with him. Mr. Alcott said it seemed to him that things were interesting to us, just in proportion as they seemed to be alive.

The next series of questions was calculated to bring out what was their taste for the arts; and there was considerable variety of taste; some were architects; some painters; some sculptors.

Who think dollars and eagles are very beautiful, and they take great delight in seeing them? One boy said he took great delight in having them.

15*

Who like carriages and splendid equipage? One said I
like sleighs. Another said, I like to be inside of them.
Who like beautiful clothes, dresses? None. Those may
stand up who would not play with beggar boys, even if
they were good, because of their looks? Several rose;
and Mr. Alcott said that many of those who were standing
up, would make the beggar boys worse probably; so it was
very well. Who would play with beggar boys, if they
were good? Several rose with great emphasis. Who
would not play with colored boys, if they were ever so
good and well instructed? The same boys rose as did at
first. I am afraid your minds are colored with prejudices,
said Mr. Alcott; and that you would darken their minds
with your faults. So it is very well. The rest laughed,
and when those sat down, rose up, and said they would
play with black boys, if they had cultivated minds.

What if you were blind, and could not *look out* upon
things at all; would there be any thing left to make you
happy? He said this to the little girl analysed. Yes,
inward things, said the little girl. What inward things?
Thoughts; feelings; a good conscience, &c. were named.
Who are most truly blind, those who cannot see inward
things, or those who cannot see outward things? Those
who cannot see inward things. You know when we talked
a while ago, we said something about *a net* which catches.
Things, perhaps, are a net which catches us sometimes.
Perhaps some of you are caught? I should like to see one
person caught, said a little boy. Should you, said Mr. Alcott, like to see a boy, whose eyes and ears are so caught
by *things*, that his mind is all taken up, and never looks
inward? Yes. Well there he is! said Mr. Alcott, holding
a looking glass before him.

He then turned again to the little girl. Which power
had you better use, the power of outsight or of insight?
The power of insight. Why? Because it sees the real
things. What are those things which the outsight sees?
Shadows of real things. Now each one think, said Mr.
Alcott, what idea you have in your mind from this conversation? One said insight is better than outsight. Another

said inward things are better than outward things. Is that an idea in your head, or a feeling in your heart? I don't know, said she.

Suppose you saw a man born into this beautiful world, and all his life long he was running round to catch bubbles, every one of which broke in his hand? They all laughed. Or a man running after his shadow; and he went on with several similar analogies which made them laugh. Such are the persons, he said, who live for outward things, instead of inward things.

Who says play is a bubble? Some held up their hands. But play is a very proper exercise in its place. Who says pleasure is a bubble? All held up their hands. Yet it is a bubble that it is innocent to look at a little. Is love a bubble? No. Is happiness? No. Is the soul? No. Is heaven? No. Is immortality? No. Who says they have no doubt about inward things, but about outward things there is an uncertainty? Several did.

Mr. Alcott then said, we will close with some words of Jesus, words which he said when he lived in a body like ours. Lay not up for yourselves treasures on earth, where moth and rust do corrupt, and thieves break through and steal; but lay up for yourselves treasures in heaven,—in the inward world,—where moth and rust do not corrupt, nor thieves break through and steal.

May 6th.—Mr. Alcott called the class to analysis, for the last time. He said we had now gone through the scale; but it had often been changed since we began, for almost every week had improved it. He then drew their attention to the one which was now on the black board; and said that only the arrangement was altered; for the same subjects were brought up by both scales.

We began with love; and then went to faith; and then to conscience, speaking of obedience, temptation and will; and then to the appetites, affections, and aspiration of the soul; and then we went to the mind, and spoke of imagination, and judgment, and insight. To-day I intend to talk a little more about insight; and I shall read what Jesus Christ says about it. He says we should not strive to get outward things which may be stolen and corrupted; but we should strive to get things within, which cannot be taken away, because they are God's; for what we love will take up all our exertions.

He here stopped and said that one of the boys in this school had said that he did not know before he came to this school, that he had any inward eyes; but now he felt that they were open. They began to guess who it was, but they did not guess the right one. Mr. Alcott said that many of them, when they came, were blind, were in midnight; and then he went on reading different passages of the gospels. He ended with the light of the body is the eye; What eye? This eye, said a little boy of five. That is the body's eye; What is the spirit's eye? That eye which can see every thing that it wants to see, and which can see God; the body's eye cannot see what it wants to, but the spirit's eye can. And Mr. Alcott, I think that when we are asleep, the spirit goes out of the body, and leaves the body dead; and bye and bye it goes back again, and makes the body alive again. But is the body entirely dead, in sleep? said Mr. Alcott. Why, perhaps a little spirit stays in the body to keep it alive. But the spirit generally goes out, and sees and hears with its inward eyes and ears, and that is dreaming.

Such of you as think, said Mr. Alcott, that the spirit acts in instinct, may hold up their hands. No answer. As soon as a baby is born, it cries; it seems to be astonished to find itself in the world, amidst so many things it does not know, and which are so unlike itself; not one thing it sees, or one word that it hears, does it understand. It cries——By instinct, interrupted one of the children. Yes, said Mr. Alcott, and it moves its hand to take hold of the sun, or fire, or whatever it sees; for it does not know how far off things are, or what will hurt, and what will not. Is there instinct in a baby's first motions? Yes. Does the spirit act in instinct? Yes. Does the spirit act when it loves its mother? Yes, a good deal, said one. Does the spirit act in appetite? Yes. Does the spirit act when it sees and feels something beautiful? Yes. What is that action?

Aspiring. Does the spirit act in thought? Yes, for the body cannot think. Thought, said Mr. Alcott, is the ladder by which the soul climbs up to heaven, or back to itself. Instinct, and appetites, love, and faith, go out from the soul. Thought goes back to the soul. By insight we go into the soul and see what is in ourselves. By judgment we compare thoughts. How many have insight? But a few thought they had. One of the most thoughtful said, a very little. Who do not go *in* for whole days? Two boys, one a lazy boy of eight, another a new scholar of five, held up their hands. Who cannot live a week without being taken captive and carried into the inward or spiritual world? No answer.

Who, every night, before they go to sleep, go inward and think that what is within is better than any thing out? Many. Who think of this over again, in the morning? Several. You know that Jesus said, there was a fountain in there of living water, which springs up into everlasting life. What is this fountain? The spirit.

We talked about dreaming a good while ago; who among you, dream? Several. Most of you dream when you are awake, you see things vaguely, and dimly; not as if they all belonged together, but as if they were in disjointed pieces.

How many of you think God can be discovered with the eyes? None. Such as think you can see his works only with your body's eyes; and that He himself is to be found by looking within, with inward eyes, hold up your hands. All did. How many of you look within enough to know a good deal about God? None. How many do not? All. How many think it is hard? One indolent boy held up his hand. How many think an idle person can see God? Some. It was here found that some confounded idleness with repose; when all comprehended it, they all said no idle person could see God; and made the same answer to the questions, How many think an intemperate person can see God? An obstinate-willed person? An angry, passionate person? A person living for the outward? A liar, deceiver? There was some talk about the difference

of liking truth in others, because it is convenient to ourselves; and loving it, so as to speak and act it. Who think
that those who love truth will probably know most of God ?
All. Who think that those who deny themselves; who
try to control their feelings, even their love, will know most
of God ? All. Such as think they cannot love God without being willing to die and lose their body, hold up their
hands. All did. Such as think that to find God, we must
keep all our nature in its right place; our spiritual part, our
faith and love; our mind; our body ; that no part should
be asleep; that all should be like the child aspiring, (he
pointed to the cast ;) hold up their hands. All. He then
went on, making remarks on each of the scholars, and saying what parts of the nature of each were asleep. This
took a good while ; but it was not lost, as it brought the subject home.

He then spoke of the effect of the passions: how, in the
drunkard, appetite swallows up all the nature ; how, in the
avaricious, the love of riches swallows up all the rest of the
nature, &c: but when the Spirit swallows up all the rest of
the nature, nothing is destroyed, but every part is strength-
ened and purified, and put in the right place.

Who think that we must know ourselves, in order to know
God? All. Who thinks he cannot know God, till he
knows himself a great deal? All. Who think that they
can know God by studying outward things? None. What
are outward things? Shadows of inward things, said the
little girl, who was generally the subject of analysis. The
representation of the mind, said a boy of nine. Who was
called the image of God? Jesus Christ, said the whole
school. Yes, said Mr. A., the outward world is the image
of the perfect mind ; and the perfect mind of Jesus Christ
was the image of God; and his soul was all spirit, and his
spirit was one with his Father's, as he said. Who think
that until we study ourselves, we cannot study outward
things to much advantage? Many.

Mr. Alcott then remarked that many naturalists who never studied themselves, but studied outward things, did not
believe in any spirit; and some who believed in spirit, yet

did not think it was the most important, and did not therefore believe in Christianity, or what Jesus Christ taught
about spirit. Others have gone out into the outward world,
thinking it was a shadow of the inward, and followed on
until they found themselves, and then God. One boy said,
if I study botany, can I go on from it and find God? Mr.
Alcott explained, but I could not hear him, as he walked to
a place, where he stood with his back to me. Some remarks were made on the Free Enquirers, calculated to produce charitable feelings towards most of them.

Upon what subject have these analysis lessons taught you?
Upon ourselves. Yes, upon your inward selves, upon spirit. Perhaps some time next winter, I shall get some one
who knows such things better than I do, to come and teach
you about the human body,—your outward selves, how
your eyes are formed and adapted for sight; and your ears
for hearing; and your stomach for digestion ;—who will
like to hear this? All held up their hands. Which do you
think you should like best, to hear about the construction of
your bodies, or about your spirits? Spirits. You prefer to
talk of inward things rather than outward things? Yes.
Who think the analysis has taught you a good deal about
yourselves? All. Who think it has taught you a good deal
about the meaning of words? All. I intend you shall
learn outward things too: I shall get people to come and
tell you about many outward things which I do not know
much about myself. I can teach better about the inward
things. The next quarter I am going to teach you about
inward things, not in yourselves, but in another,—a perfect
being.—In Jesus Christ? asked some. Yes; we will not
analyse, but study Jesus Christ ;—how many will be glad to
do this? They all held up their hands. How many have
learned something from the analysis,—they are very sure;
they know it? Almost all held up their hands. The rest
were tired and not attending. How many are sorry these
lessons are over. Several. Some said they were glad the
next subject was coming. Who would like to hear the
record of all the analysis read? All.

Mr. Alcott then recurred again to the scale, and said he would read it; and if they did not understand it, they must say so.

THE DIVINE SPIRIT Quickens and Irradiates the HUMAN SPIRIT, in the REVELATIONS OF CONSCIENCE, through		
Aspiration of Soul in Faith;	Conspiration of Will in Obedience;	Inspiration of Mind in Thought;
Felt through Sensibility.	Exerted through Reason.	Seen through Intelligence.
in Love. Desire. Instinct.	in Self-apprehension. Self-direction. Self-crucifixion.	in Insight. Imagination. Judgment.

After this was done, he said that he supposed this scale was now drawn in their minds : and he began to obliterate the word *instinct*, which he said they all understood. As he obliterated each word in a certain order, they signified by their remarks that they understood them, excepting the words which had not been talked about. First, he obliterated the column of the Soul ; then that of the Intellect ; and then that of the Will ; leaving the Revelations of Conscience, which were naturally referred to the Divine Spirit, that stood above as the Source of all.

GENERAL PRINCIPLES OF EDUCATION.

I am well aware that the foregoing record is an entirely inadequate representation of the interesting communications between Mr. Alcott and his pupils; but if I have not failed utterly, some interest has been excited, kindred to that which the careful and frequent visiting of his school always inspires —to know the general principles on which his methods are based, and the results which he has in view. At the risk, therefore, of being called metaphysical, a phrase which seems to be designed, when used in common parlance, to deter all enquiry into causes and the principles of method, I shall proceed to make a few remarks, by way of key to unlock the treasures of childhood, which is the business of education. But in doing this, I do not intend to leave the ground of observation and experience, where every mother finds herself, if she is at all spiritually-minded.

There is nothing in true education which has not its germ in the maternal sentiment; and every mother would find more of the spiritual philosophy in her own affections, if her mind would but read her heart, than could be obtained by years of study in books. It indeed requires thought to get possession of principles, as well as to act upon them, and it is necessarily metaphysical thought, when the subject of attention is a child, whose essence is beyond the physical nature; but every intelligent woman who will make the effort, finds, on analysing her own mind, that she knows more of metaphysics than she does of any thing else.

These remarks are not made, however, to introduce any great metaphysical disquisition. Nothing is to be attempted here, but a few hints, by way of theory. But, in writing the humblest essay, on a subject involving universal relations, the colloquialisms of small circles must be abandoned in a degree, and more general words found and used. And, when an inadequate philosophy, long prevailing, has adulterated in many different ways, the natural language of the heart and imagination, it is especially necessary to newly

16

wash, in the ' undefiled wells' of feeling and thought, whence
language first arose, those strong and forcible mother-words
which grew out of the philosophy of innate ideas, and
which, since its decline, have been obscured and kicked
aside, as unregarded ' pebbles, in the dusty wheel-ruts of
custom.' Yet it is very true that the use of any words systematically, gives an air of science to very familiar knowledge, that may savor of a pedantry of which the writer is
utterly unconscious.—But enough of preliminaries.

Every thing in education depends on the view taken of
the soul. What is the soul? is the question; and, will not
every mother, who has watched the infant from its cradle,
respond to the following propositions, by way of answer
to this question?

The feeling of existence, before a shadow has fallen from
matter and circumstance upon that breath of the Almighty
which makes man a living soul, must necessarily be Happiness.

And the instinct of something else, whether being or
thing, conforming as it must do, to that which is within,
can only be kindly, the germ of Love.

And the action from within outward, — must therefore be
Faith, since what is expected is according to what is known;
and when nothing is known but Happiness and Love, nothing else can be expected.

But Happiness, Love, and Faith, in their first form of Feeling, are active principles; therefore there is no passiveness
in the nature of the soul. Its passiveness is a production of
the Will, and the Will is a growth.

When action begins to be reflected upon, and those original feelings are seen to be great Ideas, impulse becomes
self-conscious, and self-conscious Impulse is Will.

But the spirit is placed in the midst of matter, of which
it has no Idea ; for that is an acquisition which it gains in
this world. The process of gaining the notion of matter,
is temptation.

Human Will soon finds itself limited, for there is only
its own direction, in which any human spirit can go, to find
the Individual perfection allotted to it in the Infinite Plan.

Faith is deceived until it is realized as the evidence of things unseen ; Love is disappointed, until it finds the spiritual ; and Happiness is disturbed until all is righted again. In short, human life is obstruction, and obstruction gives, or is the idea, of the material world.

Temptation must come to all spirit, in order to its development ; that is, the material world, and circumstances growing out of outward limitations and obstructions, must deceive Faith, disappoint Love, and disturb Happiness, in a degree. But only in a degree, since the material world is finite. " I have overcome the world," said the perfected ; and the most imperfect, have principles within them, which must survive, conquer, and triumph over matter.

Now, in order that this life, conquest, triumph, may be from the beginning, the soul must be assisted by sympathy of other souls. Souls must make common cause ; in other words, human influence, or education, instead of taking the side of the material world, must take the side of the spiritual. This will lead those who superintend education, first, to keep up the reality of Happiness to the child's heart, by leading him out to observe happiness as a fact. He should be taught the signs of joy, wherever they exist, and different as they may be ; he should be led to sympathize with it, whether manifested in the insect, or the most advanced human being. He should not be able to doubt that there are those who find it their satisfaction to contribute to his own happiness; and that even in the pain a wise love inflicts, there is an ultimate regard to his welfare. All natural beauty, as an expression of God's happiness, may subserve this end. The first stage of true religion, perhaps, is necessarily pantheism. And babyhood is the right time for pantheism. It will die out, and give place to Christian theism, as individuality is realized.

The realisation of Happiness, involves the second principle of education ; for it promotes the action of Love. When we lead a child to see the happiness within and around him, we are giving him a true perception of our love, and leading himself through an experience of it, for every thing which his eye rests upon. In this part of education, let us be careful to pamper the body as little as possible. It is the spirit of a child which is to be loved and sympathised with; and he should hardly be allowed to think of his body, except to govern and deny those instincts which appear in it. It makes a child selfish, and materialises him, to let his love find yours through his and your body. As he recedes from the nursery, his love should find a more intellectual and spiritual expression continually.

Thirdly, this realising of Happiness, and action of Love, encourages Faith along its dark path. Faith should also be cherished in education, by our endeavoring to find out, on general principles, what the child should expect; what the Providence of God, unshadowed by human arbitration, would afford; and avoiding to disappoint expectations which our love and goodness have raised. It is the office of matter and circumstance to disappoint. Let not the spirit which the soul meets in the human being, be matter to him; let it be spirit, inspiring. A child's faith has much to encounter, having spirit for his standard and meeting matter. Let him learn that spirit is infinite, even in the human being; that he gains, in proportion as he trusts; and he will forever *aspire*.

But it is the next principle of growth which is, perhaps, the most obvious work of education, for its action is more dependent on the assistance of others. The principles of human nature, its Happiness, Love, and Faith, must be thought out into consciousness. The consciousness of an active nature evolves Will, Will is strong in proportion to consciousness. Let it not be crushed, or perverted, in being taught to obey. It has been happily said, " a man is a river; on every side there are obstructions, but in one direction the infinite is open." In opposing a child's will, show him that the action to which you call him, though it may be inward, is greater than that from which you call him.

These principles in education are very general, but they are the frame-work of all others. The parent or teacher should be in a right line with the Creator. When men are to each other the mouthpiece of those fountain Ideas, Happiness, Love, Truth, Beauty—then, and not till then, will human nature be redeemed. It will be no longer of the earth, earthy; but the Lord from Heaven.

The teacher of a school can seldom receive a child from the hands of its parents, in that condition into which the clear apprehension and persevering application of the above principles would bring it. Yet sometimes we are so fortunate as to do so; and such is the admirable arrangement of checks and balances in that divine social institution of Family, that it is astonishing to find how much of the true method of inspiration, is acted out by true-hearted men and women, who never speculated. These happy accidents preserve children several years, and a teacher who has the advantage of receiving pupils young, generally finds the majority of his pupils, at least in our community, in a very hopeful state, in which to begin. The child comes to him to be intellectually trained. And this is his main object, it is true. But this is not to be accomplished, by regarding his intellectual nature alone; for such a course produces a dismemberment, which is death to every form of life, æsthetic, intellectual, and moral. The teacher should enter into the place of the parent, and breathe into the child the same inspirations.

The word inspiration applied to the action of human beings on each other, is perhaps new. But the action itself is old, and is very inadequately expressed by giving an active sense to the word sympathy, whose real signification, by its etymology, is passive. The very reason, probably, that inspiration, the active operation of sympathy, has not been recognised and named as a principle of education, is because it is so universal; just as the principle of attraction escaped the notice of all observers of nature, until the days of the practical Newton, though its phenomena had been exhibited in every motion of the universe since the creation.

From the beginning of time, the action of human beings on each other has been in proportion to the inspiring power of the one party, meeting the sympathies and aspirations of the other. Temper and conduct, expressed by tone and manner, convey feelings and sentiments, or rather, wake them up in the souls to which they are addressed, as truly as

16*

words convey ideas, or wake them up in the understanding. Common language abounds with idioms which involve this universal fact. Common life abounds with
particular facts which prove it. The waiting-woman who
was accused of witchcraft, because she made the Italian
Countess do whatever she chose to ask her, replied, in her
own justification, that it was only the natural influence
which a strong mind has over a weak one. Almost all
willing obedience in human society, and even much that is
not willing, but seems instinctive, may be referred to the
same cause. How few pursue the right, merely because
they see it! How easy is it to do what those we venerate
or love desire us to do! What life does the same proposi-
tion receive from the lips of an earnest speaker, as fell cold
and powerless from one who repeated it by rote, and did
not send it from the intimate convictions of his soul! In
fact, human life, in all its relations, is but a varied exhibition of this principle of action. All movement, progress,
the spirit of every age, is but the result of it; and it is
because the loftier souls of men have the power of waking
up a spirit kindred to themselves, which otherwise lies
slumbering unconscious of itself, that they become the
prophets of future times. No great era but must have had
its prophets, whether they uttered the prophecy in words
or not; for there must have been men to bring it about
who elaborated its spirit in the silence and depth of their
own souls.

But the inspirations of men have a various moral character. That was a very good one, by which Lycurgus
induced all the rich people of Sparta to divide their lands
and become poor, for the sake of the body politic. But
there must also have been inspiration, and not a little, from
that mind or those minds, that, having devised the system
of the Asiatic religious polity, had the power to make it so
universally accepted, that it was established; though it
does violence to so many of the feelings of men. It was
inspiration from the mind of Peter the Hermit which turned
all Europe in a crusade upon Asia. It was inspiration that
produced the adoption of the Monastic system. So there

is much inspiration in domestic life of a most deleterious character, and many families are moulded by a will which is not moral, though it is too plainly productive of Will in others, not to be admitted spiritual.

There is however, a step down from the spiritual world which may be taken; and this is done in education and legislation, (which latter is but the former applied to adults,) whenever the method of inspiration is abandoned for that of mere physical force. The result is imbecility and weakness. It is also the ultimate result of all the spiritual action, which is not governed by the moral power.

The power of inspiring depends on our own, and others' original depth of feeling; but the character of our inspirations depends on the right regulation and direction of our feelings. If we feel for ourselves rather than for others; or for a few rather than for the many ; or for things rather than for beings; and inspire our little ones and others with such a disproportionate and falsely directed spirit, " it were better that a millstone were hanged round our necks, and we were cast into the depths of the sea." And when a parent loses faith in the power of his own soul to influence, and of his child's soul, to receive the influence of his spirit, and puts his ultimate trust in a rod, or a rule, or a formula of doctrine, his child, as far as he is mastered by them, is injured vitally. He may become deceptive in self-defence, or utterly imbecile in will, unless he resist the authority altogether, which latter alternative endangers all that is faithful and beautiful within him. It is of the last importance, therefore, to have the spiritual power pure and moral. The parent or teacher should make it his first business to know himself; for most surely he will transmit his moral character by inspiration to his child, in just such proportion as circumstances allow him to have any influence, and the child has any sensibility. The time came when the generous spirit died out of the institutions of Lycurgus, and then Sparta was a military despotism. The men who devised the religious despotisms of Asia have long since died, and left institutions and idols that have degraded the race below men. St. Francisco, St. Dominique, Ignatius de

Loyala, have passed away, with their fervent piety, their disdain of bodily privation, their self-sacrificing spirit of martyrdom; and left their well-meant rules to crush the spirit of men.

It is not however enough that the guardian of a child's mind himself understands, what is the nature of soul; and what is the true method of assisting its development. The child himself must, from the beginning, be made to co-öperate, by having his attention turned inward as early as the era of responsibility begins; that is, as soon as he is capable of right and wrong action. When is this era?

The time comes when every human being begins to act on himself. Supposing the most favorable case; that the child has been in a sympathetic atmosphere; that it has received all the inspirations after which its nature has aspired ; that its unfolding understanding has been met by wise instructions, he may yet do wrong. When his understanding is sufficiently developed, to see that he is an individual, and one of the agents by which himself is to be inspired and directed, he will have a sense of a duty which he owes to himself. And after having fairly felt and seen this duty, if he neglects it, he sins.

If sin then is the failure of the soul in its duties to itself, the first object in moral education must be to leave no interval of personal power unenlightened by self-knowl-edge. What is the human germ of never ending exist-ence; is the first question which is to be brought before the mind of the child. Is this germ matter; insensate, unthinking, involuntary, finite, lifeless matter, of which sensation, thought, volition, are mere modes, like form, or results of motion, like sound, and to which the Creator may superadd, as an attribute, eternal life? Or is it LIFE, from the fountain of life ; feeling, thinking, willing, acting, by the same necessity of nature by which God loves, knows, creates; and to which matter is but a temporary accident.

This is the question between the material and spiritual philosophy : and the materials of judgment are within the sphere of any sound-minded child, whom we consider ca-pable of right and wrong; as we trust has been proved to those who might incline to doubt it, even by the foregoing imperfect record of Mr. Alcott's school.

It may be seen from the genius of the primitive languages, that the oldest philosophy of the human race was spiritual. The yet unmaterialized fathers of mankind, seeing that Eternal Life cannot have beginning more than end; that Human Will may and often does overcome matter, by triumphing over pain and death; that Thought can only be born out of Sensibility; and that Sensibility is the opposite of matter, did unhesitatingly declare that the human germ is Spirit, bearing the relation to the body in which it is manifested, that the Creator bears to the material universe, which, all-glorious as it appears, is but a dark representation of Himself. Thus, the Hebrew language so completely identified God with the will of man, as to cease to convey truth to minds which lost the philosophy that should comprehend, and the virtue which should explain it. "The corruption of the best is the worst;" and morality was lost in the east in religionism; and family government was expanded into despotism; and spirit itself petrified into matter;—an everlasting warning, which is not sufficiently regarded by subsequent generations.—The theoretical philosophy of Anaxagoras was the reassertion in Greece, of the religious philosophy of the east. Mind is God, said the great teacher of Pericles and Socrates. And hence sprang up in Athens, the practical philosophy of *know thyself.* If the human being is a generation of that Spirit which preceded the existence of matter, (so reasoned Socrates,) then a consciousness of its own laws, i. e. of itself, must be the point from which all things else are to be viewed; and without affirming any thing, he began to inquire himself, and to lead others to inquire, into the distinction between the accidental and the real. He analysed the theory of obedience to the will of the gods, and found that man had within him a power of questioning the right of even that power which calls itself divine: for he has a standard within, by which the pretensions of power are to be analysed and weighed. And he leads to the conclusion that man need not obey any thing but Goodness; since in allegiance to Goodness, he is able to suffer martyrdom with satisfaction. Did not Socrates, in this, discover God, and the human spirit's union with Him, in that bond, which all the powers of this world might not break ?

By the path of this practical philosophy, this pursuit of *self-knowledge*, which is but another word for *psychology*, since *self* is used by Socrates in the general sense of *soul*, Plato went up, and beyond the ground of Anaxagoras and the Oriental Philosophy. As God, (so he reasoned,) contemplating his own unfathomable essence, manifests his contemplations by the outward world which is his mirror and his speech, so the generated spirits, which partake his being in all but self-consciousness, must become conscious of themselves and of their eternal sonship, by evermore using the outward world as a remembrancer, to wake up feeling after feeling, and thought after thought, in their own unfathomed being. To go inward, and become fully conscious of what goes on there, and to verify it in action, is therefore the Alpha and Omega of a true life.

And Bacon has only carried out this old Platonism in one direction, when he has spoken of all outward objects as exponents of the Laws—that is, Ideas, or spirit of God. Accidental coincidences, he admits, may favor, and to minds fully alive, perhaps suggest Ideas, yet he very plainly declares that the experimental philosophy, to answer its end, must proceed from ever-renewing theories in the mind of the experimenter. Wordsworth has but carried out the same old Platonism in another direction, when he has spoken of the Primal Sympathies, "which having been, must ever be," wedding the soul to nature, with a dowry of beauty and joy, which must be felt to be understood.

And whence, indeed, comes that Love which may not be gainsayed, existing in certain souls, towards particular departments of nature, but from the soul which draws its laws and sympathies from the Being who created all the departments of external nature, as symbols of Himself? Has it been the accident of habit, which has made martyrs in every field of science, as well as of humanity ? or has it, indeed, and in truth, been a conscious partaking of the joy

of the Creator, from the soul's finding its own development in the intellection of the Laws, deduced from the
department of creation it impulsively explores?

But all this is the spiritual philosophy—that is, it all
expresses that the Soul is an emanation from the Infinite
Spirit; consisting of Principles, or absolute beginnings of
never ending movements; and the whole of the above
ground can be traversed by a sound-minded child, whose
nature has not been injured by the influence of the adult.
This philosophy does not exist merely in a scientific
form. It has not only always pervaded more or less, the
poetry of nations; but it speaks to all human sensibility and intelligence the language of the heart in the
person and words of Jesus Christ, who himself embodied
it, the Word made flesh. A spiritual oneness of Jesus and
God has never been denied by any sect of religion. In his
person, the humanitarian, as well as the trinitarian believes,
that the infinite was incarnated; that the universal was
felt; that time and space, and all practical difficulties in the
development of the mind were seen through; that pain
and death were overcome; that the Father's business, as
far as it was committed to him, was finished; and that he
has taken his place with the Father, as a source of pure
inspirations to other men.

Yet no sect of religion has asserted with sufficient distinctness the great truth which makes all this practical;
namely, that all other souls are potentially what Jesus was
actually; that every soul is an incarnation of the infinite;
that it never will think clearly till it has mentally tran-
scended time and space; that it never will feel in harmony
with itself until its sensibility is commensurate with all
beings; that it never will be fully alive, till, having finished
the work given it to do, it has passed through the grave.
This, however, is the philosophy of Christianity; and
therefore the philosophy of education.

Nor is it only for moral education, that self-analysis and
the study of " the truth of our nature " in Jesus Christ, is
indispensable. It is no less beneficial, as the first step of
intellectual education. The soul itself, when looked on as

an object, becomes a subject of scientific classification, in its
faculties and operations. And the perpetual renewal of
Mr. Alcott's diagrams has been found to preclude the idea
of a stationary science of the mind, while they give the
desirable idea of systematising our knowledge of it, for the
time being.

But the obvious and simple way of giving children an
insight into the the science of mind, (themselves,) is by
teaching them their own vernacular tongue in the spelling
book. In order to understand the most common words, in
all the varieties of application of which each word is susceptible, both the mind and outward things must be quite
extensively known. Children come to feel this, by means
of the defining exercises, upon which Mr. Alcott immediately puts all his scholars. It has been seen that he is in
the habit of calling on each scholar to illustrate the word,
in some original or remembered sentence. Figurative applications are generally the first that come out. He one day
began with the youngest of thirty scholars, to ask for illustrations of the word brute; and there were but three literal
answers. A brute was a man who killed another; a
drunken man; a man who beat his wife; a man without
any love; but it was always a man. In one instance it was
a boy beating his dog. Which is the brute, said Mr. Alcott,
the boy or the dog? The boy! was the answer of the little
girl, with the gravest face. Here is an opening, therefore,
for speaking of the outward as a sign of the inward, and
giving life to nature and circumstance, as well as language.

The lessons on self-analysis, also, are not merely of a fine
moral influence, in showing the grounds of self-estimation,
and of righteous judgment of others, but in laying a foundation of accurate knowledge of language in its most spiritual vein. It has been seen how the life of Christ is used
as the standard in self-analysis; but Mr. Alcott has arranged
the Gospels of this Life, in such a way as to illustrate the
whole Career of Spirit on earth; and this he intends now to
go upon, and read, with conversations, in place of the lessons on self-analysis. Parallel lives, showing, here and
there, approximations to this ideal, or even wanderings from

it, are to be given in connexion, affording variety of illustration.

Biography is the right study for the young. But there is very little biography written, which gives an insight into the life of the mind, and especially into its formation. It is only occasionally, that we find a philosopher who can read other men's experience; and to whom the incidents of a life are transparent. But for the purposes of education, there should be biographies of the childhood of genius and virtue, on the plan of Carlyle's Life of Schiller, and the review of Lockhart's Life of Burns. Autobiography will however increase, as men grow enlightened enough by the revival of the spiritual philosophy, to look upon themselves as objects, without egotism, and to consider the facts of a soul's development, as the best gift which philanthropy can contribute to the cause of general improvement.

To supply the want of biography, Mr. Alcott relies a great deal upon journal writing, which is autobiography, while it hardly seems so to the writer. To learn to use words, is a ready way to appreciate their force. And while Mr. Alcott presents this exercise as a means of self-inspection and self-knowledge, enabling the writers to give unity to their own being, by bringing all outward facts into some relation with their individuality, and gathering up fragments which would otherwise be lost; he knows he is also assisting them in the art of composition, in a way that the rules of Rhetoric could never do. Every one knows that a technical memory of words, and of rules of composition, gives very little command of language; while a rich consciousness, a quick imagination and force of feeling, seem to unlock the treasury; and even so vulgar a passion as anger, produces eloquence, and quickens the perception to the slightest inuendo.

Self-analysis, biography, and journal-writing, leading therefore, immediately, into the knowledge of language, are as truly the initiation of intellectual as of moral education. And language has ever stood in the fore-front of children's studies. Although, the ancient languages, first took their place in that early stage of education, which they now

17

occupy, when they were living languages, and necessary for the purpose of any reading whatever, they have retained the same position, notwithstanding many disadvantages which they have involved, because of the good effect which has been experienced from the concentration of attention upon the vernacular words by which the Latin and Greek words are translated; and from the acquisition of the spirit of one's native language, by the recognition of its idioms in contradistinction to those of other languages.

No thorough method of studying one's native tongue, independently of learning another, has been practised; and it may be freely admitted, that to study another language is better than to study none at all. But it would have a much more creative influence upon the faculties of the young, besides saving much time and distress, if the study of English on Mr. Alcott's plan, should come first; and that of the ancient languages be delayed a few years. Boys would be, generally speaking, better fitted for college at fourteen or fifteen, even in Latin and Greek, if they did not begin to learn them till they were twelve years old; always providing, however, that they thoroughly study English, by means of self-analysis, poetry, and religious revelation, up to that time. Mr. Alcott, it is true, has Latin taught in his school, with reference to fitting boys for the other schools; and it does not interfere with the prosecution of his own plans, since his assistant has long been in the habit of teaching it, with reference to such results as he secures by his exercises on English words.

These observations on the intellectual bearings of the study of language, will explain much that is peculiar in Mr. Alcott's school. And it will show that the intellectual results are never separated from the moral, and consequently never neglected. Gradually, self-knowledge becomes psychology; knowledge of language, grammar; and the practice of composition, leads to the principles of true rhetoric. Even if by removal from the school, these results are not attained under his immediate observation, he cannot doubt that they will surely come out from the principles which he sets into operation.

In speaking so elaborately of the study of the medium of communication between mind and mind, I must not be understood, however, as counseling a sequestration of children from nature. The forms of nature, as furniture for the imagination, and an address to the sentiments of wonder and beauty; and even as a delight to the eye, and models for the pencil, cannot be too early presented, or too lovingly dwelt upon. The use of pictures referred to in the early part of the Record, and the practice of drawing under regular teaching, together with the study of geography, on the plan suggested in a former portion of this volume, involve a knowledge of the general facts of natural history, such as the location of plants and animals, and their more obvious characteristics, quite sufficient for poetry, art, and religion. This, with exercises in arithmetic on Colburn's plan, is "enough of science and of art" in geography, natural history, and arithmetic, for children under ten years of age. Their understandings are to be formed, in the first place, by the apprehension of the Spirit within themselves, as a key to the Express Image of that Creator, who Himself must be seen, in order to the seeing of Nature in Him, who alone makes its Unity. For what are the Laws of Nature, but the Will of God? And what is the Will of God, but His Unity in action? The only being in human form, who has comprehended Nature sufficiently, to seem above it in its common operations, studied nothing but Spirit. But in knowing the Parent Spirit, Jesus knew all things, as well as all men.

The scientific study of Nature, however, has its place in education. And the knowledge of our own language, is the greatest aid to the study of the sciences, as well as the best preparation for the study of other languages. I have heretofore tested this in my own school. Being convinced that children were not benefitted by committing to memory text books of natural science, or even by witnessing experiments, until they have come, in the first place, to look upon the creation with the poetical and religious eye, which regards every fact as an exponent of spiritual truth, I fought off all these branches of study from my younger scholars for many years; making the sole exception of geometry which is not so much science of external nature, as contemplation of our own intellect. I found that their knowledge of words made the theory of geometry easy to them, and enabled them to master the particular demonstrations so rapidly and completely, that it was a favorite study with a whole school of thirty-five scholars, between the ages of eight and twenty, with all their various minds, that I never subjected to the slightest artificial stimulus, not even what might arise from my keeping a weekly record, or changing their places in a class. And they became expert, though in different degrees, in geometrical reasoning; even the slowest of all, a child formed intellectually as well as bodily, for the early death she met; and whom I never could carry farther in grammar, than to separate the names of sensible objects from other words, or deeper in natural history than to remember the facts that addressed her social affections, did go through the Plane Geometry with pleasure, and do all the problems with success, though not without long and faithful labor. But when at about thirteen years of age, these children were set to the study of natural philosophy; even without the advantage of an apparatus for experiments, and with no means of verification but geometrical demonstration; they made a progress which fully answered my own expectations, and has astonished every experienced person who has heard the details. It would be perfectly safe, and perhaps even better, were schools taught as they should be, that the natural sciences, together with history, should not come among school studies, but be deferred to the period of life immediately succeeding the school period. Drawing, language, arithmetic, geography, and geometry, indeed whatever can be more easily acquired by the assistance of others, should be school studies; and these train the mind to a maturity, which makes books of natural science, and of political history, easily understood, and acquired. It is very easy for a prepared mind to learn, or at least to reason at a glance upon facts, which no mere industry could apprehend in any relation to each other. This preparation is what Mr. Alcott means by spiritual culture, a term so general, that it includes moral and intellectual.

APPENDIX.

———

Specimens of Paraphrase—THE LORD'S PRAYER—*by a boy
of ten years of age.*

Our Protector who dwelleth in the heavens, reverenced
be thy title. May thy judgments come to pass. May thy
desires be complied with on earth as they are in thy dwelling place. Provide us this day with our usual subsistence.
Pardon our transgressions, as we pardon those who offend
us. Let us not stray into wickedness; but protect us from
sin. For thine is the strength, dominion and praise without
end. Amen.

From Wordsworth.

            Nature never did betray
The heart that loved her. 'Tis her privilege
Through all the years of this our life, to lead
From joy to joy; for she can so inform
The mind that is within us, so impress
With quietness and beauty, and so feed
With lofty thoughts, that neither evil tongues,
Rash judgments, or the sneers of selfish men,
Nor greetings where no kindness is, nor all
The dreary intercourse of daily life,
Shall e'er prevail against us, or disturb
Our cheerful faith that all which we behold
Is full of blessings.

Paraphrase of the above, by a boy of ten.

            Nature is ever faithful
To the spirit that adores her. 'Tis her joy
'Midst all the hours of this our being, to direct
   17*

From bliss to bliss : for she can so improve
The soul within us, so imprint
With stillness and beauty, and so protect
With elevated ideas, that neither wrongful tongues,
Impetuous thoughts, or the ridicule of selfish men,
Nor kindness where hypocrisy prevails, nor all
The irksome communion of repassing life,
Can e'er attack to overcome us, or destroy
Our inward trust that all which we perceive
Is full of Providence.

Grammatical analysis of the same passage, by the same.

Objects.	Actions.	Qualities.	Substitutes.	Relations.
years	betray	lofty	that	so
tongues	lead	evil	her	and
men	inform	rash	it	of
nature	impress	all	this	nor
heart	feed	dreary	our	or
privilege	prevail	daily	which	from
life	disturb	cheerful		for
joy	did	full		within
mind	can	never		with
quietness	shall	ever		
beauty				
thought				
judgment				
faith				
blessings				
greetings				
kindness				
sneer				
intercourse				

Specimens of composition (uncorrected) from a Journal of a little girl of ten years of age, who had not written composition before. It began six weeks after she entered school.

November 4th, 1834.—This morning, at 9 o'clock, **Mr.**

Alcott read the story of Peter Bell in poetry written by Mr. Wordsworth. Peter Bell was a pedlar, who chose to go about the country selling earthen ware. The part that I was most interested in, was about the ass, and where Peter Bell got to the dead man's house. Then in recess we went double hop around the room. After recess Miss Peabody asked us questions in Arithmetic, and then we studied Latin until school was done. I went home, and after dinner I studied my Latin lesson a little while, and then I took a pleasant walk, and got very tired, and I went to bed early.

March 30th, 1835.—This morning I got my sisters ready after I had done a few things for mother and my cousins went to school with my younger sister and my other goes alone because she has so short a way to go.

When I got to school myself I found that it had not begun. So I took my things off and sat down to warm me—but school began very soon and I was glad because I do not like to get here much before school time : I only want time to get ready to come in and make my determination not to do any thing wrong, which takes a very short time. As the clock gave the alarm I took my seat and began to write my journal when S. B. came in to speak to me so I went into the other room with her and I am afraid I staid too long so I resumed my journal—After I had finished it I wrote some words on my slate. To day being the day that we have conversation on the words of the spelling so we turned round and Mr. Alcott asked us if we should not like to spell longer words and almost all the scholars held up their hands. Then three of the boys said that they could spell all the words of one syllable that they ever heard and so Mr. Alcott took the spelling book and pronounced some of the words and they could not spell all of them. I cannot tell all of the conversation then we talked about the word clown Mr. Alcott asked all of us the meaning and the general answer was a lazy fellow and Mr. Alcott said there were some clownish scholars here and then he told us a story from the Looking Glass which I have not time to tell. If I had I know I could tell it because I have it all pictured in my mind. We talked till twelve o'clock and then we were dis-

missed.   After school I read to mother from a book which
one of my friends lent me.

In the afternoon I came to school and had a Latin Lesson which was very interesting and I think that the reason
is because I was attentive to it because no lesson can be interesting when there is not attention paid to it.

In the evening I read and played dominoes.

April 1.   This morning I did a few things for mother
and then came to school.   When I got to school I wrote
my journal.   I like this very much and I think it will learn
me to think a great deal besides learning me the various
other things which the journal affords.   We turned round
earlier than usual because Mr. Alcott is going to read from
the Bible after the last supper of Jesus as he talked with his
disciples about love.   And though I have read it a great
many times and had it read to me, I think I was more interested this time than I ever was and I think I understood
it better.   After Mr. Alcott had read it and talked a little he
placed us in different places so we could see the analysis
better.   I think Mr. Alcott is very kind to try to make us as
comfortable as he can, and is always willing to gratify our
wishes though I think we are too apt to ask questions and
to complain sometimes of the heat and sometimes of the
cold.

The analysis was on Love or Affection which was very
interesting.   Mr. Alcott asked all those that had such love
as Jesus to hold up their hands several did so and I held up
mine because I thought I had some such love.   He then
asked us if we loved every body in the world and several
other questions which we answered.

April 6th.—*   *   *   at the usual hour we turned round
and had a very interesting conversation on the words, *abject*,
abscess, *absent*, and *abstract*.   The most interesting word
was absent.   Mr. Alcott said that this word related to the
mind as well as to the body.   And he said that some of the
scholars were absent, that their bodies were here but their
minds were on the common or at home, but I do not think
mine is very often for I take so much interest in every
thing we do here that I hardly have time to let my mind
wander.

Thursday, 23rd of April, 1835. I came into school at 9 o'clock, and found that Mr. Alcott had put every thing in order; so I took my journal and wrote in it a little while, and then wrote my paraphrase in my book. At the usual hour we turned round, and as it was the day that we converse, the conversation began. It was about the example shown by older scholars. Then Mr. Alcott said, that he was going to set a table with sugar-plums and candy, and all good things for the body; and those that were apt to gratify their appetites would of course come and eat some of them, and eat till they could eat no more. And he was going to have another table for the spirit, and was going to put good books and good bread and pure water on it, for they were the emblems of truth and goodness, and those that loved the spirit better than the body, would come to that table and eat the words from the books, and the bread and water. And he guessed that they would be quite as *happy* as those that were at the other table eating and drinking and getting intemperate or intoxicated. He said a great deal more, but I have not time to write it now, and I hope what I have written will give you, my reader, (if my journal is fit to be read, I shall have readers; if I do not have many, my parents and sisters will like to read it when they find their daughter has improved, and my sisters that their sister has improved,) some idea of what we said yesterday.

P. M.—When I got to school I found the scholars in their chairs, hearing Miss Peabody read a geography lesson very interesting. After Miss Peabody had read about an hour, we took our Latin, and had a lesson in Latin grammar, which was very interesting. When I got home I found that my sisters were playing in the Court, and so I played with them till 6 o'clock, and then (as mother was out, she did not call me in,) but my conscience did, so I took my sisters into the house, and we read till mother came home, and then we had tea. After tea, I read till it was time to go to bed, and then I went.

Monday, 27th.—When I got to school, I wrote my journal, and then my spelling lesson in my book. At the usual hour I turned round, and Mr. Alcott gave me a slate and pencil for me to superintend; so I took my seat. Mr. Alcott then began to talk about the words of the spelling lesson. We talked about *atlas, atom, axis*. The word atom was the most interesting word that we talked about. Mr. Alcott said that we were all atoms once that could not be seen, but love formed our bodies, and when we die our spirits leave us, and without them we crumble away into the air, and help form other bodies. We had a very interesting conversation which occupied us till 12 o'clock, and then Mr. Alcott asked those that had been interested this morning to hold up their hand. I held up mine because I had been more interested than usual; while we were talking about the words,* one of the boys asked me if I had written him down on the slate, and I put him down before for playing, but I did not know whether to put him down or not for asking me if he had been put down, so I rubbed his name out; but next time I have the slate, I shall put down those that ask me such questions. After school, I took my brother to walk, and he said that he wanted to see the great man—I supposed he meant Washington, so I took him into the State House, and he was very much pleased with the great man as he called him.

From the Journal of a boy of eight years of age.

March 1st.—Went to school, and had a very instructive conversation with Mr. Alcott—the subject was the various modes of expression. We possess, I think, the following: *action*, and *writing*, and I am not sure but what *words* belong to this class also: and these, I believe, are the most mighty and sublime. Washington, I think, had great power over his thoughts, by expressing them with actions, and Milton, and Byron, by their writings. Next to these modes of expression, I think, comes the art of *sculpture* and *painting*. What happened in the course of the morning and afternoon I will not relate. In the evening I read in *Smellie's Natural History:* One part pleased me very much, and which I had

---

* She says in another place, " it is almost always pretty difficult to tell what word is most interesting, because they are all so very interesting."

thoughts of mentioning here, but at present I have not the book to refer to, neither have I a sufficient quantity of words to express in appropriate language.

Sunday 2nd.—To day I did not feel as if I wanted to go to church—however, I did go, and now I am glad of it; for there I heard a most important and interesting sermon in which Mr. *** spoke of the many *sensual idols* of this world, and which most people worship as their God—their father—their protector—their every thing; and thus they worship, what false what gross ideas. Instead of worshipping a great, true and invisible God, they take hold of the things of sense and have that as their idol, and when we try to prevail upon them to worship a higher, better, and more powerful God, they turn away and say no! we do not believe there is any other *God; we must have sense,* and that is everlasting. In the afternoon I finished Mr. Alcott's book of Natural History, the author of which I have mentioned in my preceding chapter. After this I read in Peter Parley's *Tales of Africa, and Sea;* but the short parts that I read, was all about prisons, and robbers, and pirates, and such things, which I dislike very much; and which made my reading very gloomy and uninteresting. But as I had no other book to read, and as I did not want to be idle, I read this.

Monday 3rd.—I accomplished the drawing of the map of Delaware, and putting the most important parts, concerning this small state in my book to-day. I also drew the map of the four *Middle States* united, in which I think I succeeded in drawing them to my satisfaction. The above occupied nearly all my time at school, to-day, except the conversation I had with Mr. Alcott, in which he told me that he had only one *fault* to find with me at school—that was, that I answered questions which he addressed to others. This fault, I will try to overcome, as I find I have others. Part of this afternoon and evening, I took much interest and satisfaction, in writing in my journal.

Tuesday 4th.—Finished my selections of the *Middle States,* which I wrote in my book. Then drew the map of

Maryland, and put important parts concerning it on my slate. After school, Mr. Alcott read to us a very interesting story—the name of which I do not remember. In the afternoon, I wrote a chapter of the *Biography of Columbus*—that part where he was making known his Theory. In the evening, I read some, and did several other things. My account of what happened at school to-day, is very short, I know; but the reason of this was, because my studies there were not as interesting as they generally are.

Wednesday 5th.—Put in my book the *Biography* which I wrote yesterday. Mr. Alcott gave us a lesson in reading —my voice, I think, is very little cultivated; but I am trying to improve it; and I hope I shall succeed. One thing I forgot—that was a story which Mr. Alcott read to us before school, which I think was called *Clouds* and *Sunshine.* I can not appropriately express what this taught us, or I would. I spent the evening in reading in the News-Papers, and writing in my Journal, which I took great pains with.

Monday 24th.—At school Mr. Alcott read a story called "A Story without an End." I do think your allegories, Mr. Alcott, are a great deal more instructive, but not so picturesque and mysterious. I like that part best where he, the boy, is in the cave, talking to the fire-flies and hare-bells are ringing, and the spider spinning a curtain for him. The Dragon-fly of Thought I liked much, not only for his pleasant company, and good nature, but for his delightful stories, and amusing conversation. Mr. Alcott then desired me to give a description of what he had just read—part of which I did; but I was rather idle and lazy to-day—and that was the reason why I did not finish it. In the afternoon I wrote with much pleasure and satisfaction. My evening in reading the French Cabin Boy. I think this story entirely equals Robinson Crusoe. I have never before witnessed in any boy so much fortitude. I declare I was quite astonished. If I was in this boy's situation, I think I should set down there, and after crying a day or two, I should begin to feel hungry, and then I might get up and look about for something to eat. But it is very uncertain what I should do—therefore I shall here drop the subject and the day also.

Sunday 30th.—Mr. ——'s sermon to-day, was very appropriate—it being Easter Sunday. He spoke beautifully on the *Resurrection*. But this day I did not understand the sermon; but all sermons must not expect to be adapted only to children's comprehension. In the afternoon, I took much interest in reading the various anecdotes and tales in the News Papers. I spent the evening in writing for my Journal.   *   *   *

Sunday, April 6th.—Mr. —— selected for his text to day the fifth chapter, 44th verse of Matthew—" *To do good to those that hate you.*" I never heard so beautiful an illustration of the virtues of Christ. Mr. F. said, suppose we imagine the veil of Futurity raised before us, and we behold a Being arrayed in light, and commanding myriads of those not as enlightened as himself; and while the enraptured stranger was viewing this majestic sight, he hears a small still voice, saying—this is what ye may become, and what ye may do in the next world. Mr. —— said that we all had a picture similar to this one, implanted in our own minds. And we ought not to let sin over-cloud and dim its glowing colors; and when it did, we should have imagination near to re-touch the fading tints of the once beautiful picture.

Letter to Mr. Alcott, from a boy of eight years of age, dated Philadelphia, February 23rd, 1834.

DEAR SIR: I received your letter with great satisfaction; the good advice you gave me, I will try to remember and profit by. That inward ray of immortal life, which you have so minutely described, I understand to mean conscience, though I do not always obey its influence. The comparisons in your letter, I think were very good—the one that struck me most forcibly, and which I have before mentioned in my journal, was the Looking-Glass of Circumstance, which I think, meets the subject. In this letter you have fully convinced me, that we should not too often commit the dreadful sin of seeking all good *without*, and not beholding it *within* our imagination.

18

My journal I am very much interested in. I have tried very hard, in my last week, to please your desires—though the chapters are short, and badly spelt; this last fault, and many others, I have and will try to overcome. One great desire of mine is, to learn to express my language better than I do; and your school, Mr. Alcott, is the best for this purpose. There, we are not forced to talk about subjects we do not understand, and know little or nothing about; but our conversation is generally what we can understand, and what we can ourselves easily explain, and when it is not thus, you always explain it to us. I expect to hear from you soon. Yours truly.

Another letter from the same boy, dated May 24th, 1834.

Dear Sir, During the now departing holidays I have not felt near so happy as in general ; my Journal has not been well written or composed, and I have altogether felt very much behindhand. I have exercised a great deal of pro-crastination, and have frequently been in the most ungovernable passions. I feel that I cannot be left to myself, and long for school to open again—there I have full employment, and feel that I am doing right; but when I am at home I am always wanting to play, and then I hurry off the thing that I am doing with so much rapidity, that it is not fit to be seen, and when I go out to play, I have no pleasure, for my conscience is continually telling me that I am indulging in what is wrong, and that I ought to be reading, writing, or doing some useful thing, and I feel the truth of its warning voice, and still I do not obey it, and I will say to myself for instance O never mind, I can do that this evening, and when evening comes, I want to read, or do something else, which I like better; and so I put it off every day; it becoming more of a burthen to me, and at last, I do not get any thing done without somebody forces me to do it. But I will not continue this letter any longer, for it is full of *regrets*.

I remain your ever obliged pupil.

The following is from a boy of five, written with a pencil, dated Philadelphia, March 24th.

My dear Mr. Alcott: How glad I should be to see you. One night I wrote a letter, and I think you would like to hear it. I think your school is the very best I ever went to. I like the story of young Carlo, and little Henry, and Pilgrim's Progress.

Extracts from a letter of a girl of eight, who had been under Mr. Alcott's instruction for a year.

OCTOBER 18th. * * * * There is one question I have wanted to ask you for sometime; but I was afraid you would think me too inquisitive. I must ask you at any rate —that question is, *how do we get truth?* Will you tell me in your next letter, and tell it in as few and simple words as you can. I wish you would begin with another of the Three Books; let us take *self.* * * * * * Though you expected me to fill a sheet, I cannot; for I have written all my thoughts.

A letter from the same, dated October 23rd.

Mr. Alcott: I liked your answer to my question, *how do we get truth;* but I want to know if you can express it in fewer words. I do not think you could express it in simple words, or more simply than you did.

Do you think that if you tried very hard and did nothing else, you could write good poetry? The reason I ask you this is because, yesterday I asked you if you thought the "Three Books" which I put in my "Mental Gems," was a Gem, you thought it was pretty well, for one who had had so little practice; and I thought from that, that you thought, if you had more practice you could write much better poetry. Did you not tell more *what truth is*, than *how to get it?* But it helped me to understand your answer better. I cannot help wondering how this winter will be spent. I had better employ it to the best advantage, as I expect I shall go away from your school in spring. I do not think that I shall ever find a school that I can like as well as this; though other people like other schools, because they learn more lessons. I think that we learn many lessons, but of a different kind. Experience is as much our teacher as you are; you teach us how to learn from her.

You said that the Three Books are the Books of Man, Nature, and Revelation—do you not mean by Man, *the human heart*, and by Revelation, *the Bible?*

There is one thing I want to tell you—that is, when I ask you the meaning of a word, and you tell me, I always remember it better than when I look in the dictionary.

When you said " Truth was the gem that floats in the waters of experience," I understood you very well.

I have not written on one subject, but many. I wish you would ask me a great many questions.   Your Scholar.

Extract, dated October 26th.

*   * You found some fault, in conversation, with your own thoughts when you said truth was the gem that floats in the clear waters of experience; for you said " a gem would sink, and not float ;" but I could imagine it to do so. I think if you were to look carefully into all comparisons, you could find a good many faults, even in those that seem most beautiful. After that, you speak of truth lying at the bottom of the fountain of experience ; I think this is better.

Extracts might be multiplied, but there must be a time to stop. Some original fables, biographies, &c., may be found in three articles of Mr. Alcott's, on the *Principles and Methods of Intellectual Instruction, exhibited in the exercises of young children,* published in the Annals of Education— in the numbers for January and November of 1832, and the number for May, 1833.   No specimens presented in those numbers, are from scholars older than ten years; and all specimens both in the Annals of Education, and in this Appendix, are uncorrected exercises of the children.

FINIS.

Printed in the United States
94852LV00002B/49-57/A